Family and the State in Soviet Lithuania

Library of Modern Russia

Advisory Board:

Jeffrey Brooks, Professor at Johns Hopkins University, USA
Michael David-Fox, Professor at Georgetown University, USA
Lucien Frary, Associate Professor at Rider University, USA
James Harris, Senior Lecturer at the University of Leeds, UK
Robert Hornsby, Lecturer at the University of Leeds, UK
Ekaterina Pravilova, Professor of History at Princeton University, USA
Geoffrey Swain, Emeritus Professor of Central and East European Studies at the University of Glasgow, UK
Vera Tolz-Zilitinkevic, Sir William Mather Professor of Russian Studies at the University of Manchester, UK
Vladislav Zubok, Professor of International History at the London School of Economics, UK

Building on Bloomsbury Academic's established record of publishing Russian studies titles, the Library of Modern Russia will showcase the work of emerging and established writers who are setting new agendas in the field.

At a time when potentially dangerous misconceptions and misunderstandings about Russia abound, titles in the series will shed fresh light and nuance on Russian history. Volumes will take the idea of 'Russia' in its broadest cultural sense and cover the entirety of the multi-ethnic lands that made up imperial Russia and the Soviet Union. Ranging in chronological scope from the Romanovs to today, the books will:

- reconsider Russia's history from a variety of interdisciplinary perspectives.
- explore Russia in its various international contexts, rather than as exceptional or in isolation.
- examine the complex, divisive and ever-shifting notions of 'Russia'.
- contribute to a deeper understanding of Russia's rich social and cultural history.
- critically reassess the Soviet period and its legacy today.
- interrogate the traditional periodizations of the post-Stalin Soviet Union.
- unearth continuities, or otherwise, among the tsarist, Soviet and post-Soviet periods.
- re-appraise Russia's complex relationship with Eastern Europe, both historically and today.

- analyse the politics of history and memory in post-Soviet Russia.
- promote new archival revelations and innovative research methodologies.
- foster a community of scholars and readers devoted to a sharper understanding of the Russian experience, past and present.

Books in the series will join our list in being marketed globally, including at conferences – such as the BASEES and ASEEES conventions. Each will be subjected to a rigorous peer-review process and will be published in hardback and, simultaneously, as an e-book. We also anticipate a second release in paperback for the general reader and student markets.

For more information, or to submit a proposal for inclusion in the series, please contact:

Rhodri Mogford, Publisher, History (Rhodri.Mogfrod@bloomsbury.com).

New and forthcoming:

Fascism in Manchuria: The Soviet-China Encounter in the 1930s, Susanne Hohler

The Idea of Russia: The Life and Work of Dmitry Likhachev, Vladislav Zubok

The Tsar's Armenians: A Minority in Late Imperial Russia, Onur Onol

Myth Making in the Soviet Union and Modern Russia: Remembering World War II in Brezhnev's Hero City, Vicky Davis

Building Stalinism: The Moscow Canal and the Creation of Soviet Space, Cynthia Ruder

Russia in the Time of Cholera: Disease and the Environment under Romanovs and Soviets, John Davis

Soviet Americana: A Cultural History of Russian and Ukrainian Americanists, Sergei Zhuk

Stalin's Economic Advisors: The Varga Institute and the Making of Soviet Foreign Policy, Ken Roh

Ideology and the Arts in the Soviet Union: The Establishment of Censorship and Control, Steven Richmond

Nomads and Soviet Rule: Central Asia under Lenin and Stalin, Alun Thomas

The Russian State and the People: Power, Corruption and the Individual in Putin's Russia, Geir Hønneland et al. (eds)

The Communist Party in the Russian Civil War: A Political History, Gayle Lonergan

Criminal Subculture in the Gulag: Prisoner Society in the Stalinist Labour Camps, Mark Vincent
Power and Politics in Modern Chechnya: Ramzan Kadyrov and the New Digital Authoritarianism, Karena Avedissian
Russian Pilgrimage to the Holy Land: Piety and Travel from the Middle Ages to the Revolution, Nikolaos Chrissidis
The Fate of the Bolshevik Revolution, Lara Douds, James Harris and Peter Whitehead (eds)
Writing History in Late Imperial Russia, Frances Nethercott
Translating England into Russian, Elena Goodwin
Gender and Survival in Soviet Russia, Elaine MacKinnon (transl. and ed.)
Publishing in Tsarist Russia, Yukiko Tatsumi and Taro Tsurumi (eds)
New Drama in Russian: Performance, Politics and Protest, Julie Curtis (ed.)
The Culture of Samizdat: Literature and Underground Networks in the Late Soviet Union, Josephine von Zitzewitz
Making Ukraine Soviet: Literature and Cultural Politics under Lenin and Stalin, Olena Palko
Family and the State in Soviet Lithuania: Gender, Law and Society, Dalia Lienarte

Family and the State in Soviet Lithuania

Gender, Law and Society

Dalia Leinarte

BLOOMSBURY ACADEMIC
LONDON • NEW YORK • OXFORD • NEW DELHI • SYDNEY

BLOOMSBURY ACADEMIC
Bloomsbury Publishing Plc
50 Bedford Square, London, WC1B 3DP, UK
1385 Broadway, New York, NY 10018, USA
29 Earlsfort Terrace, Dublin 2, Ireland

BLOOMSBURY, BLOOMSBURY ACADEMIC and the Diana logo are
trademarks of Bloomsbury Publishing Plc

First published in Great Britain 2021
Paperback edition published in 2023

Copyright © Dalia Leinarte, 2021

Dalia Leinarte has asserted their right under the Copyright, Designs and
Patents Act, 1988, to be identified as Author of this work.

For legal purposes the Acknowledgements on p. ix constitute an
extension of this copyright page.

Cover image: Dior model Kouka Denis appears in the Soviet Union for an officially sanctioned fashion
show visiting the GUM department store in Moscow, Russia, 1959.
(© Howard Sochurek/The LIFE Picture Collection/Getty Images)

All rights reserved. No part of this publication may be reproduced or transmitted in any
form or by any means, electronic or mechanical, including photocopying,
recording, or any information storage or retrieval system, without prior permission
in writing from the publishers.

Bloomsbury Publishing Plc does not have any control over, or responsibility for, any
third-party websites referred to or in this book. All internet addresses given in this
book were correct at the time of going to press. The author and publisher regret any
inconvenience caused if addresses have changed or sites have ceased to exist, but
can accept no responsibility for any such changes.

Every effort has been made to trace copyright holders and to obtain their permissions
for the use of copyright material. The publisher apologizes for any errors or omissions
and would be grateful if notified of any corrections that should be incorporated in
future reprints or editions of this book.

A catalogue record for this book is available from the British Library.

Library of Congress Cataloging-in-Publication Data
Names: Leinarte, Dalia, author.
Title: Family and the state in Soviet Lithuania : gender, law and society / Dalia Leinarte.
Description: London ; New York : Bloomsbury Academic, 2021. |
Series: Library of modern Russia | Includes bibliographical references and index. |
Identifiers: LCCN 2021004247 (print) | LCCN 2021004248 (ebook) |
ISBN 9781350136090 (hardback) | ISBN 9781350136106 (ebook) |
ISBN 9781350136113 (epub)
Subjects: LCSH: Family policy–Lithuania–History–20th century. |
Families–Lithuania–History–20th century. | Women–Lithuania–Social
conditions–20th century. | Lithuania–Social conditions–1945–1991. |
Lithuania–Politics and government–1945–1991.
Classification: LCC HQ638.9 .L45 2021 (print) | LCC HQ638.9 (ebook) |
DDC 306.85094793–dc23
LC record available at https://lccn.loc.gov/2021004247
LC ebook record available at https://lccn.loc.gov/2021004248

ISBN: HB: 978-1-3501-3609-0
PB: 978-1-3502-5489-3
ePDF: 978-1-3501-3610-6
eBook: 978-1-3501-3611-3

Series: Library of Modern Russia

Typeset by Newgen KnowledgeWorks Pvt. Ltd., Chennai, India

To find out more about our authors and books visit www.bloomsbury.com
and sign up for our newsletters.

Contents

List of Tables	viii
Acknowledgements	ix
List of Abbreviations	x
Introduction	1
1. Soviet family policy	7
2. Marriage and divorce	47
3. Parents and their children	109
4. Household	135
Conclusions	157
Notes	165
Bibliography	199
Index	211

Tables

1.1	Assistance paid to single mothers and mothers of large families, 1944–6	38
1.2	Assistance paid between October 1944 and 1 December 1946	41
2.1	Marital age in Lithuania, Vilnius, 1946–75	57
2.2	Newlyweds under the age 20 per 1,000 marriages, 1980–90	72
3.1	Birth rates in Lithuania, 1950–88	110
4.1	Cars in the Soviet republics, 1977 and 1985	141

Acknowledgements

The process of researching and writing this book spanned over a decade. In the course of this long journey almost all parts of the book were presented to the Association for Slavic, East European, and Eurasian Studies (ASEEES); the British Association for Slavonic and East European Studies (BASEES) and the Association for the Advancement of Baltic Studies (AABS). Multiple panel discussions held during these international venues for Eastern European and Soviet studies were crucial in shaping and transforming the manuscript into what it is now. However, every research also requires serene and solitary space and time. This was kindly provided to me by the Vytautas Magnus University, my home institution. I am grateful to all the academic spaces which inspired and enhanced my research as well as gave me a chance to finalize it.

Substantial parts of the manuscript are based on archival sources, in particular documents stored at the Lithuanian State Historical Archives. I am thankful to its professional and willing staff for their kind support and assistance.

Originally written in Lithuanian, the book was subsequently translated into English. I was enormously lucky to have had the manuscript translated by Jūra Avižienis. I am indebted to her for reaching the English reader. I am also sincerely thankful to Rhodri Mogford, Bloomsbury's publishing editor for Russian studies as well as Laura Reeves, and especially Tom Stottor, the former I.B. Tauris editor in history, who believed in my work and trusted the manuscript.

Finally, my deep gratitude goes to my daughters, Dalyte and Emilija, and their families. Born in the last years of the Soviet rule, they are both the subjects of my research as well as knowledgeable readers.

Abbreviations

ATS	Automobile and tractor stations
LCP CC	Lithuanian Communist Party Central Committee
CP(b)	Communist Party (Bolshevik)
JBAM	Jūra B.'s Personal Archive
LCP(b) CC	Lithuanian Communist Party (Bolshevik) Central Committee
LCSA	Lithuanian Central State Archive
LKP(b) CK	Lietuvos Komunistų Partijos Centro Komitetas
LSSR	Lithuanian Soviet Socialist Republic
LTSR	Lietuvos Tarybų Socialistinė Respublika
MARS	Manuscript Department of the Wroblewski Library of the Lithuanian Academy of Sciences
MGB	Ministry for State Security of Soviet Union
NBRS	Rare Books and Manuscripts Unit of the National Library of Lithuania
OSBMLFSM	Office of State Benefits for Mothers of Large Families and Single Mothers
RSFSR	Russian Soviet Federative Socialist Republic
RTFSR	Rusijos Tarybų Federacinė Socialistinė Respublika
SSRS	Sovietų Socialistinių Respublikų Sąjunga
USSR	Union of Soviet Socialist Republics
VKP(b)	Visasąjunginė Komunistų Partija (Bolševikai).

Introduction

On 15 June 1940, the Soviet Union occupied the independent Republic of Lithuania, and two days later, the Red Army marched into the other two Baltic states, Latvia and Estonia. The occupation of the Baltic countries was followed by the imprisonment and mass deportations of hundreds of thousands. A total of 131,600 civilians were deported from Lithuania and resettled in the far reaches of the Soviet Union. The deportees included families, women and the elderly; every tenth deportee was a child. From 1941 to 1953 alone, more than 50,000 women and 39,000 children were deported, and on 2 October 1951, during a single night, 3,992 Lithuanian families were deported (15,041 individuals). A total of 156,000 inhabitants of Lithuania were sentenced and incarcerated in Soviet prisons; approximately every tenth GULAG prisoner was a Lithuanian national. Mothers and their small children were also locked inside prison cells in their homeland: from 1946 to 1952, Lithuania's Šilutė labour camp held 620 children and their mothers; among the children, 194 were born there.[1]

The war was accompanied by one of the most painful chapters in Lithuanian history, the Holocaust. In the period of just a few months, 80 per cent of Jews living in Lithuania were killed. In all, Lithuania lost approximately 196,000 Jews during the Nazi occupation.

The occupation, genocide, deportations and emigration to the West radically changed the sociopolitical face of Lithuania. In 1963, the last Lithuanians were released from forced deportation and prison; however, when they returned home, they found themselves without rights, without property because it had been confiscated and in many cases without family as their families had been torn apart. Each of the hundreds of thousands of victims of the Soviet regime experienced the terror differently, but no less tragically. Together with citizens who had avoided deportation and imprisonment, they were all survivors of the regime and targets of totalitarian ideology.

Soviet family policy and propaganda unavoidably affected every Lithuanian demographic. Mandatory work by men and women for the state, coordinated free time and extracurricular activities for their children, centralized distribution of summer vacations, often incompatible with one's spouse's time off, reduced the available amount of family time. This is not to mention that the average citizen's everyday routine also required a lot of effort. Under universal shortage conditions, household chores were attended to at the expense of time parents and children could otherwise spend together. Women in particular were forced to deal with a drastic change in lifestyle. After 1945, the Soviet government integrated women into the workforce and turned them into social activists. In 1956, women made up 45 per cent of the workforce, and by 1964, they comprised 49 per cent.[2] In the Soviet Union, the family was not the watershed between the public and private spheres. Quite the contrary, wives-mothers-workers served the socialist state and the ideology of the regime.

The idea for this monograph was born while I was working on the oral history study *Adopting and Remembering Soviet Reality* (2010) on the experience of Lithuanian women of the Soviet era. Years of conducting interviews revealed that the respondents' memories about family life played a small role in their life narratives. This surprised me because in the Soviet state, women were responsible for the home and devoted a considerable amount of time to the family and household. Pauses and incoherent narratives about the family could not be explained simply as gaps in memory, hesitation about speaking or traumatic experience. On the contrary, women spoke in detail about the tragic post-war years, the deportations to Siberia and the deprivations they all suffered. They similarly spoke vividly about political events during the years of Gorbachev's *glasnost*. However, the respondents could barely remember their family life. Why were family memories of women who had lived through the Soviet years dull, fragmentary and poorly individualized? What did Soviet family policy and ideology espouse, and how did it affect the everyday life of average families? These essential questions are what this book attempts to address. The book claims that the state regulated most aspects of family life, leaving meagre space for individual family members' initiatives or commonly shared family time.

There are four chapters in the monograph. The first, 'Soviet family policy', analyses the circumstances surrounding the founding of the Work Among Women Division and the party structures through which gender equality in Lithuania was implemented. Based on archival material, the chapter reveals how women's activism and unpaid labour were used to rebuild the war-ravaged economy and strengthen the Soviet regime. A new epoch of gender equality began in the mid-1950s in Lithuania when women's rights and their social situation began to be evaluated and measured solely through numbers and statistics. Gender equality reports stressed that women in Soviet Lithuania took part in aspects of professional life, which in interwar Lithuania had traditionally belonged to men: medicine, education and commerce. According to the Lithuanian Soviet Socialist Republic (LSSR) deputy minister of health, among 2,389 physicians in Lithuania, 1,682 were women. Similarly, statistics on the growing number of female members of the Communist Party and Comsomol were also considered an indicator of gender equality: in 1953, among communists in the district of Tauragė, 30 per cent were women, and among the Comsomol, young women made up 53 per cent of all members.[3] The chapter also reconstructs in detail state assistance to mothers of large families and single mothers governing boards and their divisions' activity in Lithuania between 1944 and 1952 and discusses the Soviet government's first attempts to reconcile women's work and the family. The mission of the governing board was to enact the 8 July 1944 decree of the Presidium of the USSR Supreme Soviet *On State Assistance for Pregnant Mothers, Mothers of Large Families and Single Mothers, On Strengthening Support for Mothers and Babies, On Bestowing the Honorary Title Mother-Heroine, the Order Mother's Glory and the Medal of Motherhood*, and discusses why the programmes of the governing boards and their divisions providing support for mothers of large families were ineffective and unsuccessful. The book's first chapter also analyses the laws providing support for the family, in effect until 1990.

The book's second chapter, 'Marriage and divorce', uncovers legal provisions on marriage and divorce. The USSR Marriage and Family Code of 1936 came into effect in the territory of Lithuania automatically and was effective until 1969 when the Lithuanian Supreme Soviet (*Aukščiausioji Taryba*) adopted the new Marriage and Family Code of 1969. Soviet law and ideology tried to consolidate the provisions of Soviet marriage and family in several ways. Firstly, it consistently propagated the idea that only registered civil marriages could be happy ones. Soon after the end of the war, Lithuanian newspapers and magazines were filled with articles and 'letters from readers' about marriages that supposedly ended in divorce because one of the spouses was religious and had avoided civil registry. Religious marriage was considered inappropriate on the grounds that happiness in the family was left to be ensured by God. According to Soviet propagandists, religious marriages caused spouses to reject individual responsibility for their personal destiny and happiness. In the 1950s, Soviet ideologues were still waging a battle against prospective spouses who practiced religion. In 1957, the newspaper *Komjaunimo tiesa* (Comsomol Truth) summarized its readers' letters and published the article 'Ar tai tikroji, tvirta draugystė?' (Is This a True, Solid Friendship?) Citing readers' letters to the newspaper, the article appealed to friendship and love as well as attempted to provide readers with the cliches of Soviet marriage and included the following: 'After being demobilized from the Army, Peter came to Telšiai. The couple met again and understood that they could not live without one another. But what kept them apart this time? Well, it was the same thing all over again. Along with national differences, their parents had provided them with religious ones as well.'[4]

What were the Soviet motives for marriage and what kind of romantic love did Soviet propaganda propagate? The chapter reveals the Soviet government's efforts at moulding romantic love with a totalitarian ideological framework and using it to serve the state's family policies. The chapter provides an overview of the concept of romantic love in interwar Lithuania. The cultural modernization of interwar society placed ever greater importance on the sentiment of romantic love. Mutual romantic feelings became not only an indelible part of the popular literature but were also perceived by women and men as the symbiosis of soulmates. Romantic love aimed to guarantee harmony within the marriage and set the foundation for familial happiness. On the contrary, the Soviet propaganda presented passionate romantic love as a dangerous and overall abnormal human state. Soviet propaganda declared that family happiness and romantic love were not identical concepts and suggested that love should not be the foundation for marriage. The concept of Soviet love was formulated within Stalinist and Khruschevian family policies. It sought to simplify sexuality and identify sexual experience with reproduction. By the end of the 1950s, the press was waging a propaganda campaign against any manifestations of sexual life.

The second chapter analyses all registered divorce cases and decisions of the Supreme Court of Soviet Lithuania for the period 1945–89. For the first time in historiography, it uncovers the motives for divorce and the possibility of rebuilding lives in its wake. When civil registry was instituted in 1940 in Lithuania, it opened up the possibility of resolving marital discord and unhappy marriages through divorce, undoubtedly corresponding to the desires of modern society. The divorce proceedings at the Soviet People's Court and Superior Courts were a relatively formal affair, especially during the first post-war years. On the other hand, the courts were directly influenced by Communist Party leadership and various Soviet organizations. For this reason, rulings were often affected by the party bureaucracy and the patriarchal stereotypes prevalent in society. The chapter asks how divorced couples dealt with dividing up living space if the Soviet laws regulating the allocation of housing for citizens forbade the purchase or sale of state-issued living space.

The third chapter, 'Parents and children', discusses women's attempts to reconcile their full-time employment with household and childcare responsibilities. The chapter argues that in a society in which a significant amount of time was spent dealing with constant material shortages, within the context of insufficient childcare institutions and an insignificant role for fathers, childcare was dealt with using traditional nineteenth-century peasant society norms and informal Soviet-era-reality-dictated strategies. The chapter presents the hypothesis that childcare in Soviet Lithuania frequently facilitated emotionally distant parent and child relations and did not encourage child's individuality. Up to the end of the 1970s in Soviet Lithuania, the network of kindergartens and day-care centres was incomparably poorer than in any other Soviet bloc country. In the 1950s in the USSR, 80 per cent of mothers of working age who had young children worked, and only 13 per cent of children aged 1 to 6 attended preschool institutions. In 1965, this number had grown for children living in cities, reaching 22.5 per cent, whilst less than 12 per cent of children living in rural areas attended kindergartens or day-care centres. The book asks what strategies for childcare did parents choose if the preschool network only began to fully meet the needs of parents in the early 1980s.

The book's third chapter, 'Parents and children', also examines the legal regulation of maternal and childcare leave. The Soviet government offered its assistance along three main lines: it granted paid maternity and childcare leave and also provided free medical assistance and financial support for single mothers and mothers of large families.

The fourth chapter of the monograph, 'Household', reveals how under universal shortage conditions, the everyday family life was improved upon using informal strategies. Average citizens who were unable to make use of professional, party contacts and established privileges, or informal *blat*[5] relations, attempted to solve their material problems by writing letters and lodging complaints to government representatives or newspaper editorial boards. The authors of the complaints had no intention of informing on anyone or having them punished. By writing, they simply hoped to solve their everyday life problems and lessen their family's material deficiencies. At the same time, government officials and journalists receiving and reading the letters understood themselves as defenders of the interests of ordinary citizens. The authors of the complaints often were women who did not have husbands in high positions or exclusive social relations themselves. The chapter looks at the 1964–74 correspondence between a disabled woman and a correspondent working for the main official newspaper *Tiesa* (The Truth).

The fourth chapter also discusses the mass construction of residential housing in Lithuania and the centralized distribution of housing to the population. The design and establishment of typical mass construction micro-districts was considered one of the greatest achievements of the Soviet government. As mass urbanization began, the problem of housing in Lithuanian cities became acute: in 1945, in the capital Vilnius the population was 145,000. By 1959, it had grown to 236,000, and by 1979, it had reached nearly half a million.[6] From 1951 to 1976, 700,000 inhabitants had moved from the villages to the cities. In 1945, the urban population was 15 per cent; by 1989, it was 70 per cent. In 1948, a construction trust was founded in Vilnius. At the same time, construction firms and building material plants were established in other Lithuanian cities. The first prefabricated concrete block buildings in Vilnius were built by the Vilnius Home Construction Factory in 1959, and in 1962, the first residential micro-district, Žirmūnai,[7] was developed in Vilnius. In 1974, after nearly ten years, the Lazdynai micro-district was completed in Vilnius with four separate shopping centres, cultural centres and children's kindergartens. From 1956 to 1965, throughout the USSR many micro-districts were built, and 108 million inhabitants moved into the new apartment complexes.[8] But despite the massive construction projects of residential buildings, for many people of Lithuania, an apartment of their own remained an unrealizable dream. In 1970, approximately 70 per cent of newly-weds began their new lives living in the home of one of the spouses.[9] But wherever the families called home, they tried to arrange their home and lives according to the modern and aesthetic lifestyle advertised in the Soviet magazines and newspapers.

The monograph was researched using various primary and secondary sources, both published and unpublished. A good part of the archival material used in this book is being published for the first time. This is the first analysis of divorce cases from LSSR Supreme Court between 1944 and 1989, material from the LSSR Ministry of Labour and Social Welfare (regarding support for families and large families), laws issued by the LSSR People's Commissar of Finance and Finance Ministers, as well as individual archives of epistolary materials. Oral history sources make up a different category. The book cites qualitative interviews that the author conducted between 1998 and 2005 with women who lived through the Soviet period. Along with other secondary sources, the book makes use of census data from 1959, 1979, 1989, as well as Soviet-era newspapers and magazines from 1944 to 1989.

1
Soviet family policy

The beginnings of gender equality

After surviving the 1940 annexation of Lithuania and the Second World War, the people of Lithuania soon faced a second Soviet occupation and post-war upheaval. Many once again experienced coercion, exile, loss of loved ones, and every one without exception became the target of Soviet propaganda. Women were in an especially sensitive situation because the regime expected their prompt affiliation and transformation of their customary way of life. In pre-war independent Lithuania, it had been rare for mothers raising children to work full time beyond the confines of the family home, but the Soviet state demanded that all men and women work and conform to the image of a socially engaged citizen. The first communication – that henceforth women would be required to do work useful to the state – was disseminated immediately after annexation. On 15 August 1940, the newspaper *Vyriausybės žinios* (Government News) announced the *Lithuanian Marriage Law*, which was lifted wholesale from the USSR. In the section on divorce, the law required minor children to be financially supported by both parents. In the case of the parents' inability to come to terms, the court would decide on the amount of child support to be paid.[1] Thus women were required to find gainful employment if they wanted to maintain custody rights after divorce.

The period 1951–2 saw the liberalization of Stalinist labour laws that rendered it illegal to leave one's job without government permission; however, by April 1956, independently initiated leaving of one's job was no longer considered a criminal offense by the Criminal Code.[2] But, in place of this law, the Lithuanian Republic's Criminal Code criminalized unemployment without justification and in this way enforced women's employment. Unemployed men and women were designated with a special term: *individuals, avoiding work useful to society and living anti-socially as parasites*. In 1952, Criminal Code Articles 155 and

73/2 added prostitutes to the category of parasites and vermin. The law however targeted only those women in prostitution who did not hold an official job and who made their living exclusively from sex work.[3] Eventually, women who had nothing to do with prostitution but who nevertheless did not hold official jobs began to be associated with prostitutes. If women and girls frequented a given restaurant without male chaperones, and if their attire and make-up were flashier than that of the typical Soviet woman, they would inevitably expect to be questioned by the *militsiya* as possible prostitutes. And if the woman in question spoke a foreign language, she would be hard-pressed to avoid the attention of the KGB.[4] Moreover, in 1958, the Presidium of the Lithuanian Soviet Socialist Republic (LSSR) Supreme Soviet[5] approved a resolution regarding the 10 April 1957 decree *On Criminal Liability for Petty Speculation*. The resolution mentions women charged with speculation arrested for repeated offenses of selling food products and clothing by which they secured a living for themselves.[6] In 1966, criminal responsibility for speculation of individuals aged 16 years or older was made more severe.[7] The criminalization of speculation as an informal economic activity also diminished opportunities for avoiding work in a state-run industry.

Cheap labour, which Lithuanian women provided, was essential for rebuilding the war-ravaged agricultural sector and for speeding up collectivization. The universal employment of women in Soviet Lithuania was implemented with the help of the Criminal Code and propaganda campaigns to encourage women to work as much and as effectively as possible.[8] Propaganda played a role in achieving gender equality in this case. After the 1917 Socialist Revolution in Russia, the Bolsheviks pursued universal employment using the slogan of gender equality to fight against women's 'backwardness and illiteracy'. After the Second World War in Soviet Lithuania, the universal employment of women was carried out within the battle against the bourgeois family, which had ostensibly imprisoned women in the home. The rhetoric of Soviet gender equality was also used to promote women's liberation from the slavery imposed by the bourgeois family. The Soviet government planned to transform the traditional family so that it could serve the socialist state by quickly mobilizing women in the rebuilding of the agricultural sector and implementing collectivization as well as spreading Soviet propaganda. On 20 March 1948, the LSSR Council of Ministers adopted the resolution *On Establishing Collective Farms in the Republic*, which marked the beginning of the creation of collective farms in the republic. In early 1949, 4 per cent of landholding and landless farmers from independent Lithuania had joined collectives, but by the end of the year, the percentage had reached 62.4 per cent. The rapidly expanding collective farms needed additional labour.

Nevertheless, pre-war stereotypes about 'communist polygamists' and *homo sovieticus* in neighbouring Russia hindered the large-scale incorporation of Lithuanian women into the new Soviet way of life and prevented active participation in the party and professional activities. Women in post-war Lithuania were convinced that members of the Bolshevik Party were inevitably drunkards and polygamists; they automatically associated these stereotypes with the state and party apparatus being established in Lithuania. In the towns, women spread rumours that 'as a rule, almost every second communist has 2–3 wives. This is a fact.'[9] The women worried that the amoral work environment would negatively affect their Catholic upbringing. When M. Kaunaitė, one of the first Soviet women activists, travelled throughout Lithuania giving lectures promoting gender equality, her lectures angered and even frightened her listeners. The women were afraid that after several such lectures by Kaunaitė, they might be transformed into 'great Bolsheviks and atheists'.[10] Disdain for the new regime was evident. The Lithuanian Communist Party Central Committee (LCP(b) CC) instructor in her letter to LCP(b) CC First Secretary Antanas Sniečkus wrote that in one collective farm, the director himself had turned one of their 'Red Corners' into a cattle shed, that is 'he had provided lodging there to someone who had sectioned off a corner for himself, and in the rest of the barn, he kept a goat and chickens; above them on the wall, he had hung up portraits of "our leaders" along with other propaganda posters'.[11]

Despite the widespread enmity, the propaganda on gender equality and the New Soviet woman was intense and disseminated across all of Lithuania. Every month, ever larger groups of women were forced to participate in the agitprop meetings and seminars and to listen for many long hours to the propositions of the new politics. The invasion of the new ideology unavoidably influenced women's behaviour and world-view. Even communist activists were surprised when in the middle of the winter of 1947, at 6.00 am, as voting began for local workers' deputy committees, they noticed a mother holding a 3-month-old baby in her arms outside. The woman explained that she kept seeing a poster depicting a mother with her baby in her arms standing next to the ballot boxes, and she wanted to look like her.[12] Indeed, the Soviet government used visual as well as verbal propaganda to indoctrinate Lithuanian women, dedicating financial and human resources, as well as the already established structures for implementing gender politics. The following section examines how this functioned and what results it achieved.

The LCP(b) CC establishes the Work Among Women Division

The Work Among Women Division was created in August 1945 by the LCP(b) CC. The department was charged with realizing Soviet gender equality policies in the Soviet republic. Shortly thereafter, local Work Among Women Divisions were founded in every one of Lithuania's twenty-three counties, and women-organizer positions were established in its 365 rural districts. In the central Work Among Women Division, three positions, namely one supervisor position and two instructor positions, were paid with state budget funds. The county-level departments were allocated one full-time director's position and one instructor's position. Kaunaitė was appointed director of the Work Among Women Division's central office. In 1950, after they had completed the administrative and territorial distribution reforms in Lithuania, the LCP(b) CC approved the new Work Among Women Division positions. After the 1950 reforms eliminated Lithuania's counties and rural districts, four regional Work Among Women Division departments were created, each with a director and instructor position. In addition, Work Among Women Division positions were created within the Ministry of Agriculture, as well as in district and town executive committees and automobile and tractor stations (ATS).

By 1950, all the necessary positions in the Work Among Women Division had been filled, of which 216 were financed by the state budget:[13]

- Two positions within the LCP(b) Central Committee
- Eight positions in the four LCP(b) regional committees
- Four positions in the four LCP(b) city committees
- Eighty-seven director positions within the eighty-seven LCP(b) regional executive committees
- 113 positions within the political departments of the 113 ATS
- Two directors' assistant positions within the political department of the Ministry of Agriculture charged with issues pertaining to women

Nevertheless, the most significant category of the Work Among Women Division was composed not of full-time public servants, but of the so-called women-delegates, whose work was voluntary and unpaid. According to reports filed by Kaunaitė, there were sixty-two directors and instructors in the Work Among Women Division regional departments in 1948, whereas there were over 11,000 unpaid women-delegates throughout the republic.[14] In 1950, that number was close to 20,000.[15] It was this army of women that was meant to affirm that gender equality policy was successfully being implemented in Lithuania and had mobilized thousands of activists.

One of the greatest impediments to the activism of the Work Among Women Division departments in the provinces was the poor education of its staff. Before the 1950 administrative reforms, three workers of the Alytus county department had only a fourth-grade elementary school education, one had not completed elementary school and only one had a high school diploma.[16] The departmental staff in the provinces also complained that they had not been instructed on the goals and tasks of the Work Among Women Division. The departmental directors were regularly sending the central office director, Kaunaitė, written requests for instructors or permission to go to Vilnius, the capital of Lithuania, themselves in order to clarify their respective department's goals and strategies. In 1948, the Kaunas county departmental director, Nakaitė, wrote to Kaunaitė: 'Please, Comrade Director, allow me to come talk to you regarding this work. Many things are not clear to me, and I cannot make sense of them on my own. I would be very grateful for your advice.'[17]

The principal complaints coming from the provinces were related to the management of the project, undefined operations and confusion regarding concrete strategies for implementing gender equality policies. Soon it became clear to them all that the Soviet government equated gender equality with women's work in all the agricultural and industrial sectors of Lithuania that were being revitalized. The LCP(b) Central Committee was expecting the Work Among Women Division departments to intensively advocate for the principles of Soviet gender equality, involving women in socialist competition, organizing women's work on the fields of the newly establishing and resource-scarce collective farms and harvest programmes, obliging them to participate in the nationalization of the republic's wealth and encouraging them to identify cases of looting of socialist property and to provide the KGB with information on Lithuania's anti-Soviet partisan movement. The local departments were also encouraged to hold informational meetings about the Soviet government's strides in achieving women's rights, inspect nursery schools and creches, manage benefits and assistance to mothers of large families and single mothers, provide help for the lonely and elderly, elect delegates to the Soviet and LSSR Executive Committees, subscribe to and disseminate Soviet publications, coordinate activities in the arts, eradicate women's illiteracy and actively read suitable Soviet books.

Yet, in order to realize the LCP(b) CC's disparate and multiple plans, the Work Among Women Division departmental directors and instructors first had to assemble an ideologically trustworthy organization of women organizers and activists. This task was undertaken with enthusiasm and on a massive scale. By autumn of 1945, meetings were being organized for the country's female factory workers and villagers about the significance of Stalin's constitution for women. Propagandists explained women's roles in Lithuanian life and their tasks in establishing a new Soviet society. In Rokiškis county, during the month of October 1945 alone, there were eighty-four massive rallies and sixty-four lectures with 2,561 women participants. In February 1946, the Panevėžys county department similarly organized twenty-nine rallies with 6,890 women participating. That same year, there were ninety-four propagandistic commemorations of International Women's Day at Panevėžys area factories, offices and schools, with 24,191 women participating. The following year, 1947, in Panevėžys county, 300 agitprop meetings were held with a total of 22,260 participants. The Rokiškis county female instructors and organizers managed to hold an additional twenty-eight meetings, offering lectures about the new role of women and their part in building a socialist society; 1,000 women attended these lectures.[18]

Agitprop meetings were especially focused on explaining what Soviet gender equality meant. Director Kaunaitė would stress that the notion of gender equality in Soviet society had nothing to do with the fight between men and women being waged in enemy capitalist countries. Not having encountered Soviet or Western gender equality until occupation, post-war Lithuanian women could hardly grasp what the difference between Western feminism and Soviet gender equality might be. Obviously, the propagandists did not bring up the feminist battle initiated in the UK at the time for equal wages for men and women. Soviet gender equality was without exception geared exclusively towards women's situation and their changing role in family and public life. Soviet gender politics did not foresee, nor did it strive for, equal rights for men and women or for the elimination of discrimination against women. Quite the contrary, any equating of the situation of women and men was forbidden and was safely quieted at departmental meetings of the Work Among Women Division. Charged with speaking out publicly about women's rights and their situation in Soviet Lithuania, lower ranking members and activists were quite often met with accusations from the director of the central office. This is precisely what happened to the Šakiai county delegate, farmer and activist Mackevičienė. According to the director, Mackevičienė was doing the right thing in endorsing Šakiai county women candidates for local people's deputy councils. However, as Kaunaitė indicated, Mackevičienė was mistakenly asserting that women candidates were better than men because 'they do everything better than men'. In her comments to the audience, Mackevičienė claimed that women were more honest and more experienced, while men were only capable of drinking, smoking and 'making a mess' of things. Kaunaitė stressed that farmer Mackevičienė's view of men was mistaken at the core and that it had to be changed according to the principles of Soviet gender equality.[19]

A portion of the meetings were dedicated to what was called 'the political education' of women and involved explaining provisions for elections to the USSR and LSSR Supreme Soviets and organizing political education circles; these included a brief Visasąjunginė Komunistų Partija (Bolševikai) (VKP(b)) course on history and the Soviet constitution. In December of 1945, sixty meetings of this type were organized in Rokiškis county alone. The meetings run by local departments were not just ideological in nature. Because the Work Among Women Division instructors and women delegate-activists were trained for physical work in the newly established agricultural and industrial companies, a portion of the meetings was also dedicated to practical problems. Twenty-one meetings in June 1948 in Alytus county discussed women's contributions to the harvest. Some meetings, in response to LCP(b) CC requirements, were dedicated to hiring women at various levels of leadership for economic and ideological work: chairs of district executive committees, secretary positions, reserve collection agents and local store managers as well as Work Among Women Division department instructors.[20]

Informally, women's councils which were being established in Lithuania starting in 1948 were also under the purview of the Work Among Women Division.[21] Women's councils would elect a president and secretary; however, their work was unpaid and for this reason, the women's council activities were coordinated by the Work Among Women Division employees. Women delegate-activists and women's council activists became a massive force for women's indoctrination and organization. In 1949, in Kretinga county, 960 women-delegates belonged to the Work Among Women Division departments; there were eighty-eight women's councils with a total of 516 members. That same year, these women in Kretinga county organized 500 meetings which were attended by 12,500 women participants. In addition, two women's conferences took place in Kretinga county. Throughout the county, there were seventeen women's arts clubs, twenty women's groups for analysing agricultural artel laws and five women's groups for eradicating illiteracy.[22] In 1946, the Seventh Lithuanian Communist Party (b) Central Committee plenary boasted that there had been 348 county-wide meetings. In all, 12,950 women had participated, of whom 4,200 were registered as Work Among Women Division delegate-activists. In 1946, 11,000 delegate-activists were chosen from throughout Lithuania. And in 1950, the Vilnius district alone counted 6,000 registered women delegate-activists. There were 6,562 members in 1,089 women's councils in the Vilnius district. The same year, 1950, there were 4,221 women's councils throughout the republic. One can only imagine how many thousands of activists were included in their ranks.[23] The women's councils had fewer members than the so-called women delegate-activists. This is because the women's councils were made up of better-educated women, for example, teachers, doctors and midwives. Meanwhile, for the women delegate-activists it was more important that they be numerous and massive. In 1946, among the 533 Biržai county women delegate-activists, there were 115 illiterate women, 40 self-educated women, 92 who had completed only a few elementary school grades, 275 delegates who had completed elementary school and 11 who had completed some secondary school levels.[24]

Collectivization

In 1948, *kolkhoznik* Senkuvienė gave a talk at the Work Among Women Division meeting. She claimed that the Western press was warning of poor wheat production in Soviet Lithuania and that supposedly the wheat would not be harvested due to labour shortages in the *kolkhozes*. Senkuvienė publicly assured her listeners that the women of her birthplace in the Mokolai district would assume the equal rights that they were being granted and 'refuse to allow such a dishonour'. In other words, they would volunteer and work without pay to make sure that the most important harvest work got done on time.[25] Although the elected women at the massively attended meetings were called 'delegates' or 'women-activists', their purpose was in fact physical or heavy labour on the farms. Unpaid labour at various institutions in the war-scarred nation and ordinary physical labour by women were true goals of gender equality policy in Lithuania. Gender equality and its challenges were without exception a woman's issue; men did not participate.

In the name of equality, women worked the most disparate jobs. They went to the villages in brigades helping mothers of large families and widows of Soviet Army soldiers who had perished in the war with the harvest. Some women activists would spend up to a month in the villages on such missions. They not only worked in the fields, but they also organized the so-called red carts, the mandatory delivery of grain to the state. Woman delegate-activist Apolonija Babickienė worked in one village for five days, organized a red cart and delivered 3,600 kilograms to the obligatory delivery station and 3,000 kilograms of grain to the Fatherland Fund. Women-delegates and the participants of the first Lithuanian collective farm convention were the first to hand over their own family cows, sheep, pigs and poultry. In 1949, in the *volost* of Kavarskas, women established twenty-five livestock farms, donating their personal family wealth. In the Soviet republic, gender equality for women meant joining the Stakhanovite movement and meeting draconian expectations upon the regime's encouragement. Women stoically produced 350 per cent of monthly norms, emphasizing that 'these days' one female worker does 'the work of two men'. In 1948, there were thirty-nine female Stakhanovites registered at the Vilnius light industry factory named Sparta. Women-delegates like actual *kolkhozniks* did not receive compensation for their labour. LCP(b) CC First Secretary A. Sniečkus admitted that the situation at the collective farms was dire. For a single day's work, a worker received 1 kilogram of grain. In 1953, approximately half of the *kolkhozes* in Lithuania did not pay their workers in cash for their labour.

A large group of women delegate-activists was assigned to help the mothers of large families, nursery schools, the elderly and families of Soviet veterans. The delegates provided assistance to families with many children according to the instructions of the 1944 Public Assistance to Mothers of Large Families and Single Mothers Board. As the board was regularly short on full-time, permanent employees, the women-activists fulfilled this function for free. In the villages and small towns, these enthusiasts promoted the *8 July 1944 decree* issued by the Presidium of the Supreme Soviet of the USSR *On State Assistance to Pregnant Women, Mothers of Large Families and Single Mothers; On Enhanced Care for Mothers and Babies; On the Establishment of the Honourable Title 'Mother-Heroine', the Glory to Mothers Order and the Establishment of Medals to Be Awarded to Mothers*. They made lists of mothers of large families and single mothers and encouraged them to draft formal applications for assistance. With the cooperation of employees of the board and women delegate-activists, during the period September 1945–April 1946, they identified 158 mothers of large families in Klaipėda county; these mothers in turn received 322,580 roubles. On average, large families received 2,041 roubles, however, whether the entire assistance made it into the families' hands is not known. Often the funds were not paid out to the mothers directly but were deposited into their bank accounts while the women received worthless government bonds. There were instances of the mothers' documents being forged whilst the money was paid out to fictional mothers.

The Work Among Women Division department instructors and women delegate-activists were also likely not compensated for their work at birthing centres, nursery schools, orphanages and nursing homes. The women reported that the nursery schools they inspected were in a sorry state, the children neglected and the quarters unsanitary. In 1946, the Tauragė county Work Among Women Division department instructors arranged a visit by two rural district social workers to a home for the elderly and disabled. Upon learning that the elderly were hungry, the women had 326 kilograms of various food products delivered. The Tauragė county executive committee also sent the women to the county's orphanage, ordering them to create a commission consisting of twelve women and to inspect the orphanages. The delegates found the home cold and unheated, and the food being served was inadequate. The women knitted thirty-eight pairs of gloves and fifty pairs of socks and brought them to the children.

The Soviet government allocated the most significant assistance to the families of wounded Soviet Army soldiers, and the women delegate-activists were brought in to do this work as well. Delegates were elected to represent the *volosts*, parishes and larger factories. These delegates were responsible for providing assistance to the families of wounded veterans of war and victims who had suffered at the hands of the Lithuanian partisans. In this case, the women with social work experience assumed the functions assigned by the Council of the LSSR People's Commissars for Securing State Provisions and Housing for Military Families which was established in 1944. The women distributed material assistance accordingly. In 1946, records indicate that 1,022 families were receiving this assistance. The delegates visited 700 families and distributed 35,000 units of American charity clothing. A total of 668 families received vouchers for a total 2,749 meters of fabric and 847 pairs of shoes. The delegates also gave out 370 vouchers for various products household items and 683 vouchers enabling recipients to purchase ready-made clothing. They distributed grain, lard, sugar and flour to veterans' families. Although the Council of the LSSR People's Commissars for Securing State Provisions and Housing for Military Families had state funding and human resources, and governing boards had been established by city, district and county executive committees, the elected delegate-inspectors and rank-and-file delegates did not receive any financial compensation for their work.

The Work Among Women Division department instructors and women delegate-activists attempted to secure financial resources 'for rebuilding the people's economy' and 'for revitalizing the agricultural sector'. It is not known how much they were able to raise, but the activists went from village to village seeking donations. More was expected from wealthier farmers: 'Average farmer' Izabelė Levickienė from Simnas *volost* gave them 3,000 roubles, and 'pauper' Adelė Blažaitienė donated 150 roubles. Full-time staff and activists of the Work

Among Women Division departments were encouraged to sell subscriptions to Soviet publications and to buy subscriptions themselves as well, thus ensuring Soviet newspapers would get sold out. The women sold the newspaper and magazine subscriptions and books by Soviet authors for a predetermined sum. At a women's meeting in Alytus county in 1948, delegate-activist Makauskienė committed to distributing Soviet periodicals during the month of December for 1,100 roubles. Unfortunately, nobody wanted the literature she was offering, and Makauskienė did not meet her quota. But in the same county, in Butrimoniai *volost*, the delegates were successful in selling forty-five copies of the official newspaper *Tiesa* eighty copies of *Valstiečių laikraštis* (The Farmers' Newspaper), 100 copies of the local newspaper *Tarybinė Dzūkija* (Soviet Dzūkija), twenty copies of the newspaper *Komjaunimo tiesa*, and six copies of the Russian-language newspaper *Sovietskaja Litva* (Soviet Lithuania). Women were encouraged to read Russian authors; lists included books like Sholokhov's *The Don Flows Home to the Sea*, Fadeyev's *The Young Guard*, Tolstoy's *Anna Karenina* and Malov's *With All My Heart*. Reading Soviet books was also organized and planned. In 1953, a Šiauliai district department report on levels of progressiveness and education of the women of the region cited a woman who had read sixty recommended Soviet books over the course of eight months.[26]

Towards doing propaganda work, Work Among Women Division departments committed themselves to holding two agitprop meetings per month. Homemakers were some of the most desired participants of these meetings, which encouraged the women to leave their homes, get government-paid jobs and become politically active. But in general, each department came up with as many different and convincing ways possible to influence homemakers into changing their lifestyle. In 1946, Tauragė county homemakers were invited to the LCP(b) CC hall in Tauragė, and in this unfamiliar environment, they listened to a lecture about how they could ensure that their republic would achieve the goals of its five-year plan. The women delegate-activists also organized programmes for eradicating illiteracy and ran reading and writing circles. In 1948, a Marijampolė county Kalvarija *volost* circle was recognized for teaching twenty-two illiterate women to read.[27]

The activism of Work Among Women Division department organizers and delegates was a completely new experience for Lithuanian women and required a considerable amount of time and energy; however, it wasn't just the exhausting activism, jobs in factories, offices and collective farms, and the difficulty of juggling all this with household labour for their own families that marked post-war women's lives: their male colleagues did not value the ideals of gender equality, and the society belittled women activists and quite often was openly hostile towards them.

Men, women and class conflict

Although gender equality was official Soviet government policy, it was not supported by rank-and-file party members or government functionaries, especially men. Not only did proponents of gender equality not find agreement, support, useful advice or help, but quite often their colleagues openly belittled and humiliated them. During joint district central committee meetings, party secretaries would discuss everything but women's issues. Many Work Among Women Division department directors were also deputy political department directors, but their supervisors ignored their female colleagues and did their best to discredit them and their work. If their assistants travelled to the provinces on matters related to the Work Among Women Division, their supervisors would mark them absent from work. Although the Work Among Women Division was an official part of the Soviet government structures and administratively belonged to the LCP(b) CC and acting committees, political department directors typically just ignored them. Work Among Women Division directors and instructors reported that political department directors not only did not help them in their work, but often hindered them. The Panevėžys county Troškūnai *volost* party organizer belittled all the units' initiatives and called the activists hags (*bobos*). The women who toiled in the fields for no pay were given the poorest equipment which made it practically impossible for them to meet their quotas.

The new functionaries of the Soviet structures were annoyed by women's challenges to patriarchal stereotypes. In addition, activists and Work Among Women Division staff began to actively and diligently discuss the so-called maladies of Soviet life: theft, fraud, negligence and incidences of corruption, often engaged in by their own supervisors. When a commission of the Krekenavas *volost* women delegate-activists from Panevėžys county discovered 30 kilograms of stolen sugar in their cafeteria and notified the local party organizer about this, he became livid. Shouting, he berated the women: 'I'll send you to the prosecutor if you keep sticking your nose in other people's business like this.'[28] And in Mažeikiai county, Židikai *volost*, party organizer Gabalis outright refused to associate with the employees of the Work Among Women Division. On 20 July 1946, he was invited to give a talk at a women's conference. Some participants had travelled 10–15 kilometres from various villages, but Gabalis didn't show up. At the end of July, he was asked to organize a meeting for the Work Among Women Division employees in Mažeikiai, but he never ordered horses for the carriages resulting in some organizers having to travel on foot, some upwards 29 kilometres. And the party organizer from Veiviržinai, in response to a newly elected organizer's request to help host a meeting, responded: 'Outrageous. If I go, I'll hold the meeting myself. I have no interest in keeping company with those hags.'[29]

The new party functionaries' behaviour towards the women activists was arrogant and inappropriate. Some even assigned the women tasks that they themselves feared or avoided. In addition to providing assistance to mothers of large families and the elderly, the women activists were forced to investigate the theft of state wealth and deal with farmers who were hiding their wealth. Homemaker delegate-activists were tasked with reporting and clarifying financial improprieties in store book-keeping to the local government. Thanks to the women's audits, employees newly appointed by the regime lost their positions; they were punished, and their cases were brought to the prosecutor. Because the Work Among Women delegate-activists knew the people living in the surrounding villages and parishes, they were obliged to investigate farmers' hidden animals and grain and to inform on them. The delegates of Debeikiai *volost* in Utena county made plans to 'out' the *kulaks* and locate their hidden wealth. Each of the delegate-activists of the *volost* committed to finding at least one hidden cow per month and promised to reveal information about the anti-Soviet partisans still underground in their region.[30] They also inspected milk collection centres, making sure the milk was not being diluted with water.

During the peak of the partisan war, some women delegate-activists were encouraged to work as informants for state security. In this capacity, the activists once again called on the help of other women. In 1948, in Alytus *volost*, delegate Monika Uscilienė gathered information from the village women about the partisan stronghold in the village of Karklynai in Raudonikiai *volost*. Uscilienė immediately informed the Ministry for State Security of Soviet Union (MGB[31]) staff about this and accompanied them to the village. As one would expect, they found a group of men who had come from the forest. As the report states, one of the men was shot, but the others managed to run away. The report also indicated that Uscilienė helped provide information about many other matters of importance to the regime.[32] Other women participated in the nationalizing of the Lithuanian population's private property, and in some cases, they even appropriated the property of those being deported to exile. In 1948, the Anykščiai county Work Among Women Division department director brought out a chest full of items confiscated from the villagers; she took for herself a coat, Persian rug and dishes.[33] These women's service to the regime was not unobserved by Lithuanians actively resisting occupation; the women were thus risking the lives of their families as well as their own. The women activists' dissemination of Soviet propaganda, work in the Soviet administrative structures, loyalty and help to the government, informing on partisans and direct assistance to Soviet security organs led to resentment and hatred by civilians and partisans alike. Many of the women activists were badly beaten and their hair was cut short. Ten women activists became targets of the partisans and were assassinated.

The end of gender equality

The extreme gender equality policies of the post-war period in the Soviet Union were enacted under economic and political turmoil and the women's activism was exploited for difficult and often dangerous work. In 1955, the LCP(b) Work Among Women Division and its departments in the rural districts and cities was shut down, their functions handed over to the LCP(b) Communist Party Propaganda and Agitation Department. The elimination of the division and its departments marked the end of the active pursuit of gender equality policy in Soviet Lithuania. The work of the women organizers, delegates and other activists had nonetheless achieved its goal. The number of women actively engaging in the new Soviet reality increased by the day; the women were not only driven by fear, but by duty and an inner need to be active citizens and to work outside the confines of the home. In 1948, Neveravičienė, an ordinary *kolkhoz* worker in Alytus *volost*, reporting on a whole array of completed tasks, realized that she had undertaken the work because of encouragement she'd received at the women's meetings. In her words: 'I met my public obligations 100 per cent. I brought in 50 kilograms of grain above the quota, and 100 kilograms of potatoes ... I also bought a Soviet book for 20 roubles. And I invite all women to buy at least one book.'[34]

Laws enacting the universal employment of women remained on the books and were continually corrected and improved until the collapse of the USSR. The *27 May 1961 decree of the Presidium of the Lithuanian SSR (LSSR) Supreme Soviet* ordered that individuals avoiding work should be moved out of their place of residence and punished with corrective measures, such as the garnishing of 10 per cent of their wages. If these individuals continued to refuse to work in the service of society, the LSSR Penal Code provided for imprisonment and mandatory corrective labour. In the following and subsequent years, the

Presidium of the LSSR Council of Ministers intensified the battle with men and women classified as parasites, living antisocially several times. In 1970, the LCP(b) CC and LSSR Council of Ministers' resolution appointed city and district executive committees to systematically target unemployed 'parasites', to find them quickly and to put them to work. It is thus not surprising that the number of working women in Lithuania continued to increase. In 1959, in Soviet Lithuania, 66.3 per cent of all adult women were working outside the confines of the family home, while in 1979, the number of women working full-time had increased to 83.3 per cent.[35]

The shuttering of the Work Among Women Division marked the abrupt end of the period of Stalinist gender equality policies. But it also marked the beginning of formal gender equality policies in Lithuania, whereby women's accomplishments in various sectors began to be evaluated exclusively through numbers and statistics. This tendency began in the post-war era, when Soviet ministries were required to provide statistics on women and the Work Among Women Division used these figures to author reports about enacting gender equality in the republic. At every level, the reports viewed gender equality very narrowly as merely formal statistics on the number of women specialists: '1,682 of 2,389 doctors were women', or the increasing number of Communist Party members who were women: 'in 1953, 30 per cent of all communists in the Tauragė district were women, and women made up 14 per cent of the newly joined party members in 1953. The ranks of young women in the Komsomol were greater, making up 53 per cent of all members.'[36]

Throughout the life of the Soviet state, *gender* remained a fundamental category of Soviet ideology, although gender equality policies in public and private life applied only to women. From the very beginning of gender equality, this Soviet policy's goal was to free Lithuanian women from the confines of the 'bourgeois' family in order to transform them into a large, and until then, unexploited source of labour power. The regime never attempted to change the foundations of patriarchal stereotypes about men's and women's roles.[37] The bureaucratic Soviet system was aggressive towards all citizens; however, women experienced double burden and double discrimination. In government work, women were paid one-third less than their male colleagues, and when they came home, the tasks of homemaking awaited them: long hours of housework, childcare, and, often, violence which the state refused to recognize. By the end of the 1960s, women across the Soviet Union, received approximately 60 per cent of men's wages and this percentage did not change until the 1990s. Opportunities for women to participate in decision-making were frozen in a formal quota system. The number of women members deputed in the LSSR Supreme Soviet never changed. In 1967, women comprised 32.4 per cent; in 1971, 32.33 per cent; in 1975, the number was 34 per cent; and in 1980, 35 per cent.[38]

The legal foundations of public assistance to families

The 8 July 1944 decree of the Presidium of the USSR Supreme Soviet of the USSR adopted the decree *On State Assistance to Pregnant Women, Mothers of Large Families and Single Mothers; On Enhanced Care for Mothers and Babies; On the Establishment of the Honourable Title 'Mother-Heroine', the Glory to Mothers Order and the Establishment of Medals to Be Awarded to Mothers*. The ruling was automatically incorporated into the Lithuanian legal system immediately after the war and became the first law in Soviet Lithuania that provided aid to mothers. It lengthened maternity leave to seventy-seven calendar days, offered financial aid after birth, aimed to expand the kindergarten-nursery network and established mother and child medical clinics. On 1 April 1956, the Presidium of the USSR Supreme Soviet further lengthened pregnancy and maternity leave from 77 days to 112 calendar days. In other words, all mothers, with the exception of *kolkhoz* workers, were granted eight fully paid weeks of maternity leave before birth and the same number of weeks afterwards. The 1944 decree was not universal however. It provided only one-time or monthly payments to mothers of certain categories. Single mothers, for example, received one-time or monthly payments for each child, beginning with the first. Mothers of large families and widows received only one-time payments beginning with the third child, and monthly payments starting with the fourth. Monthly payments began when the child reached 2 years of age and were halted when the child turned five. In Kaunas in June 1945, payments to mothers of large families and single mothers were given out to only 193 women; of these 90 per cent were workers.[39] In the case of the death of the mother, the husband or legal guardian would continue to receive payments. The press criticized this law's inefficiencies including delayed payments or awards and backlogs in processing the mothers' identification booklets required for receiving aid; there were also instances of overpayments.[40] The *18 March 1954 decree of the Presidium of the USSR Supreme Soviet* once again emphasized the importance of timeliness in awarding medals and orders to mothers of large families, as well as the honorary title 'Mother Heroine'.[41] Although the issuing of orders, medals and honorary titles should not be considered direct assistance to families, the mothers who received these awards gained rights to certain social benefits.

In terms of getting financial assistance to mothers, the law was not effective because mothers of large families and single mothers were not the primary beneficiaries of needed aid in Lithuania. The *8 July 1944 decree* did not provide financial assistance to families raising one or two children, and two-children families were indeed the most common in Soviet Lithuania. Quite often, the press was silent on this matter and would discuss the law as universal, concerning itself with the social welfare of all mothers and their babies. In actuality, assistance even to large families was meagre throughout the Soviet era. Until the close of the 1970s, the material condition of large families was considerably worse than that of families with one or two children. Because the newspapers, radio and TV trumpeted Soviet government assistance, the rest of society was convinced that these families enjoyed exceptional conditions and rights to special privileges, including access to special stores and special access to state-distributed apartments. But in reality, only 10 per cent of large families interviewed confirmed the above assumptions to be accurate. A more realistic view of the everyday reality of large families shows that, essentially, a large proportion lived close to poverty level. Only 62 per cent of large families had their own apartment; 56 per cent of parents spoke of a negative view of large families by the society as a whole.[42]

On the other hand, and this was critical, the law mandated the administration of medical clinics for all expectant mothers and mothers raising small children. Every clinic housed a so-called milk kitchen, which provided complimentary food for babies up to four months.[43] This universal healthcare for mothers and their infants was also considered public assistance to families. The law provided that all expectant mothers living in cities – from the sixth month of pregnancy to the fourth month of nursing – could expect additional food provisions: butter, sugar, grains and milk. The law also provided a lump sum payment to all new mothers for their babies' material needs: mothers of babies born in the city received a one-time payment of 120 roubles, while mothers of babies born in the villages received care packages containing no fewer than ten textile and industrial items.[44] The procedure for mothers of large families and single mothers was different; they received their products individually. Mothers of large families and single mothers enjoyed several additional social benefits besides financial assistance and product packages: their rent, childcare and nursery school payments were reduced.

The *8 July 1944 decree* sought to increase the number of childcare facilities for preschool-aged children. In the fall of 1944, there were 119 preschools in Lithuania. In 1947, there were 192, which were attended by about 7,500 children.[45] Nonetheless, it was not until the beginning of the 1980s that the more or less universal provisions for creches and preschools in Lithuania were instituted. There weren't enough preschools, and the Soviet press had no qualms about discussing this well-known fact. In 1947, in Kaunas, the second largest city in Lithuania, there were only five creches with a total of 260 beds. Yet, 2,349 mothers with the right to a one-time payment and monthly assistance after birth (i.e. single mothers or mothers of large families with three or more children) were registered in Kaunas.[46] The situation did not improve. In 1954, the principal LCP newspaper *Tiesa* wrote that there were practically no plans for establishing preschools in the republic's *kolkhozes*.

Adapted Soviet legal acts that guaranteed assistance to families of veterans who died at war were by no means effective in providing aid to the Lithuanian families of the time. Lithuania had fewer war-scarred regions and fewer war widows. The 28 October 1944 Presidium of the LSSR Supreme Soviet decree established a Military Families' Public Assistance and Housing Procurement Executive Board Under the Council of the LSSR People's Commissars. The board's departments were established under the executive committees at the city, district and county levels, and, after the 1950 Administrative Reforms, at district-level executive committees. The board and its departments were charged with providing pensions and benefits to families of the Soviet Army and Navy rank-and-file and commanders. The board was concerned with securing employment and well-being for the military family members.[47] Eight years later, on 7 March 1952, the Presidium of the LSSR Supreme Soviet adopted the resolution *On Supplemental Public Assistance for the Families of Veterans Wounded or Perished in the War*. The resolution provided that, at their request, the families of fallen Soviet Army soldiers and Soviet partisans should be provided with employment by 1 June 1952. The resolution also required families of fallen soldiers of the Soviet Army be accommodated with apartments without queue, with all renovations taken care of, and the families' general well-being attended to.[48] But this law too only applied to a small number of Lithuanian inhabitants. Men born between 1875 and 1915 typically married at age 33. We can assume that a large number of those who fought in the Soviet Army and died at war were young and unmarried men. Thus, assistance to families of those who perished in the war would be significant, and real assistance in Soviet republics where human losses were incomparably higher than those suffered in Lithuania and where the average age at marriage was lower. It is precisely in Slavic republics such as Russia, Belarus and Ukraine where traditionally the age at marriage is much lower than in Lithuania. To a great extent, the law was useful to Soviet Army soldiers from other Soviet republics who were transferred to live in Lithuania after the war.

Social assistance for families of soldiers who had died at war was administered for twenty-five years after the war. On 4 June 1970, the LSSR Council of Ministers passed a resolution regarding further improvements to housing for fallen soldiers' families, although the veterans' children by that time were already adults and part of the workforce. Point by point, the resolution unequivocally created an exceptional situation in society for these families. The very first point of the resolution required not only that the families of fallen soldiers be provided with apartments, but also that, within a two- to three-year span, their housing conditions be improved.[49] Social assistance for the families of fallen soldiers was the principal task of the permanent Social Welfare Commission of the LSSR Local Deputies' Councils. Such permanent commissions were established by the *21 July 1951 resolution of the Presidium of the LSSR Supreme Soviet*. At first glance, the permanent social welfare commissions' regulations had declared that the purpose of the resolution was to provide assistance to all Lithuanian families. Yet, point thirty-four of the statute required that the social welfare commission assist only the families of fallen Soviet soldiers. Paragraph (a) required the commission to procure pension payments for the families of fallen Soviet soldiers, and paragraph (c) ensured that the families of fallen soldiers would indeed receive the benefits the law provided for them.[50]

Assistance to needy families with disabled children

On 29 August 1965, the LSSR Supreme Soviet adopted the resolution *On the Free Transportation of Schoolchildren Residing in Rural Areas*. The resolution provided schoolchildren with the right to transportation to and from school via shuttle bus, intercity and local trains and *kolkhoz* transport.[51] However, on 12 January 1966, the LSSR Council of Ministers' resolution greatly limited the children's right to complimentary transport. Point four of the ratified resolution stipulated that pupils could travel on the previously mentioned means of transportation only during the schoolyear and only if there were free seats available. Pupils were forbidden from taking advantage of this benefit en route to cultural institutions or excursions. They were also forbidden from carrying luggage except for books or educational materials. In addition, free transportation was only valid within a 20-kilometre zone. Some of the limitations were exempt if the child lived on the grounds of a boarding school for the needy or a general secondary school dormitory. In such cases, the pupil could return to the dormitory on workdays as well as on holidays, was also allowed to have larger bags on their person and could travel distances in excess of 20 kilometres.[52]

On 3 December 1965, the LSSR Council of Ministers' resolution *Regarding Measures for Further Increasing Food Production to Ensure That Children Are Fed* authorized city and district executive committees to coordinate free meals for young children from large and needy families. Although free infant formula was introduced on 11 March 1960 by a resolution adopted by the LCP(b) CC and the Lithuanian Council of Ministers, the 1965 ruling provided additional free meals.[53]

In 1967, for the first time social assistance to families raising children with disabilities was considered. On 7 December of the same year, the LSSR Council of Ministers adopted the resolution *On Monthly Allowances for Those Disabled Since Childhood*. Although the assistance payments were meagre, totalling barely more than 10 roubles, the ruling was notable as it actually acknowledged the existence of such families and set the stage for further development of the legal framework.[54] The benefits were paid when the disabled child turned 16 and were considered to be his or her unemployment compensation. The press apathetically depicted the resolution as 'generous assistance to families'. This assertion was obviously disingenuous, because the actual amount of the benefit was spelled out: 'They [disabled children] are paid a monthly benefit of 16 roubles when they turn sixteen.'[55]

Trends in public assistance to families in the early 1970s

Besides maternal and pregnancy leave and childcare protections, laws ensuring universal financial assistance to families were passed only thirty years later. In 1970, two resolutions that ensured material and basic financial assistance to teenagers who had lost the guardianship of either one or both parents were adopted. The 30 March resolution *On Providing for Students Attending Vocational, Technical and Specialized Secondary School Who Are Orphans or Who Have Lost Their Parental Guardians* established norms for orphans regarding footwear, clothing, food and an additional monthly allowance of 5 roubles.[56] Moreover, the LSSR Council of Ministers' resolution *On the Payment of Assistance to Students of General Secondary Schools, Grades One Through Eleven, Having Lost the Primary Breadwinner in Their Families* guaranteed financial assistance until the child completed secondary school, regardless of whether he or she was of age 18.[57]

Through the 1 June 1970 ordinance, the Soviet government not only recognized mothers as children's caregivers and educators but also acknowledged that fathers too received social assistance. The LSSR Ministers' Council ordinance *On Reductions in Child Support for Fathers While Their Child Is Not Attending Childcare Institutions during the Father's Annual Holiday* was a revision of the 1948 law which provided for an exemption only during mother's annual vacation.[58] In the early 1970s, other areas of family social assistance, until then considered peripheral, began to be addressed. The 30 October 1973 LSSR Council of Ministers' ordinance *On the Regulation of Room and Board for Pupils Attending Boarding Schools for the Needy* restructured the fees paid by parents for room and board. From then on, fees were waived if the child missed five days of school in a row due to illness or vacation.[59] This ordinance demonstrates that through flexible fee structures, the Soviet government was trying to improve social assistance to families by encouraging various forms of assistance. Beginning 1 December 1973, for the first time in thirty years, female collective farm workers had the right to the same maternal benefits and the same pregnancy and maternity leave as office workers and manual labourers.[60] The 25 August 1974 Presidium of the USSR Supreme Soviet edict introduced universal financial assistance to children of all low-income families.

The administration of summer holidays for children and adolescents was a significant and fairly effective form of universal social assistance to families. On 2 April 1973, the LCP(b) CC, the LSSR Council of Ministers and the LSSR Council of Trade Unions adopted the joint resolution *On Measures for Further Improving the Management of Summer Recreation for Children and Adolescents*. The resolution confirmed the responsibility of its executors. Responsibilities were shared by various ministries in charge of children's recreation: the Ministry of Education oversaw the work of summer camp directors and educators; the LCP(b) CC and the Ministry of Higher Education and Specialized Secondary Education supervised the senior 'Young Pioneer' leaders and platoon leaders; the Ministry of Higher and Specialized Secondary Education and the Ministry of Education supervised the music programme directors; the Ministry of Higher and Specialized Secondary Education and the Committee on Physical Education and Sports supervised physical education directors and swimming instructors; doctors reported to the Health Ministry; and qualified cooks reported to the Ministry of Commerce and the Lithuanian Union of Consumer Cooperatives.[61] It appears that the abundance of supervising agencies did not create confusion and the administration of student recreation in Soviet Lithuania was one of the most successful initiatives for providing social support to families. Indeed, during the early 1980s, approximately 400,000 children spent their summer holidays at pioneer camps, recreation centres and preschools. Nearly half received complimentary travel vouchers; others were partially subsidized. Families with two or more children, children of single mothers and boarding school students received preference for travel vouchers to the summer camps. In 1985, 436,000 children were accepted to summer camps; in 1978, there had been only 353,000.[62]

During the final decade of the Soviet Union, two government resolutions on universal social assistance for families with children and on protections for maternity were adopted. On 11 May 1981, the LCP(b) CC and the Lithuanian Council of Ministers approved the resolution *On Means for Increasing State Assistance for Families with Children and Improving the Demographic Situation in the Republic*. The resolution attempted to stabilize the consistently declining birth rate; it provided parental leave for up to one year, paying 35 roubles per month, and guaranteed the right to unpaid leave until the child was 18 months old. It also ensured a monthly payment of 20 roubles to single mothers until their child reached 16 years of age. The resolution, which went into effect in 1982, further expanded the network of preschool institutions and summer Young Pioneers camps, lengthened the school day and expanded after-school programmes and also included plans to expand boarding school and orphanage networks as another form of assistance to families and orphans. Starting in 1985, the resolution would apply to single fathers raising more than one child under the age of 12. In 1987, the resolution *On Improving the Ability of Mothers to Reconcile the Responsibilities of Work and Home* was adopted. Women raising children under the age of 8 were entitled to work part time. On 22 March 1989, the LSSR Supreme Soviet legalized by decree eighteen months of paid parental leave and three years unpaid leave but maintaining seniority. Monthly benefits were increased to 50 roubles during the care of the child until he or she was 12 months old and 35 roubles, until 18 months; an amount 70 roubles was allocated for disabled children until the age of 16.[63]

After the 1990s, the independent Lithuanian republic sought to lengthen maternity leave and increase monthly benefits. On 8 March 1991, the Lithuanian government adopted the resolution *On Benefits to Women Raising Children Under the Age of Three*. Although the title referred only to mothers, the resolution provided assistance to working parents, mothers or fathers. Parents caring for children until the age of 18 months were compensated with a monthly allowance equal to 100 per cent of minimum wage, and 50 per cent of minimum wage for children not attending any preschool institutions until the age of 3.

The administration of social assistance to mothers of large families or single mothers

On the 1 January 1944, the LSSR People's Commissariat for Finance was re-established and within its confines the Office of State Benefits for Mothers of Large Families and Single Mothers (OSBMLFSM) began to function. The goal of the agency was to ensure financial assistance, guaranteed by the *1936 Soviet Family and Marriage Code* which had automatically gone into effect in the Lithuanian territory, to the women of these two groups. However, its actual mission was the enforcement of the *8 July 1944 decree* of the Presidium of the Supreme Soviet of the USSR *On State Assistance to Pregnant Women, Mothers of Large Families and Single Mothers; On Enhanced Care for Mothers and Babies; On the Establishment of the Honourable Title 'Mother-Heroine', the Glory to Mothers Order and the Establishment of Medals to Be Awarded to Mothers*.

The OSBMLFSM and its local branches was the principal institution which provided Lithuanian mothers of large families and single mothers financial assistance. M. Kymantaitė was appointed its first director; her mission was to design its organizational structure, hire employees, and set the activities of the office in motion. Among other initiatives, the new director organized the first training session in Vilnius for the staff of the OSBMLFSM branches.[64] Kymantaitė's initiatives, however, were not appreciated and the Soviet and republic leadership were consistently unhappy with the OSBMLFSM's work in Lithuania. The 10 May 1950 USSR Finance Minister's decree removed Kymantaitė from her responsibilities and on 1 June 1956, the office itself was dismantled, and its functions transferred to the LSSR Ministry of Social Welfare. The unproductive and chaotic functioning of the OSBMLFSM was not only due to staff shortages, incompetence and simple dishonesty. The main reason it failed was the automatic and formal transposition of the Soviet *8 July 1944 decree* to Lithuania, a law which had little bearing on the contemporary demographic realities, hopes and historically formed traditions and values of the Lithuanian family.

The *8 July 1944 decree* was a fundamental law of the USSR, in force in every Soviet republic, providing for lump sum and monthly cash benefits to mothers of large families and single mothers. But the law was not universal. Single mothers received one-time, lump sum and monthly benefits upon the birth of each child, starting with the first one. Mothers of large families and widows received their lump sum and monthly benefits only upon the birth of their third child; their first two children were not eligible. With the birth of the third child, the mothers received 400 roubles in a one-time, lump sum payment. Upon the birth of the fourth child, they would receive a lump sum payment of 1,300 roubles and 80 roubles per month thereafter. Upon the birth of the fifth child, they would receive 1,700 roubles and 120 roubles per month, respectively; 2,000 roubles and 140 per month for the sixth; 2,500 roubles and 200 per month for the seventh; likewise, 2,500 roubles and 200 per month for the eighth; 3,500 roubles, 250 per month for the ninth; and likewise, 3,500 roubles and 250 per month for the tenth child. Every child henceforth was guaranteed a one-time payment of 5,000 roubles and 300 roubles per month.[65] It was expected that the new benefits law would guarantee assistance to the neediest families. But the transfer of the *8 July 1944 Law* to Lithuania was not effective because the republic's demographics differed from those of other Soviet republics, particularly Central Asia.

The *8 July 1944 decree* was dedicated to providing assistance to families raising more than three children because the state only guaranteed monthly benefits starting with the fourth child. However large families had never been the norm in Lithuania. The number of children in interwar Lithuanian families resembled the typical nuclear family. The families of farmers or urban workers were slightly larger (on average, 5.2 and 3.2 children per family, respectively) and fewer in white collar worker families (2.6–3.4 children per family).[66] Starting with the onset of the Second World War, the birth rate in Lithuania consistently decreased. If, before the war, there had been 23.5 births in a typical Lithuanian village of 1,000 inhabitants, by the end of the 1940s, the number of births per 1,000 inhabitants was down to 16.1. Although in Russia the birth rate had also begun to decline before the war, it nonetheless remained greater than that of Lithuania. In 1926, in Russia, the relative birth rate was 6.38, meanwhile in 1923, in Lithuania, it approached 3.4. In 1936, the relative birth rate in Russia fell to 4.74, while in 1937, in Lithuania, it was down to 2.6. Ten years after the war, in 1959, in the Lithuanian capital Vilnius, the relative birth rate was only 1.8.[67] The birth rate in four collective farms in various regions of Lithuania from 1951 to 1953 recorded the following results: only one in four collective farm families had an average of 3.2 children. In the remaining three *kolkhozes*, the average number of children per family was, respectively, 2.6, 2.1 and 2.7.[68] These numbers attest to the fact that, on average, mothers had the right to claim state financial assistance upon the birth of their third child in only one out of three collective farms, and this assistance amounted to one lump sum payment.

In 1951, Lithuania's population was 2.3 million, that is almost 10 per cent lower than in 1945.[69] Interviews indicate that, in post-war Lithuania, married couples did not plan for more than two children. In 1947, in Lithuania there were 24,600 marriages and 59,700 newborns.[70] Not counting babies that didn't survive to see their first birthdays, in 1947, the average number of children per family was 2.4. Thus, only a very small percentage of Lithuanian families had the right to claim the lump sum financial assistance guaranteed by the *8 July 1944 decree*, and an even smaller number of families could count on the monthly benefits starting with the birth of their fourth child.

Plans and projects

One of the first tasks of the OSBMLFSM was to inform the Lithuanian public about the *8 July 1944 decree* and its guaranteed benefits. Because the OSBMLFSM and its branches answered to the People's Commissariat for Finance (later the Finance Ministry), the latter provided general methodological instructions on how to most effectively carry out this project. On 6 October 1945, the LSSR Deputy Commissar for Finance Jonas Genys warned that, according to his sources, some OSBMLFSM branches were only going through the motions of informing county and city residents about the financial support available to mothers made possible by the law. According to Genys, the workers were waiting for the mothers to find out about their rights on their own and then apply for assistance. He advised the staff to discuss the law with local newspaper editors, encouraging them to publish information about the benefits and honorary awards available to mothers of large families.[71]

Each OSBMLFSM branch initiated its own set of methods and means to disseminate information about the benefits. The OSBMLFSM branch in the city of Vilnius proposed calling together every building manager of every district in the capital and explaining the *8 July 1944 decree* to them. They also talked about passing out posters that publicized the law to the building managers and commissioning them to make lists of mothers of large families and single mothers in order to explain the decree to them individually. The Vilnius branch also planned to release informational literature in the newspaper and to involve union members in disseminating information about the law. There were proposals to provide local *militsiya* department chiefs with posters and ask them to discuss the law with their subordinates. Posters were to be hung up in women's medical clinics, creches, nursery schools and hospitals.[72] In 1946, the Šiauliai county OSBMLFSM branch anticipated assistance from local women's councils. The branch planned to call a meeting of activists from women's councils in their *volost* to instruct the activists about the importance of the law.[73] In 1947, the Prienai county branch's instructions were urgent; they required all women with the right to assistance be identified for the period from 25 November 1947 to 20 December 1947; meanwhile, the law was to be explained to mothers of large families and single mothers in executive committees and district labour councils.[74]

Several times a year, the OSBMLFSM board would organize three- or five-day seminars for branch staff. Director Kymantaitė would normally invite the senior inspector-auditor to the 'briefings' in Vilnius. She would advise them that attendance was mandatory and that seminar participants should not forget to bring their food ration cards because 'they would not be served meals in Vilnius'.[75] From 1944 to 1952, the schedules and programmes of the seminars never varied. Enacting the mission in the provinces was likely a challenge for the board and its branches, and workers always brought up the very same problems: first and foremost, their attempt to promote the benefits programmes more intensively. Seminars were also dedicated to drawing up quarterly work plans and the benefits payment process – although the latter had not changed since the very establishment of the board in 1944. The seminars also touched on individual instances of benefits payments as well as clerical work in the organization.[76] Parallel with the seminars, medals and orders would be awarded to mothers of large families. An anniversary seminar celebrating three years since the *8 July 1944 decree* was held between 7 July and 10 July 1947. Director Kymantaitė and the LSSR Ministry of Finance Party Organization Secretary Bašlakovas gave the keynote address. In his remarks about the anniversary, Bašlakovas highlighted the importance of the office and urged its staff to work 'like Kalinin: quickly, honestly, fairly and without falling prey to bureaucracy'.[77]

Promoting the *8 July 1944 decree* was a regular part of the OSBMLFSM's agenda. The LSSR Finance Ministry would report on their progress promoting the law among the populace directly to the Presidium of the LSSR Supreme Soviet. In 1946, the LSSR Deputy Finance Minister J. Genys,[78] in his report to Chairman of the Presidium J. Paleckis, wrote that from 8 July 1944 to 1 July 1946, on the occasion of the first and second anniversaries of the law, they had advertised on the radio; published eight articles in the republic-wide press and six articles in the local press; held informational meetings on the law at factories and apartment building offices; printed 5,000 posters and distributed them in the villages; and organized formal ceremonies to honour the mothers.[79]

Designing quarterly work plans was an equally important part of the agenda of the OSBMLFSM and its branches. Every branch would prepare slightly different plans but they all were grounded in the same principle of socialist planning, that is their projections of the number of mothers to be supported and awarded with medals were hypothetical. In 1946, the Vilkaviškis county branch's fourth quarter work plan anticipated 150 cases of mothers who would be receiving financial assistance and 100 to be receiving medals. The branch's work plan also estimated that they would be interviewing fifteen mothers in their homes and conducting information sessions on the *8 July 1944 decree* once a week at the birthing centres.[80] In the same year, the Šakiai county branch's fourth quarter work plan focused more on awards for large families. The Šakiai branch's plan anticipated giving out awards to forty mothers in October, and another thirty in December.[81] The 1947 third quarter work plan for the central office of the OSBMLFSM was funded in roubles: in the third quarter, the plan budgeted 500,000 roubles for mothers of large families and single mothers. Of this amount, 150,000 roubles would be paid out in July; 150,000 in August; and 200,000 roubles in September. The Office also committed to presenting ninety mothers with honorary orders and medals.[82]

There can be no doubt that the number of beneficiaries projected by the OSBMLFSM's quarterly plans seriously complicated the office's day-to-day work because they were forced to locate the number of mothers of large families and single mothers that their plans had projected for. The normal Soviet economic practice of falsifying indicators in this instance was no easy task because the plans referred to actual citizens and there was no way to ignore 'living' indicators. The LSSR Finance Ministry, after perusing the OSBMLFSM governing board's 1946 third quarter work plan, had no significant comments, but they did note that it lacked 'socialist competition and rationalization proposals'.[83] In other words, the quarterly plans had to anticipate ever-improving results and reflect the ever-increasing number of celebrated mothers of large families. The OSBMLFSM soon learnt how to respond to such criticisms and demands by the Soviet government to improve fourth quarter work plan indicators. The LSSR Finance Ministry observed that Director Kymantaitė had not gone to Šiauliai where, according to the 1946 fourth quarter work plan, she was supposed to inform mothers about their rights to assistance. In response to accusations, Kymantaitė explained that the office's inspector, Dobužinksas, who was administering the same quarterly plan in a different city, Tauragė, had been detained there, his work taking longer than expected. Thus, Kymantaitė explained, Dobužinksas had met their quota of hours spent in political canvassing in Šiauliai as required by the quarterly work plan.[84]

However, from 1947 on, the Soviet and republic governments were requiring increasingly more detailed quarterly work plans from the OSBMLFSM and its branch offices. Accordingly, the Jurbarkas branch's work plan foresaw regularly investigating the files of mothers of large families in order to keep track of the women who were not collecting assistance, and to visit their homes to find out why. The staff of the Pagėgiai county branch committed to locating thirty additional mothers of large families eligible for benefits per month.[85] Accordingly, the number of falsified cases in the mothers' files increased: deceased children as well as babies who had never been born were included in the counts. After 1947, the work plans shifted their focus to giving out awards to mothers of large families. The pretext for this requirement was a report given at the LSSR Supreme Soviet Presidium awards by the director of the accounting and registration group. The report also claimed that since the law went into effect in 1944 until 1947, in the counties of Alytus, Biržai, Lazdijai, Trakai, Rokiškis and Zarasai, and the cities of Klaipėda and Panevėžys taken together, a mere 855 mothers had been recognized, and that was not enough. The report also noted that 'during the past fourteen months' only six mothers of large families had been located in Alytus county. The report evaluated the work of the OSBMLFSM and, in particular, provided negative feedback on Director Kymantaitė's work. The Presidium of the LSSR Supreme Soviet criticized the county and *volost* executive committees who were required to periodically confirm the number of mothers located and honoured according to the quarterly work plans of the OSBMLFSM branches; however, they did not do this. The Presidium demanded that the mistakes be corrected and the medals be given out to the mothers immediately.[86]

Payment of benefits: Confusion and plunder

Thus, how were the benefits distributed? And what were the fundamental failings of the OSBMLFSM and its branches that hindered their ability to administer benefits to families?

The OSBMLFSM staff were urged not to wait for the mothers to take it upon themselves and apply for financial assistance; the staff were to compile their own lists of single mothers and mothers of large families. Then, according to the lists created under dubious circumstances, the mothers were encouraged to write formal requests for assistance. With each mother's request in hand, the staff would open up an individual's case, mark the number of children living with their mother and their ages (children living separately were not counted when determining assistance). The children's birth certificates were checked against local vital records offices and *militsiya* departments. Each case had to be validated by the county, *volost* and city executive committees, and starting in 1950, by appropriate regional and district executive committees as well. Once approved, the OSBMLFSM branch would issue an ID card, on which OSBMLFSM staff would mark the date and amount of assistance issued. Upon receipt of the money, the mother was required to sign her name in the register which was stored in the branch office. The staff member in turn would cross-check the mother's signature in the register against the one in her individual case file (in the branch office files). The actual payment could be issued directly from the executive committee or by the local bank.

This, at first glance a simple procedure, was soon mired by bureaucracy and problems such as organized looting of the state's funds. The first step in the process was already problematic: the compilation of lists of mothers. On 31 December 1945, the head of the Kėdainiai county executive committee finance department jointly holding the position of director of the OSBMLFSM branch in a note to the central office explained that he was unable to make lists of mothers because the *volost* executive committees had not sent him the information he needed.[87] On 20 December 1945, A. Sinaiskis, LSSR Deputy People's Commissar of Finance, urged all finance departments of all counties: 'Hurry up and provide us an accounting of all mothers not receiving assistance. Serious penalties will result to those not providing this information by 25 December.'[88] Panicking, the branch staff flooded the OSBMLFSM central office with lists of surnames of mothers of large families. But in reality the mothers' surnames were supposed to remain in the files of local finance departments or the already established OSBMLFSM branches. The central office in Vilnius had only requested numbers: the number of mothers receiving assistance and the number of mothers eligible for assistance but to whom it had not yet been disbursed. After the above-mentioned Sinaiskis's appeal, the central office began receiving long lists, not only of mothers' surnames, but also their children's names and dates of birth. The office returned these lists, explaining that the Vilnius officials had no need for the mothers' surnames; it was local personnel who needed them in order to administer the payment of benefits.[89]

The office's provincial branches created many bureaucratic roadblocks for those receiving assistance. The LSSR Finance Ministry reported that before administering benefits, the Kupiškis district branch staff were illegally eliciting information on the mothers' morals and behaviour.[90] The Tauragė district branches were not only extracting references about each applicant's moral character; applicants were also being forced to fill out questionnaires created by the staff themselves along with numerous additional documents. Because of the growing paperwork and bureaucracy, applications to the Tauragė district branch were taking ten to twelve months to process; however, officially, according to the Rules of Procedure, mothers' applications for benefits were to be processed within two weeks. The Vilkaviškis county was also asking applicants to fill out made-up questionnaires.[91] In 1946, a major audit of the OSBMLFSM branches in Tauragė, Švenčionys, Utena, Prienai, Varėna, Kaišiadoriai, Trakai and Alytus counties and the savings banks in Tauragė, Švenčionys, Utena and Lazdijai determined that the branches did not have copies of the mothers' signatures. The branch personnel were also not requesting vital statistics bureaus to notify them about deceased children (they simply trusted the mothers' words), which had created a precedent for paying out benefits on behalf of deceased children. The audit also revealed that mothers receiving cash benefits at savings banks were being forced to deposit their benefits at the bank or buy bonds.[92] And the savings bank in Utena had been fabricating queues so that the mothers would have to pay bribes. The bank in Lazdijai had no queues, but they had run out of cash and the women were forced to wait several months for their money.[93] The Kretinga, Utena, Trakai and Zarasai savings banks were also always short on cash. The mothers, after travelling 50–70 kilometres, would return home empty-handed. The county savings banks in some instances required the mothers to buy bonds or would have their money transferred into savings accounts without their permission; the mothers would be handed savings booklets rather than cash.[94] In Zarasai and Telšiai, the city *militsiya* would refuse to issue documentation attesting to changes in the number of children, thereby preventing receipt of assistance.

But it was not only bureaucratic roadblocks, but also envy for families receiving financial benefits and negligence on the part of the OSBMLFSM that prevented mothers of large families and single mothers from receiving assistance. Quite frequently, the money was simply misappropriated or stolen. The easiest way to cheat the system was through benefits paid out for 'dead souls', that is, for non-existent or deceased children. In 1949, an audit determined that the staff at the Kaunas county branch were concealing children's deaths and were supposedly continuing to pay assistance to their mothers. Overpayment for deceased children in the Kaunas county alone cost 56,748 roubles. What is not clear from the audit records is whether the mothers were also privy to the fraud and whether they were taking their share, or if the branch staff were simply forging their signatures. Children's death certificates of 1944, 1945 and 1946 make clear that in October and November of 1948, benefits were being paid for children who had died several years prior. In the same Kaunas county branch, there were cases in which the mothers were paid benefits for children who were no longer eligible.[95]

Similarly, the staff of the Alytus branch of the OSBMLFSM were allowing mothers to submit children's birth certificates that had obviously been altered or 'fixed'.[96] In 1948, Pagėgiai county savings banks were sometimes paying out benefits without the mother's signature or identification booklet – in other words, to anyone at all.[97] On the other hand, some OSBMLFSM branch staff were overly zealous and inextirpable. Such was the Lazdijai county OSBMLFSM branch staff member Giedraitis, who categorically refused to authorize assistance without the mother's signature, even when he knew that the woman was illiterate and could only sign with an x. As the audit shows, such mothers were left with no benefits.[98]

In 1947, a significant fraud case was discovered in the Šilutė county OSBMLFSM branch. During the years 1946–7, the branch's inspector-auditor and senior accountant had misappropriated 355,709 roubles from monies that had been allocated for cash benefits. The funds were acquired in various ways: payments were issued for dead children, non-existent children and fictional mothers. In these cases, the staff used the letter x in place of mothers' signatures. The audit determined that the mothers had received a share of the benefits issued for dead children. This fraudulent scheme involved even more officials. During a regular financial audit at the Šilutė county OSBMLFSM branch, the inspector 'did not notice anything suspicious' although the money had already been stolen. On the contrary, the inspector had praised the two branch staff members who had looted the funds for their excellent work. After the inspector left, the funds at the Šilutė branch continued to be stolen for another six months. It was determined that 392 fictional mothers' accounts had been fabricated to facilitate the fraud.[99]

The deliberate fraud, looting and incompetence led to financial problems for the OSBMLFSM branches. Assistance was overpaid, underpaid or there wasn't enough money to pay out benefits. On 20 May 1950, in Mažeikiai county, the amount of money overpaid amounted to 67,453 roubles.[100] And in 1948, in Pagėgiai county, the amount was 25,080 roubles. Only a small portion of the overpaid funds was returned to the savings banks. In 1950, in Joniškis county, 14,015 roubles were overpaid, but only 2,520 roubles were returned.[101]

Confusion regarding single mothers

Various stereotypes predominant in Russian and Lithuanian society hobbled the work of the OSBMLFSM and its branches. The *8 July 1944 decree* had allocated funds to single mothers; however, as the project was implemented, it became clear that neither Lithuania's branch staff nor the actual recipients of the benefits could clearly explain who belonged to the category 'single mothers'. The ill-defined category created confusion in the branches and became yet another reason for providing benefits to women ineligible under the auspices of the law, or denying benefits to eligible women. In Lithuanian society, single mothers were understood to be women abandoned by their husbands and thus raising their children on their own. However, in its essence, the *8 July 1944 decree* emerged from the liberal interpersonal relations developing between men and women during the 1917 socialist revolution in Russia. Up until 1936 in Russian society, the state had provided care for single (never married) mothers, while Lithuanians found it hard to understand how a woman raising a 'bastard' could be financially supported by the state. In post-war Lithuania, it would be hard to find a significant number of single mothers (never married) that the OSBMLFSM branch staff eagerly budgeted for in their quarterly plans. In 1944, in all of Lithuania, there were only six single mothers (See Table 1), and in the summer of 1946, in all of Kaišiadoriai county, there were only thirteen single, never-married mothers.[102]

According to their own understanding, the OSBMLFSM branch staff distributed benefits to women who had been abandoned by their husbands, and not to single, never-married women as the law provided. This is borne out by data recorded on 23 February 1948 by the Kėdainiai county OSBMLFSM branch; on 20 February at the Tauragė savings bank; on 21 November 1950 in the

Table 1.1 Assistance Paid to Single Mothers and Mothers of Large Families, 1944–6

Year	Amount Allocated To Single Mothers	Amount Allocated To Mothers of Large Families	Amount Paid (in Roubles)	Amount Paid (in Roubles)
1944	6	177	3,000	245,000
1945	1,232	17,076	642,450	27,085,142
1946	5,873	28,169	5,078,300	60,124,834
Total:	7,111	45,422	5,723,750	87,454,976

Data collected by OSBMLFSM, submitted to LCP(b) CC Women's Division. Reported by M. Kymantaitė, 15 February 1947. LCVA, F. R.-164, Ap. 14, B. 8, L. 3.

Joniškis branch; and on 11 October 1951 as seen in the report compiled after an audit in the Rokiškis branch.[103] The 1949 audit of the Pasvalys branch concluded the following: '[F]inancial assistance continues to be provided to single mothers regardless of whether a father's name is included on the child's birth certificate.'[104] According to the *8 July 1944 Law* it was illegal to register the child's biological father's surname on the birth certificate if the marriage was not registered in the civil records and the child's mother also did not have the right to bring an action to establish paternity or request child support before the court. Thus, if the mother and father agreed to indicate paternity in the civil record, the single mother gave up her right to financial assistance. The intimidated and confused staff of the Lithuanian office stopped paying financial benefits if the child's birth certificate included a father's surname, even if in actuality the woman did not live with the father and she actually was a single mother.

Shortly thereafter the USSR Finance Ministry issued a special, separate resolution, regulating 'single motherhood' for the Lithuanian OSBMLFSM. The Soviet Ministry declared the Lithuanian OSBMLFSM null and void, forbidding the payment of benefits to single mothers if a father's name was recorded on the child's birth certificate. Ministry officials explained the following complex series of tenets:

1. If the marriage is not registered, but the child's parents cohabit in a single household and share in child-rearing responsibilities, no assistance will be provided.[105]
2. If the marriage is not registered, but the child's father lives with the family, however he is not part of the household and does not share in child-rearing responsibilities, the assistance may be provided.
3. If the mother has been abandoned but is not officially divorced, no assistance will be provided.
4. If the child's father is recorded on the birth certificate but the marriage was never registered and the couple do not cohabit, assistance will be provided.

In Lithuania, these labyrinthine interpersonal relationships were difficult to comprehend. The Biržai county branch director reported to the central office:

> We repeat that at our branch, we have just one single mother whose children's birth certificates have a father listed, but the mother was not and is not in a registered civil union and does not live with the child's father and they do not share a household. Her name is Tatjana Grečkina, and we do provide her with financial assistance.[106]

In April 1950, in Lazdijai county, 150 single mothers who did not share a household with their children's father were identified.[107]

The category of single, never-married mothers was increasing. The tendency was recorded, even if it was by Kymantaitė's imprecise data. In 1945 in Lithuania, 1,232 single mothers received assistance in Lithuania, and the following year, 1946, there were 5,873 mothers (See Table 1.1). Perhaps the number of unmarried mothers raising children independently was growing in Lithuania in general. Or perhaps the Lithuanian population were accommodating themselves to the opportunities for assistance offered by the Soviet system, and they were thus intentionally falsifying their marital status.

Financial assistance for mothers: Results and statistics

In reports sent to the OSBMLFSM central office in Vilnius, branch directors were consistently complaining that they did not have precise information about mothers and the sums paid out to them. This is why the central office of the OSBMLFSM and its branches had different numbers of mothers who received financial assistance and those who were honoured with awards. A report to the central office by the Panevėžys county executive committee finance division on the assistance paid out in 1945 indicated that there might be approximately 350 mothers eligible for assistance in the county. However, the report included an addendum stating that the branch did not have precise information about mothers of large families.[108] Lack of information about the population was to be expected as the first census in Lithuania would be completed only in 1959. Besides, the numbers of women receiving assistance were enhanced due to corruption in the organization and anxiety about not meeting quarterly work plan goals. In the early years of the office's functioning, the number of benefits distributed as well as their amounts were enhanced merely because of overpayments which were regularly fixed by the auditors of the OSBMLFSM branches. These tendencies are clearly reflected in the statistics for the years 1944–6 provided by Kymantaitė, director of the OSBMLFSM, in reports to the LCP(b) CC's Women's Division (Table 1.1) and in the LSSR People's Commissar of Finance A. Drobnys's report by county to First Secretary of the Communist Party of Lithuania Sniečkus (Table 1.2).

As the tables demonstrate, the number of mothers receiving assistance during the 1944–6 period as reported by LSSR People's Commissar of Finance Drobnys,

Table 1.2 Assistance Paid between October 1944 and 1 December 1946

Counties	Mothers Receiving Assistance	Amount of Assistance in Roubles
Alytus	778	1,171,000
Biržai	387	616,000
Kaunas	947	2,253,000
City of Kaunas	559	777,000
Kėdainiai	496	777,000
Kretinga	679	650,000
Klaipėda	23	-
City of Klaipėda	23	62,000
Lazdijai	433	438,000
Marijampolė	994	1,758,000
Mažeikiai	344	507,000
Panevėžys	430	1,018,000
City of Panevėžys	153	1,011,000
Raseiniai	781	405,000
Rokiškis	246	-
Šiauliai	785	1,610,000
City of Šiauliai	217	800,000
Šakiai	350	438,000
Švenčionys	512	800,000
Tauragė	453	539,000
Telšiai	709	1,178,000
Trakai	840	1,433,000
Ukmergė	828	1,070,000
Utena	387	593,000
Vilnius	1,103	3,038,000
City of Vilnius	366	-
Vilkaviškis	506	738,000
Zarasai	467	768,000
Total	14,796	24,448,000

Data collected by Report given by A. Drobnys, LSSR People's Commissar of Finance, LCP(b) to the First Secretary of the Communist Party A. Sniečkus on the implementation of the *8 July 1944 decree*, on 1 February 1947. LCVA, F. R.-164, Ap. 14, B. 5, L. 1.

is significantly smaller (14,796 mothers receiving benefits) than that reported by Kymantaitė (52,533 mothers receiving benefits, combined single and mothers of large families). The numbers reported to the central office by individual provincial branches, and the numbers reported in Drobnys's report to the First Secretary of the LCP Sniečkus are also different – they are significantly smaller or considerably greater. In 1945, the city of Panevėžys branch reported that there may well have been forty-four mothers of large families eligible for assistance in their city. The branch director wrote that they had collected the mothers' surnames at the office of vital records and then 'went door to door and informed the above-named mothers about their eligibility'.[109] Meanwhile, Drobnys's figures show that the number of such mothers in Panevėžys during the period 1944–6 was significantly greater: 153. The Kaunas county branch reported that in 1946, they had found 3,129 mothers of large families.[110] According to Drobnys's data from Table 1.2, during the entire period from October 1944 to 1 December 1946, the Kaunas county branch had 947 mothers of large families and single mothers combined.

The data on the number of mothers receiving assistance varied according to different reports by the tens or even hundreds and they were constantly being revised. Thus, the Biržai county branch reported figures for 1945, adding thus: 'As of today, we registered 516 mothers and have already accommodated 403 mothers. Another 113 mothers due to their ineligible number of children or ages are not eligible for assistance.'[111]

The OSBMLFSM gets phased out

From the very beginning, the main office of the OSBMLFSM had difficulty managing the branches and could not ensure smooth functioning. The provincial branches complied with the office's directives quiescently or not at all: they did not compile lists of mothers of large families or single mothers; they did not submit their quarterly work plans or disburse benefits in a timely manner; and they were careless in their administration of accounts of mothers receiving assistance. For their part, the branches did not seem pleased with the work or the directives of the Vilnius office. At times, not only did branch directors not comply with Kymantaitė's instructions, but they gave her instructions instead. In response to a letter from Pagėgiai in July 1946, Kymantaitė replied as follows: 'I am returning Document No. 1235 from 10 July of this year and kindly request that you please stop sending such ignorant communications to the central office. You are required to provide us with your work plan for each quarter ... not to pontificate on how the office should be run.'[112]

In turn, the office was consistently being criticized by upper levels for inadequately implementing the *8 July 1944 decree*. On 13 April 1945, the Director of the LSSR People's Commissar's Commission M. Gedvilas signed a draft order on the incompetence of the OSBMLFSM's work. In it, he urged the office to complete the development of the branches and warned them to stop dragging their feet in issuing benefits, to compile lists of mothers of large families and single mothers in the cities and villages and to require the *militsiya* to issue documentation detailing the number of children per family and their ages.[113] The LSSR Finance Ministry similarly called attention to the continuing inadequacies of the office on numerous occasions. After a routine audit of the Ukmergė county branch, Deputy LSSR Finance Minister Genys in a 14 November 1946 report found that approximately 30 per cent of the mothers' files were riddled with errors; the branch office did not have the mothers' applications for assistance on file nor had the applications been signed; the savings bank was consistently short on cash for the sums needed, and because of this, the mothers from the most distant *volosts* were travelling great distances multiple times to the county savings banks and executive committee offices. It was also observed that the applicants were not being treated politely, and if that wasn't enough, the Ukmergė county government's workers' union and local press knew absolutely nothing about the *8 July 1944 decree*.[114] In 1946, an audit of the Kėdainiai county branch revealed that the staff did not know how much assistance to distribute and as they issued payments, they were either overpaying the women by several thousand roubles or underpaying them. The audit determined that the overpayments were not returned to the savings bank nor were the mothers compensated for the shortfalls. The LSSR Finance Ministry claimed that the director of the branch had washed his hands of the tasks assigned to him or was leaving everything to its own volition.[115] After a routine USSR Finance Ministry audit and several other inspections, on 25 July 1947, by order No. 577 of the LSSR Finance Ministry Drobnys to the office Director Kymantaitė, a stern rebuke issued.[116]

On 10 May 1950, the USSR Finance Ministry evaluated the progress of the Lithuanian OSBMLFSM. According to the ministry, the issuing of benefits in Lithuania had led to confusion and the creation of an unnecessarily large bureaucracy. Because of this, the issuing of benefits was slow or wasn't happening at all. These unfavourable conclusions about the office's work were prompted by yet another large-scale case of theft of benefits. This time, the money was being stolen from inside the Trakai county OSBMLFSM branch. The unfavourable evaluation of the office's work and subsequent incidents of theft led the USSR Finance Ministry to relieve Kymantaitė of her responsibilities. On 10 May, by decree, the director of the Lithuanian OSBMLFSM was fired.[117]

The situation however did not change even after Kymantaitė's departure and the hiring of a new director. In December 1951, the new director E. Jurgaitytė announced that on 1 October, there had been many significant overpayments and underpayments in the Lithuanian branches and 145,325 roubles due to the mothers had not been issued.[118] But the amount of the overpayments was also significant. In the Šiauliai branch alone, on 1 January 1952, a case was presented to the People's Court regarding 109,380 roubles that had been stolen. Aside from the financial irregularities, a whole series of other infringements was discovered in the Šiauliai branch including unjustified delays in processing women's applications and artificial obstacles to the issuing of awards. Because of its poor performance, Lithuania's OSBMLFSM board was evaluated unsatisfactory for a second time. In an order of 1951, the LSSR Minister of Finance A. Zverev noted that the performance of the Lithuanian OSBMLFSM was fundamentally flawed. Lithuania's OSBMLFSM and its branches took heart by focusing on their achievements. In discussing the Kaunas branch's achievements, they noted that although ninety-five mothers had received their booklets late during the third quarter of 1951, only seventy booklets had been late in the fourth quarter. Thus they had reduced tardiness by over 26 per cent.[119]

The bureaucracy and obstacles in dispersing benefits by the OSBMLFSM branches and savings banks caused mothers to outright reject state financial assistance. During an audit, the Trakai branch was advised to check on some of the mothers who had refused assistance for more than six months. The Trakai branch was asked to explain these women's behaviour and draw up a report. An audit of the Joniškis district branch similarly determined that twenty-seven mothers were no longer interested in the aid that was due them and had stopped filing for it two to three years ago. In 1952, in the Šiauliai branch, it was also observed that mothers' identification booklets were still in the office drawers because the women were not coming to claim them.[120] On 1 June 1956, the OSBMLFSM was abolished, and its functions were assumed by the LSSR Ministry of Social Welfare.

The OSBMLFSM was likely the first instance of the social welfare state in Soviet Lithuania. Under Khrushchev, the building of a social welfare state was once again first directed towards women. After the Stalinist policy of gender equality had ended in Lithuania, women became part of Khrushchev's social policy which held them solely responsible for the household and family.[121] Indeed it was now incumbent upon women to realize the regime's vision of everyday life and its often impossible ideas about a new, beautiful and culturally rich standard of living. In the new ideological vision domestic work had been transformed into services provided by the state, and work and family life had been reconciled through the ostensibly available network of preschool institutions, thus enabling respectful interpersonal relationships between men and women in the family and new types of romantic relationships between men and women. None of it came true.

2

Marriage and divorce

Marriage

Creating a socialist family

Overview of the legal framework

Catholic doctrine on engagement and marriage was defined during Sessions 17–25 of the Council of Trent, held from 18 January 1562 to 4 December 1563. These doctrines were followed by Lithuanian Catholics with practically no changes until the beginning of the twentieth century. On 2 September 1907, Pope Pius X supplemented canon law regarding marriage and strengthened its legitimation. Henceforth, the factual act of engagement needed to be confirmed in writing with the couple's signatures, and the marriage had to take place at the parish church of one of the future spouses before a priest and two or three witnesses.[1] The latter procedures for Catholic marriage in Lithuania essentially did not change until the country's annexation by the Soviet Union on 15 June 1940. Within two months, on 15 August 1940, the acting president of the Republic of Lithuania signed the *Marriage Law*, which for the first time in Lithuanian history, legalized civil marriages. Religious ceremonies were not banned, although they lost their legal standing; the law stipulated that they could be performed after the civil ceremony.[2] Couples choosing only a religious ceremony and refusing to officially register their marriage faced persecution: the *Marriage Law* imposed a fine of up to 5,000 litas and even arrest.[3] The same presidential decree also enacted a *Metrics Law*.[4]

Upon ratification, the *Marriage Law* automatically rendered the majority of marriages in Lithuania invalid because they had occurred prior to the 1940 decree and were only blessed in the church. Couples who agreed to register their church marriages according to civil registration protocols were able to resolve this legal bind. To accommodate this, the Soviet *Marriage Law* retained the canonical laws' legal age of marriage, which was 16 for women and 18 for men. Exceptions were allowed for men who wanted to marry before they turned 18, as long as they were older than 18, and accordingly, women could marry before they turned 16, but they could not be younger than 14.[5] Likewise, according to the Soviet *Metrics Law* as in the canonical laws, civil marriages were required to be performed in the parish of one of the applicants. The legal conditions had been drafted to correspond to those of pre-1940 church marriages as long as they did not infringe on marital age, marriage between blood relatives, marriage laws in different jurisdictions, or in case one of the spouses was suffering from a terminal illness and so on as laid out in the Soviet *Marriage Law*.

According to the 1940 Soviet *Marriage Law*, marriage applications could be made in writing or verbally. The director of the civil records office would process the marriage within two weeks. If the director learnt of obstacles to the marriage, the circumstances had to be investigated within the two-week time frame. The law stipulated that the ceremony be attended by the director of civil records, the couple and at least two adult witnesses.[6] Under the prior canonical laws, marriages had only been recorded in the marriage register, but the Soviet *Metrics Law* required additional documentation: the fact of the marriage was recorded in the official records and on the passports of both newly-weds; if relevant, information on prior divorces was also recorded on the appropriate passport. The director of records also had to register the marriage on the couples' birth certificates, providing the spouses' given names, surnames and the place of the marriage. If the birth certificates of either spouse were filed at a different parish, the director had one day to notify the appropriate officials of the other parish.[7] The *15 August 1940 Marriage Law* would remain in effect for only a few months, but the *Metrics Law* remained on the books until 1958. Biographical interviews attest to simple civil ceremonies after the war. Julija Greičienė (born 1926) described her own civil marriage ceremony: 'We dated for half a year. Then, one fine day we registered our marriage. I felt that he was sort of cold. We left the marriage register office, which was on the first floor of the Metropolis Restaurant, and we went in different directions: he went to his job; I went to my room.'[8]

On 30 November 1940, the Presidium of the Lithuanian SSR (LSSR) Supreme Soviet issued an order on the application of criminal and civil laws of the Russian Soviet Federative Socialist Republic to Lithuania (likewise to Latvia and Estonia). The order stipulated that these laws be effective in the Baltic republics until the republics each had enacted their own laws. Thus, in December 1940, the 1936 Russian Soviet Federative Socialist Republic (RSFSR) Marriage, Family and

Guardianship Code of Laws went into effect with the official title: *The Marriage, Family and Guardianship Law Valid in the Territory of the LSSR* (henceforth referred to as the *RSFSR Marriage, Family and Guardianship Code*).⁹ The *RSFSR Marriage, Family and Guardianship Code* was appended and revised several times, first by decree by the Presidium of the USSR Supreme Soviet on 8 July 1944. A few years later, on 5 August 1946, the Presidium of the LSSR Supreme Soviet reprised the protocol by which church marriages would be made compatible with civil registrations.¹⁰ The resolution was still relevant because the majority of couples in Lithuania were not registering their church marriages with the civil registry bureaus. On 30 June 1947, the *RSFSR Marriage, Family and Guardianship* Code was appended with another decree *On the Prohibition of Marriages between Soviet Citizens and Foreigners*, which remained as a law for several years.¹¹ On 26 November 1953, the Presidium of the USSR Supreme Soviet repealed the prohibition as long as the marriage was registered within the Soviet territory. This decree was signed into law in Lithuania in 1954.¹²

Although it was expected that the *RSFSR Marriage, Family and Guardianship Code* and *8 July 1944 decree* would be temporary in Lithuania, they remained in effect with only minor additions for twenty-nine years, until 1969.¹³ On 28 June 1968, the USSR Supreme Soviet adopted the Fundamentals of Legislation of the USSR and Soviet Republics on Marriage and Family. Based on these, on 16 July 1969, the LSSR Supreme Soviet promulgated the *LSSR Marriage and Family Code* (henceforth referred to as the *LSSR Marriage and Family Code*, which went into effect in Lithuania on 1 January 1970 and remained a law until 1990.¹⁴

The 1940 Soviet *Metrics Law* expired on 20 August 1958 after the new *Instructions for Civil Registration Procedures in the Lithuanian Soviet Socialist Republic* went into effect.¹⁵ Unlike the 1940 Soviet *Metrics Law*, according to the new instructions, applications for marriage had to be done in writing; these new instructions transformed the registration of marriages into a public act. Accordingly, the marriage registration could not take place without representatives from the district (city) deputy workers' council, a work collective, trade union or collective farm in attendance. The marriage certificate would be presented by the director of the executive committee or his/her assistant. The 1958 *Metrics Instructions* repealed the mandatory attendance of witnesses at the ceremony; however, the couple was encouraged to invite family and friends to the event. The new registration instructions formalized the presentation of the marriage certificate, which was conducted as part of a solemn ceremony 'in a spacious and beautifully adorned hall'. The ritual attended by the deputy, representative of an organization as well as family and friends in a hall specially dedicated to this purpose eventually became part of a unified Soviet marriage registration and wedding ceremony. This civil registration procedure was appended in 1960. From then on, applications for marriage and the date of registration had to be announced in the local newspaper, with the state covering the costs.[16] On 23 July 1963, the same commission stipulated that in the parishes, villages and cities where there was no registration office, marriages would be registered at the appropriate district or city registry offices or departments. Once again, two pairs of witnesses were required to be in attendance; these witnesses would sign the marriage certificate.[17]

The new instructions for civil registration went into effect on 1 January 1970 along with the *LSSR Marriage and Family Code* which had been ratified in the republic in 1969.[18] The *LSSR Marriage and Family Code* and the 1970 *Metrics Instructions* remained in effect until Lithuania regained independence in 1990. The LSSR Code made the marital age requirement for both bride and groom uniform – both had to be at least 18 years of age. The 1970 *Metrics Instructions* required couples to publicly announce their intention to marry and to notify their employers or, if they were students, their educational institutions, of this fact. The couple's passports were stamped with the surname of their respective spouse along with information on prior divorces, if applicable. The *Metrics Instructions* further extended the opportunity to register church marriages that had occurred before 8 July 1944.

The continuing battle with church marriage and tradition

After the Second World War and occupation of Lithuania, as the *RSFSR Marriage, Family and Guardianship Code* and the *8 July decree* went into effect, the Soviet government began an intensive propaganda campaign against church marriages. Although religious ceremonies after civil registration were still allowed, the government's stance became aggressively negative. Couples who solemnized their marriages in church could expect negative consequences if they held professional positions of any importance. The youth and their parents of post-war Lithuania certainly considered church weddings extremely important, but they were also concerned about the consequence of marriage registration. Contrary to the law, young people wanted to consecrate their marriages in church before registering at the registry office. However, fear of persecution and criminal repercussions inhibited not only the marrying couples but their priests as well. Monika Jonynaitė-Makūnienė told of her and her husband's church wedding which took place a month after the couple's civil registration in 1951: 'If we hadn't officially registered our wedding, the priest would not have given his blessing. So, a month later, we got his blessing. My husband's sisters went to the Carmelite church to check if we really had gotten the priest's blessing, because [we were] a deeply religious family.'[19] In 1958, more than ten years after the war had ended, even after the Soviets had closed the majority of churches in Lithuania, over 60 per cent of civilly registered marriages were still being performed in church. Another ten years later, in 1968, however, due to propaganda and persecution, this number had been reduced by half: 30 per cent of all registered marriages were solemnized in a religious ceremony.

In its battle against church marriages, Soviet propaganda used fear and superstition to manipulate ordinary men and women. First, the Lithuanian population was told that only marriages registered at the civil registry office could be happy ones. Right after the war, Lithuania's major newspapers and magazines were filled with articles and readers' letters about marriages supposedly ending in divorce, in which one of the spouses had avoided civil registration. According to the publications, the desire for a church wedding was an obvious sign of immature and cavalier attitudes on the family. In 1946, one author, commenting on the divorce of a reader from Pasvalys, blamed the divorce on the woman's faith. The author shared a woman's story with readers of the official party newspaper *Komjaunimo tiesa*:

> Mama tried to convince us to go to church as well. The priest, of course, somewhat surprised, married us. Afterwards, my husband became strangely indifferent and obstinate. Before our church wedding, he had the naïve idea not to register at the records office so that his passport wouldn't have the stamp (I found this out later after our relationship had soured).[20]

The propaganda was intended to cause readers to unconsciously associate church rites with an unhappy family life and thus to renounce them.

Towards the end of the 1970s, the Soviet government turned to several other arguments to make church marriage unappealing and even repulsive. Propagandists presented couples appealing to God to assure them happiness in their marriages as infantilistic. According to the ideologues, the church was encouraging couples to be passive and unwilling to take responsibility for their own fates and happiness. A 1957 *Komjaunimo tiesa* article initiated the discussion 'On Happiness in Marriage' and an entire article was devoted to criticism of church marriages in an article entitled 'Religion Does Not Help'. The newspaper printed a story about an average Lithuanian guy named Bronius whose mother and bride Laima were trying to force him to marry in church. Bronius struggled against the women's demands, posing his own arguments in response: 'I cannot, mum', said Bronius. 'Religion says that God rewards us with happiness for our obedience. But I don't want Laima to expect that a happy marriage comes from heaven. I want us to build it together, with our own hands!'[21] The discussion also attempted to show that church marriages legitimize gender inequality because 'in the most cynical way, they belittle women and their human dignity' and reinforce women's economic exploitation. N. Solovjovas, a major Soviet family propagandist in Lithuania, claimed that church marriages essentially thwart family happiness. He added that church-consecrated marriages might beget women's patience and obedience, but not the spouses' love for one another. If the husband wants a church marriage, it means that, in principle, he is planning on marrying a slave, not an equal.[22]

Twenty-four years after the inception of civil registration in Lithuania, the Soviet press was still hard at work to improve its image. In 1964, the principal party newspaper *Tiesa* noted the twenty-year anniversary (since the end of the war) of civil unions in Lithuania in an article using powerful propagandistic cliches: 'Together, they waited impatiently for the day the registry office would open. If not for their constant demands and requests, it probably would have taken much longer for the office to open … Nervous, still unaccustomed to their duties, the bureau's staff presented the young newlyweds with Marriage Certificate No. 1, the first one issued by their office.'[23]

Soviet propaganda fought not only with religious marriages and the church's influence on marriage, but also with traditional Lithuanian family norms. The behaviour of interwar Lithuanian farmer families was in large part still influenced by nineteenth-century patriarchal norms and gender role stereotypes. In farmer society, it was nearly impossible to cheat or miscalculate the wealth of the future newly-weds during their engagement. Any non-payment of dowry in the village qualified as debt, to be remembered for life. Lawyer Petras Leonas in his memoirs notes that his mother often reminded her brother Adomas Baltrušaitis that 'he was to blame about her dowry'.[24] Nevertheless, egalitarian interpersonal relations began to have an effect on the marriage practices of Lithuania's modernizing and Westernizing intelligentsia during the interwar period. In particular, the traditional dowry lost its previous significance. In his autobiography, author Jonas Šliūpas remembered the precise amount of his wife Liudvika Malinauskaitė's dowry promised by her parents: 'it was 2000 roubles'.[25]

Although the Šliūpas family did not receive the sum they had requested, they never brought up the topic again.

In some Lithuanian families, until the end of the 1950s, the bride's dowry remained an important and indispensable element of marriage, just as it had been in traditional nineteenth-century peasant culture. Any arrears on the part of the bride's family had the potential to become the source of conflict or even divorce. In 1959, during court proceedings, a woman explained that her parents had planned her wedding according to Lithuanian traditions and as a result they suffered financial hardships. Nonetheless, her husband still demanded they pay the dowry they had agreed upon. 'They finally agreed that my father would give us 7000 roubles to help us start our life together. Immediately before the wedding, that same day, my father gave my husband 5000 roubles, and approximately 2000 roubles two months later after he had sold the family cow.'[26] The High Court approved the plaintiff's request for a divorce and ordered the husband to return the money he had accepted from his father-in-law. Indeed, some sons-in-law considered their in-laws' reneging on their promised dowries as proof that their marriages were invalid and that they had never been accepted by their wives' families. In 1947, Povilas M., who had married in 1940, complained, 'My wife's parents never accepted me as their son-in-law. After the wedding, I demanded my dowry from the defendant, but she refused.'[27] As in traditional nineteenth-century village society, even the smallest arrears of the promised amount could end in divorce of the newly formed Soviet family. In 1957, a newly-wed refused to live with his wife when he didn't receive the agreed upon dowry, a piglet. The High Court quickly approved the wife's request for divorce, basing their decision on the assertion that Soviet society does not tolerate dowries. Husbands who brought cases regarding unpaid dowries were denounced as bourgeois or behind the times. In their decisions, judges would stress that they had no basis for dismissing the suit because forcing the plaintiff to live with a defendant who holds such views is contrary to the principles of socialist morality.[28]

In pre-war Lithuanian society, women's role was associated with home and family; under the Soviet system, women's work inside and outside the home was socially encouraged. The state understood and endorsed the new roles assumed by women as their mandatory accommodation to the socialist lifestyle and voluntary assumption of a double or triple burden, because in totalitarian society women did not have the power to structurally change the patriarchal gender system and its rules.

Nonetheless, some families did challenge traditional gender stereotypes. In 1940, a husband explained to the court:

> I started to get dressed and asked [my wife] to get me my better underwear. She told me to get it myself. In hopes of gradually conditioning her to a proper, orderly married life, I tried to convince her that this was her responsibility. After all, how often do you see husbands doing women's work? She responded: 'Don't bug me with this "my responsibility/your responsibility" crap. That's how it is in your family. In my family, my father does anything we ask and we don't ever say "that's your responsibility, and this is mine."'[29]

With progressive journalists as mediators, a timid conversation was taking place in society about the need to change gender role stereotypes and attempts to reconcile work and family. Influenced by these discussions, in 1957, a wife, speaking for herself and her husband, addressed the journalists: 'Specifically, my husband and I want to know where the boundaries lie between men and women with respect to housework if both work outside of the home? Dear Editor, I kindly request that you respond to my letter. My husband too eagerly awaits your reply.'[30]

Lithuanian men and women were forced to decide certain family issues in public. As the Soviet courts, work collectives and party organizations assumed more and more issues related to family life, the regime's institutions came to be considered capable of and even required to respond to Soviet people's personal problems and to provide suitable solutions. In 1956, a defendant filing an appeal asked the court not to grant his wife a divorce and offered to work with the court in order to prove to his wife that he was worthy of her. The husband asked 'the High Court and work collective to give him a deadline for becoming a good person' and offered to introduce himself by letter to the 'entire High Court collective'.[31] Active institutional participation of the state and party in the citizenry's family life in solving intimate interpersonal problems coincided with intensive propaganda directed towards the standardization of private life in the early 1960s.

Marriage norms

In Lithuania as in the other Soviet republics, the family was the foundation of society because the absolute majority of citizens lived within the family unit. During the entire Soviet period, single, unmarried people were an insignificant demographic and were treated as a marginalized group. In 1970, men and women who had never been married made up only 7.2 per cent of the Lithuanian population: among these were 75,800 men and almost double that number of women: 148,400. Of the three Baltic republics, Lithuania registered the smallest percentage of single, never married individuals: in Latvia they made up 9.9 per cent of the population and in Estonia 12.9 per cent. In the entire Soviet Union, 91.4 per cent of all individuals lived within families.[32] In 1989, census records indicate that the total population of Lithuania was 3.69 million inhabitants of whom 1,000,002 were family units[33]. These figures indicate that the percentage of single (unmarried) individuals in Lithuania was very low indeed. In the final years of the Soviet Union, the number of single people decreased. In Estonia, men aged between 40 and 45 who had never been married made up only 2.6 per cent of the population; in Lithuania, the percentage was even smaller.[34]

Under Khrushchev, as the distinctions between public and private life were fading, the family came to be conceived as an open collective. Emotionally dependent family members' relations were called egoistic, and married couples were encouraged to create 'friendly collectives' which were made up of two parts – parents and children. Propaganda encouraged newly-weds to think about Soviet marriages as not just the purview of two individuals, but of all of society. Soviet ideologues explained that 'the spirit of and friendly competition that reigned in workers' collectives is becoming part of individual life, and it helps create happy marriages and healthy families'.[35] State family policy formed family members into individuals, each with specialized and state-supervised interests and activities. Accordingly, Soviet psychologists urged couples to avoid closing themselves off inside their families and to step outside of their husband-wife-children-parents circles. In 1970, they wrote that families are either 'open' or 'closed', arguing that nearly 90 per cent of those who seek psychological help come from closed families. They compared closed families to prison, and married couples within such families to prisoners. One psychologist argued that in happy marriages each spouse must cultivate his or her own friends and preferences. He urged wives to try to understand their husbands, allowing them to spend time with their friends, and wives too were encouraged to create their own circles of friends.[36] Psychiatrists also encouraged couples not to make their relationships overly intimate because, they claimed, such interaction infringes on individual freedom. They stressed that most husbands' and wives' needs could be satisfied only by society and that's why men must create 'male' friends' circles and women should create 'women's' circles'.[37]

During Khrushchev's Thaw, the purpose of family policy was to weaken ties among family members transforming the family into a social institution that was available to the party. In the press and literary works, the Soviet family was described in detail: husbands and wives, as well as parents and children, were advised on how to interact and spend leisure time as a family. The authors helped Soviet society solve marital problems and outlined the proper motives for marriage, showing what a happy couple looks like and what optimal number of children there should be in the family.

The idea of the family as a collective open to society was cultivated from the very beginning of every marriage. In 1958, registry office instructions obliged marrying couples to get married in public ceremonies, even though most couples at the time were more likely to opt for a simple, private wedding due to financial constraints and because of their desire for a church wedding. The new tradition was called 'Comsomol wedding' when the wedding was held and financially sponsored by the couple's employers. Apolonija Birutė Paliuliene (born in 1937) who worked as a bookkeeper at a collective farm remembered her own secret church wedding and Comsomol wedding of 1964:

> We were poor when we got married. In fact, I did have a few things – the *kolkhoz* had bought me a sofa, a table and a set of bed linens. It also gave me some meat for the wedding party. We had a Comsomol-style wedding and that was new. A month or so prior to the wedding we secretly received the church's blessing: nobody knew, but we went to the church and received the blessing because otherwise my mother would have been upset, for she was very religious. And then at the Comsomol-style wedding she danced and had fun.[38]

Soviet journalists thought that a public wedding would help reveal hidden character flaws or bad things the newly-weds had done in the past. The director of the 'Pažanga' (Progress) *kolkhoz* in the district of Rietavas proposed adjusting civil registry procedures and extending the length of time the marriage was to be publicized in the local newspaper. He also thought that the newly-weds should get their parents' permission, which was reminiscent of the canonical Catholic Church laws that had been practiced in Lithuania for centuries which had also required the parents' approval.[39]

Stereotypes also influenced the age of the newly-weds. According to the propaganda, exemplary Soviet marriages should not take place between individuals who were too young. Expectant mothers in their teens and fathers of a similar age were treated with hostility and contempt in the Soviet press. Even when couples were married with special governmental dispensations, the press would describe their prospects with dark colours, expecting their marriages, sooner or later, to fail. A teacher from Kaunas described her experience with teen marriages:

[T]he husband, a secondary school drop-out, and still in all appearances a boy, took a job at a hotel as a bellboy. His young wife became a housewife, unsure of how to spend her time, where to start. And how could she know if their parents are offended by their romantic behaviour and don't even want to talk about them, if they keep all their possessions in a rented attic room: a metal-framed bed, a wicker table, a few worn chairs.[40]

Still the state's educational and family policy encouraged a drastic reduction in marital age. In 1960, men in Lithuania typically married between the ages of 26 and 30, and women, between 21 and 25; in 1980, men were marrying when they were barely 22 to 23 years old and women, when they were 20 to 21 years old. In 1980, 48.5 per cent of marrying couples in Lithuania were between 20 and 24 years of age, and 20 per cent of them married before age 20.[41] In the villages, marriages occurred somewhat later. In 1970, men in the villages married at 26–30 years of age, and women at 21–5. According to Soviet experts, this was considered borderline 'past their prime' for both genders.[42] The decreased marital age was even more pronounced when compared with the first years after the war (see Table 2.1).

As the marital age fell and housing became scarce, inevitably a new form of family life in Soviet society was encouraged: two generations living under one roof. Such a neo-extended family was useful to the state as it instilled the concept of the family as a collective; this became yet another norm of married life. Most newly-weds' first home was a room in the apartment of one of their parents. According to data from 1970, on average, 70 per cent of new families in the USSR lived in the home of their parents right after marriage: 50 per cent with the parents of the bride and 20 per cent with the parents of the groom.[43] The Soviet press idealized the relationships between the in-laws and their common life together: 'We'll invite Mama to come live with us; she'll be with us and we'll all be happy.'[44] Often, the invitation to live in their parents' home was a wedding gift to the newly-weds. After moving in with their parents, the newly-weds would receive equal rights to the apartment as its owners. The life of two generations

Table 2.1 Marital Age in Lithuania, Vilnius, 1946–75

Gender	1946	1953	1969	1965	1970	1975
Men	30.2	28.4	27.7	27.4	26.3	23.2
Women	25.0	26.1	26.1	24.8	24.4	22.2

Source: V. Gaidys, *Visuomenės pagalba šeimai. Praktika ir problemos* (Social Assistance to Families: Practice and Problems) (Vilnius: Lietuvos TSR Žinijos draugija, 1984).

under one roof was a rather bold endeavour as the daughters- and sons-in-law would retain their rights to the apartment even after divorce. In a 1978 civil case regarding shared rights to an apartment, the daughter-in-law likened permission to live in her in-laws' apartment to an exchange of gifts between the two families on their wedding day: 'My mum, on our wedding day, in front of all the guests, presented us with 1000 roubles as seed money to help us begin our new lives, and [the groom's] father, in response to this gesture, invited us to come live in their apartment.'[45] Whether longer or shorter, married life together with parents was reflected in the interactions between the generations. The adult children felt a financial obligation to help their parents as they aged: in the late 1990s, 30 per cent of parents were receiving help from their sons' families and 10 per cent accepted help from their daughter's families.[46] The lives of two generations in the tight quarters of Soviet apartments limited the married couples' privacy and in essence presented them with very few opportunities to build their own separate individual family life.

Love and romance in Soviet society

Intimate interpersonal relations, romantic love and sexual passion did not escape normative cliches and offered a way to implement state family policies in Lithuania. Soviet love was supposed to help form appropriate reasons for men and women to marry and to offer guidance in choosing a spouse; that's why the state did not leave love to subjective, unpredictable and spontaneous emotions, and instead provided it with an ideological role. From its early years, the Soviet government used its popular Lithuanian press to educate citizens about which type of love was acceptable.

The love being propagated in Soviet society was different from that of the Western romantic tradition but also contrary to revolutionary Bolshevik 'free love'. At the beginning of the nineteenth century, Western romanticism formulated the foundations for the principles of romantic love, which today are still recognized in Western democracies as the benchmark of modern love. The French Revolution provided what was probably the biggest stimulus to the concept of romantic love. Along with equality of all people of every estate, the revolutionaries demanded the right to marriage based exclusively on love. Contrary to Medieval Christianity for which the principal value and purpose of love was God, and unlike Enlightenment rationality, in the romantic era, love became God and mission. In the romantic tradition, love was much more important and more significant than any character traits of the beloved. Romantic love became blind, but not in the sense that the Knight of Provence understood it, whose beloved's spiritual characteristics blinded her devotee. And not in the sense that the Enlightenment philosophers called out love for being deceptive because when one loves, it is impossible to understand reality. The love desired by the romantics was blind, because only irrational passion holds any possible meaning for human beings.[47]

According to the romantics, love had a single purpose: to meld with the beloved, no matter how imperfect and perhaps even sinful the beloved might be. In the romantic paradigm, any and all expressions of love were divine and good if only the lovers could meld into one another and lose themselves in the essence of the other. In this way, the transcendence they achieved could destroy the individual's isolation and alienation from the world and unite him or her with another individual, environment and ultimately, God. For Stendhal, this power of romantic love meant love without choice and without the possibility of deciding. Stendhal called it fever; for Proust it was similar to bacterial contagion.[48] Although the romantics defined sexuality as something more than the physical act, they agreed that it was possible for the absolute majority of people 'to meld into the essence of another' only through sexual passion. This is why, for the romantics, sexual sensations became an irreplaceable expression of love, and passion became inextricable from suffering. Because suffering is closely related to the maturity of the individual self, the romantics conceived of passion as one of the most important routes to understanding oneself. Having abandoned oneself to romantic love, one loves love for its own sake and for the suffering he or she experiences through sexual passion. A person knows himor herself only by risking life; that's why self-destruction through passion and suffering help one understand oneself.[49] Sexual romantic passion is not a happy love. Romance itself lives only inasmuch as love is fatal, fated and damned by life. And although passion always means suffering, it is indeed the most important experience of romantic love. Passionate romantic love is the opposite of a stable, gentle, respectful and comfortable partnership. Partnerships are much less intense because experience transformed to the everyday is no longer passion.[50] The romantics easily threw out the pledge of fidelity in marriage because a passionate romantic love is stronger than security. The twentiethcentury conflict between marriage and sexual romantic love disappeared because the modern ideals of marriage conformed with the benchmark of passionate romantic love.[51]

The Bolshevik love experiment

Bolshevik Russia was the first country in the world to try to establish government policy on sexual romantic love.[52] Free love unfettered by obligation and the union of two individuals was protected through amenable laws and became one of the symbols of the Soviet state.[53] Recognizing free love as the foundation for intimate relations, the Bolsheviks relied on Marx and Engels's ideas about the different values held by workers compared to the bourgeois family, and the different morals of communist society. After the October Revolution, the newly ratified laws were expected to guarantee and encourage new interpersonal relations.[54] The first *Soviet Marriage and Family Code of 1918* recognized de facto marriages and legalized divorce without grounds. It should come as no surprise that Russia recorded the largest number of divorces in Europe in the mid-1920s. This number was three times greater than Germany's or France's and twenty-six times greater than that in Wales or England. In 1926, every second registered marriage in Moscow was ending in divorce.[55] In 1920, the Bolshevik government legalized abortion and paid for it using state budget funds and in 1926, they ratified the *Marriage, Family and Guardianship Code*, which simplified the process of divorce even more. Applications for divorce could be mailed; the other spouse was not even notified of the court's decision. Memoirs include numerous testimonies of women with families during the third and fourth quarters of the twentieth century in Russia. The women describe how easily men would leave their children and wives in search of newer sexual experiences.[56] Elena Dolgikh gives the following account: 'We married. He was a nice person, but he later left me with our three children ... You see, he fell in love. And if he was in love, well.'[57] At the time, polygamy did not surprise anyone in Russia. Elena Ponomarenko recounts the following: 'I shouted: "Grandfather, look! He [her husband] is finally a father. We have a son!" He stood there and after a few minutes said: "You silly, silly girl. This isn't his first child. He had a daughter who died at four months. He's married." He had never told me. And here I thought he was a bachelor.'[58]

Although it encouraged sexual love as the basis for interpersonal relations, the Bolshevik government viewed the romantic 'melding of two souls' with great suspicion. This circumstance of passionate romantic love encouraged couples to shut themselves away together and for this reason they threatened the idea of collectivism. Thus, Bolshevik love was open to sexual experiences, but it refused to acknowledge the emotional tie between two people as a 'union of souls'.[59] The state believed that men and women freed from sexual tension, emotional ties and family obligations would be able to fully devote themselves to their work and the building of the new society. In order to speed up the process, party functionaries dreamt of nationalizing motherhood in Russia, with children's campuses and communal apartments run by home managers freeing women from childcare. The norms of Bolshevik love did not recognize such forms of intimacy as gallantry or flirting, likening these to the sentimental traditions of the bourgeoisie.[60] Intimate relations with former class enemies were also not tolerated and could potentially be construed as sexual deviancies.[61]

From the 1930s on, unrestricted sexual relations between men and women in the USSR were increasingly denounced along with partnerships which were not officially registered. Bit by bit, sexual romantic love as a component of family policy was removed from official Soviet propaganda discourse. In 1936, the new *USSR Family Code* recognized only officially registered marriages, made divorce procedures and outlawed abortions. Romantic sexual love was slowly transformed into 'true' Soviet love, the representations of which in art, film and literature banned and erased sexual passion and the nude body.[62] The love that propaganda made public became increasingly banal, and its expression, ever more infantile.

'True' Soviet love

In independent Lithuania (1918–40), the outlook on material relations between family members changed dramatically as new forms of interpersonal relationships were forged. In interwar society, a Western conception of marriage and family happiness was formed. Most notably, the structural and cultural modernization of the society imparted an increasingly greater significance on the sentiment of romantic love, the expression of which became important for individuals as well as popular literature. Pre-war women's magazines and novels depicted love embodied in the unity of a man's and woman's souls, the symbiosis of two hearts, the emotional and psychological concord of a husband and wife. Passionate romantic love became the basis for a happy family life and the most important reason for marriage.[63] Loving, for the interwar intelligentsia, meant absolute wholeness and an emotional and psychological bond between two people. For this reason, the beloved's social situation and different religious beliefs or political ideals were not seen as irreconcilable with passionate romantic love. In 1924, the mother of Marija Mašiotaitė wrote a disparaging letter regarding her daughter's unacceptable decision: 'If you must, go ahead and marry him, even if it has to be a civil marriage. At worst, I will approve … Maybe we'll die, so just do what you want, but I'm telling you that this is worse than death for us.'[64] In Marija's own letters to her beloved, there's not a hint of a single doubt. Every day in her letters to her future husband Juozas Urbšys in Berlin, she wrote of only one wish, to see him and to be together.[65]

Love as the autonomous unity of two souls was celebrated in lawyer Vladas Šimaitis's letters as well: 'Aldona, there is nothing more beautiful in the world than the perfect harmony of two souls.'[66] Indeed interwar Lithuanian society was starting to conceive of love as one of the most important experiences of a person's life. In 1934, Šimaitis admitted to his beloved: 'Love makes everything a person experiences on this earth possible. Whatever we achieve is only because of love.'[67]

As marital relations in interwar Lithuania became more modern, married spouses came to view one another differently. Probably for the first time in the history of the family in Lithuania, it was the beloved person's self – not material, ideological or political goals – that became the most important rationale for marriage. In 1935, Šimaitis wrote in a letter to his sweetheart: 'I want to work, I want to live, I want to struggle. All because of You.'[68] A loving interwar husband became immensely concerned with his beloved woman's comfort and well-being, for which he felt responsible. In 1930, archaeologist Jonas Puzinas, in a letter to his wife written in Heidelberg, admitted that nothing could take the place of their intimacy: 'To be alone, of course will be sad, but later I hope to bring you here and then I'll kick loneliness in the shins! When you live alone, loneliness starts to oppress you, but when I think about you and Diutis, I'm moved to tears.'[69] In subsequent letters to his wife, Puzinas described the clothing he bought for her, worried about her health, and asked 'Do you have enough money?'[70]

Married couples in the interwar period concerned themselves with the welfare of their beloved, putting great value on personal happiness in their marital relationship. Newly-wed teacher Marija Bilevičiūtė-Vasiliauskienė wrote in her diary about the sacrifice she made for the happiness and future of her beloved:

> I know that it will be hard to separate and get used to solitude [her husband was leaving for Berlin]. But at the same time I want him to go, to study, to see … he'll feel better about his life if he had the opportunity to fight more boldly for his survival. I've grown accustomed to him and I feel that he is even more dear to me than before. It's painful to part, but I want him to be happy.[71]

The supremacy and absoluteness of passionate romantic love in a happy marriage was an obvious indicator that interwar Lithuanian society was becoming more modern.

The knowledge that a happy family life and passionate romantic love were not identical concepts entered into currency immediately after the war ended, when in 1944, the conservative *RSFSR Marriage, Family and Guardianship Code of 1936* began to be implemented in Lithuania. In 1946, the Lithuanian newspaper *Komjaunimo tiesa* wrote: 'Who among the youth doesn't want a happy family life? But in the search for happiness, we mustn't allow ourselves to be guided purely by emotion. We must think rationally about our situation.'[72] The author of the article wrote that romantic love cannot be the basis for a family: 'Some say that all they need is love, but this is a deeply mistaken view. The Soviet person, building a married life should not be guided by this opinion alone. It does not justify the fundamental goal of a family: raising the next generation.'[73] Stalinist propaganda pushed passion out of everyday life and intimate relations. In the press, passion was called 'superficial and flippant treatment of the feelings of a Soviet person'.[74] In its place, the ideology introduced a new, Soviet conception of love. In the early 1950s, pedagogues in Lithuania were warning parents to protect their children from the pain and madness of romantic love. In 1954, E. Levanienė, director of the Vilnius Pedagogical Institute wrote that 'parents' and teachers' greatest trials come from adolescents and young adults falling in love. This brings more suffering than happiness to the culprits themselves. Falling in love manifests itself by sudden and acute attraction to individuals of the opposite sex. Meeting together excites them, overwhelms their mind, disrupting their common sense and orientation. Separation brings apathy, sadness, and longing. In such a state, the young person cannot study; other tasks are also difficult, but this feeling is short-lived.'[75]

During the peak of state-sponsored propaganda against sexual love, 15-year-old Bronė Sopienė (born in 1941) already had clear convictions about sexual behaviour, appropriate by Soviet pedagogical standards. Remembering her courtship with her future husband, she wrote thus:

> I was in the eighth grade when he, this eleventh grader, noticed me. Our relationship was so naïve, so innocent. I was convinced that girls my age should not kiss boys. And I lived by this, even though we were seriously involved. Even when he started university and would come to visit me, I still stood by my principles ... I was in my third year when I married him.[76]

Soviet experts convinced them that the sign of true love was a deep desire to hide it. This, according to them, was a sure sign that the love was strong and would last, ending in marriage.[77] Traces of Puritanical sex education can be found in many biographies of women at the time. Natalija J. (born 1937), in an interview, described the intimate experiences of her friend:

> I remember Onutė Knecevičienė. She came over one time and oh, how she cried! At the time she was in vocational school and Pijus had kissed her. She said to me: 'Dear God, dear God, what will I do now if a baby is born?' Onutė was from the Alytus Orphanage. I already knew that a kiss could not make a baby.[78]

Propaganda's battle with passionate romantic love as unpredictable became especially intense under Khrushchev. Although the political thaw opened up greater opportunities for cultural, artistic and scholarly expression, the sexual education of Soviet citizens was ignored. There was an attempt to convince Soviet youth that the proper time to get interested in sexual life was just before marriage. The Soviet Health Ministry encouraged teachers and parents not to interest adolescent girls in sex because, from a physiological perspective, it does not develop until they turn 20. According to ministry officials, Soviet scholarship had determined that sexual attraction and the adolescent had nothing to do with each other.[79] The popular 1962 Russian feature film *Kai medžiai buvo dideli* (When the Trees Were Large) was the screen version of this Soviet ideology: the film's protagonists Natasha and Lyonya sleep in separate beds after their wedding and have no interest in intimate relations.[80]

Under Khrushchev, sexual life was shrouded in silence and secrets; in Soviet scholarly literature, Sigmund Freud was associated with perverted lifestyles. Questions of a sexual nature began to appear in the press only at the end of the 1960s, when between 1968 and 1976 they were addressed in three new publications.[81] Nevertheless, the state's war on sexual love was met with a hostile response by some social groups. When in the early 1960s, Russian poet Jevtushenvko published a poem beginning with the line 'the bed was not made', this phrase created a sensation among the poet's admirers.[82]

Passionate romantic love was presented as dangerous and abnormal. Authors of propagandistic articles were aghast that Soviet youth were forming families and having children under the influence of this emotional affect.[83] Society and particularly the youth were warned that sexual romantic feelings inevitably led to calamities. In 1955, the chair of the Philosophy department at Vilnius Pedagogical Institute wrote in the popular magazine *Jaunimo gretos* (The Young Generation):

I remember a particular incident. One third-year female student from the Vilnius State Pedagogical University on an excursion during summer vacation met the 'ideal' young man, according to her, a 'gentleman'. Although their holiday romance did not last long, but the poor girl was so smitten that she no longer saw anything but *him*. Whenever the 'ideal gentleman' wanted something, she would bring it to him immediately, and when he got drunk with his friends and started talking about money, she gave him all of hers – she even sold her own watch.[84]

Readers invented by propaganda – or perhaps they were actual readers – sent letters to the magazine editors to inform them about the dangers that passionate love posed to marriage. M. Gamuvienė, a reader of *Tarybinė moteris* (Soviet Woman) wrote on the consequences of 'shotgun weddings':

The consequences of lightweight love are also sad … Veronika, had recently completed secondary school, and her husband was a zootechnician from a different town. As soon as he came to town, he made the rounds at the local parties, met up with our Veronika, and wouldn't you know it? Boom! He married her. The couple lived happily for six months, but then they started to bicker.[85]

Despite negative press in newspapers and magazines, men and women inevitably experienced sexual passion. At the time, propagandists explained this fact as an obstacle in the journey to 'true' love which every person must overcome. According to the ideologues, one had to be strong in order to prevail over the uncontrollable, stupid and naïve, passionate romantic love, to see it to its end, and in view of this individual victory, the Soviet person was ready for 'true' love and family. In 1955, poet Eugenijus Matuzevičius explained about the parasitic nature of passionate love: 'In life, in romance, there will be much suffering, grief, unsavoury and dishonourable behaviour. And usually, the reason for this is a flippant, simply parasitic outlook on love, on women, on relations between men and women.'[86]

Author Vytautas Petkevičius suggested that we ought not even try to avoid or hide from passionate love and suffering because no matter what, we'll still have to face it. According to the writer, in order to find relief for their sorrows in love, people will violate communist moral principles. Concerned reader Viktoras L. Baltušis offered this advice:

Trust the advice you get. You will never be satisfied anyway. You'll have to love and decide for yourself. And you will suffer disappointment and be frustrated, because love that is not experienced or lived is cheaper than a hollow knick-knack. Love detests calculations. It isn't looking for utility. It purifies. It teaches sacrifice. It forces us to stop thinking about ourselves.[87]

Lithuanian doctors were also participating in the battle with love and passion. Using medical science as his foundation, Č. Grizickas in the magazine *Mokslas ir gyvenimas* (Science and Life) claimed that in the journey to 'true' love, young people should expect a difficult road full of trials which they must endure.[88]

Propagandists warned about the number of passionate romances in a person's life. According to them, in the journey to 'true' love there cannot be 'ten or so' instances of romantic love. Quite the contrary, in their opinion, passion repeated would turn into performance, lie and, in general, no emotions will remain at all. And precisely these were what the ideologues were saving for 'true love'. Other propagandists pragmatically noted that passion repeated too many times 'repeats the very same words, oaths and duties'.[89] Eventually, a simple and clear strategy in the battle against passionate love was proposed: to limit the number of passionate love affairs, but to live them passionately, and afterwards, to forget them. It seems that the optimal recipe for decontamination after sexual romantic love affairs became to boldly experience the suffering caused by love and then to reject it. At the end of this emotional process, the Soviet youth's next step would be marriage. In 1955, the newspaper *Komjaunimo tiesa* argued that without this experienced emotional trajectory, lovers are not ready for marriage, because they have not yet gained the necessary spiritual characteristics. The author wrote:

> It seems to me that the issue is as follows: when entering into marriage according to the laws of love, young couples sometimes misunderstand it; what they call love is actually not love at all. Some might have every opportunity to start a family – they know how to love, to fall in love at first sight – yet their consciousness is still too independent, egoistic, selfish. Such persons have no right to the noble and dear emotion that we call love. They do not have the Soviet person's tremendous moral value, which we call stability in love.[90]

In propaganda films of the time, the extinguishing of passionate romantic love often coincided with the revelation of the beloved's moral failings. In the Lithuanian film *Tiltas* (The Bridge), the protagonist Rūta refuses passionate love because of her beloved's 'meagre soul' and the film's critics celebrated the film for depicting 'true love' comprehensively and with artistry. In 1957, a major family ideologue N. Solovjovas wrote about this film:

> Love is depicted masterfully in the script by Lithuanian writer Dovydaitis. Rūta, a physician, meets Romualdas. She likes him. She is prepared to be his wife. However, she cannot let go of the feelings she has for Romualdas's brother Algirdas, even though she respects him. When the war begins, Rūta sees that the

brothers are taking different paths. Romualdas dreams only of getting rich. She starts to see him as a person of weak soul. As her earlier feelings for Romualdas slowly begin to extinguish, they are replaced with a strong, conscious and bright feeling of love for Algirdas, a good person.[91]

Passionate love for the class enemy also had to be overcome, even within marriage. In the popular 1953 Russian film *Liubov Jarovaja*, the film's protagonist stifles her passion for her *kulak* husband.[92]

In Soviet culture, passionate romantic love and forming a family were two contradictory but necessary stages of a relationship. Marriage marked the end of sexual passion but opened the door to 'true' love and family. In 1956, the newspaper *Komjaunimo tiesa* published the article 'On Happy Families', in which the author distinguished between deceptive love, which one must overcome, and 'true love'. The author wrote thus: 'The majority of youth understand the development of such a complex human emotion like love too narrowly, too one-sidedly. "The culmination" is considered to be admitting one's love, while the wedding is seen as the "happy ending." '[93] The propagandists proposed waiting for love to pass and then deciding on a partner who is suitable for forming a family. An intense discussion on this topic developed between academics and writers. Although the participants in the discussion disagreed with one another, they all recognized that the content and purpose of love in socialist society was different than in the West. The professor, K. Daukšas, thought passion an unhealthy emotion which must be subdued as quickly as possible. In contrast, author Juozas Baltušis grew angry and wrote that a Soviet person's love must be passionate. But the author underscored that he was speaking about passion only possible in Soviet people and for this reason it was different from the sickly passion of the West.[94] Writers in the Soviet discourse often played the roles of 'rebellious heroes' who would organize propagandistic discussions like two supposedly opposing sides of an argument of ideas, in which ultimately the socialist values and principles always triumphed.[95]

In the early years of the post-war era, the press relied upon Russian ideologues and A. Makarenka's theory that 'love is not at all inspiration … it's an ordinary matter which must be managed'. The press also cited Clara Cetkin's thoughts about gender, calling them a vestige of bourgeois life: 'The proletariat is a rising class. It has no need for intoxication to numb it or make it nervous.'[96] At the same time, local propagandists proposed not basing marriage on love at all: 'first of all, one must put love in its place and not exalt it … Let's not put it up on a pedestal; instead let's show its true face; its powerful but sickly nature, its instability.'[97] The people of Lithuania were being persuaded that they would not create a happy family on the basis of the people's unhappiness because that would turn against the couple themselves. The youth was taught that the death of passion and sexual love is inevitable in marriage; therefore, there was no point in forming families with passion and love as their basis.[98] The state's pragmatic view on building families found an audience and indeed affected men's and women's real-life decisions. In a 1955 letter to his beloved, a husband laid out several practical plans for their marriage:

> I love you, Gražina, as my dear wife and would never wish you evil or wish to put pressure on you ... If a person loves, they can wait a few years ... For the time being, I will continue to live with Jadzė ... But if a third or fourth person were to appear on the scene to replace either of us, then perhaps it's better we don't cheat on one another. So, my angel, this is my opinion. You ask what we should do with the house? Don't sell it because if we'll be together, then we can furnish it and we'll have a place to live.[99]

Despite state and propaganda efforts, most readers still were not sure what the difference was between the first stage of passionate love and 'true love', and the press was forced to define both types of love. The authors had no trouble describing the travails and misfortunes of passion or sexual love, but they were at a loss for words to define 'true love' and expound its positive attributes. Their articles were abstract and inapplicable to real everyday life, and the authors used general phrases like 'beautiful feelings' 'enlightened and noble emotions' as well as 'emotional surrogates' as enemies of 'true love'.[100] The question became so pressing that the topic of 'true love' was treated in the editorial of the most important official Lithuanian newspaper *Tiesa*. The editors wrote thus:

> Let us judge a person's feelings based on their work and heroic deeds, which help us determine the greatness of their loving heart and the power of their ability to love, which nothing, no difficulties, no trials, no travails can defeat, disparage or belittle ... For [the Soviet people] love is not a game; it's not primitive instinct; rather, it's spiritual energy, capable of inspiring great deeds.[101]

Although 'true love' was discussed by specialists of almost every discipline, their characterizations of it were full of contradictions and were difficult to understand for Lithuania's people. The texts presented 'true' love as spontaneous, but also rational; passionate, but not blind. The authors claimed that 'true' love gave a person incredible power and was capable of imparting physical and spiritual energy on the lover, inspiring him to accomplish any task.[102] Yet, at the same time, 'true love' was depicted as incapable of suffusing a person's entire being, of being overly passionate, fatalistic and blind. Attorney T. Stungurys wrote thus:

> It's a different matter to speak of love's sickly expressions, about all kinds of crazy, blind loves, which of course must never be the inspiration for starting a family. However, a deep, true love is the necessary basis for building a family and living in harmony. One can derive a strict rule: without love, there's no need for a family. But in order for the family to be stable, love must have a real foundation: that the spouses be worthy of one another, that they have common noble goals, that their ages be compatible.[103]

The press also reminded readers that 'true love' is not merely an individual matter of the man and the woman. Just as 'art for art's sake' was dangerous to Soviet ideology, love without purpose could not exist in a socialist society. A pedagogue wrote: 'The love and friendship of Soviet youth is not just their personal matter. Friendship demands active, creative assistance and participation in the building of communist society.'[104] The propaganda warned that the Soviet person must grasp the secrets of love, otherwise they risked remaining uneducated and uncultivated. In 1964, an article in the magazine *Švyturys* (Lighthouse) wrote: 'Great treasures reside in music and the visual arts. If you don't love, you will never fully understand a symphony and you will forever see paintings only through the eyes of a craftsman.'[105]

Although the press urged readers not to trust in passionate love and to use rational criteria in selecting one's spouse, they also criticized marriages made for material reasons. Author Mykolas Sluckis, writing on marriage, argued that material difficulties make the young family only stronger. He insisted that the standard of living in socialist Lithuania 'does not demand that emotions be subjugated to material calculations'. With great bombast, the author depicted 'deep feelings' and 'true love' but like other Soviet Lithuanian artists participating in this discussion, he opposed passionate love and propagated 'carefully thought-out' feelings and marriage. In the journey to the true socialist family, Sluckis even offered Stakhanovite asceticism, calling material well-being 'bourgeois relics and exploitation of people'.[106]

At this time, Lithuanian men and women were therefore endlessly worried about whether they were capable of recognizing 'true love' where there must not be sexual passion, and which was disciplined. Confused protagonists of feature films (e.g. the 1960 Russian film *Is It Really Love?*) admitted to not understanding the purpose of intimate relations, thinking that perhaps they had missed the opportunity to have true feelings because they were unable to identify them. It seems that the propagandists themselves were incapable of answering these questions. In 1965, the editorial board of the magazine *Jaunimo gretos*, in response to the question 'What is "true" love?' of reader Dainius who was tortured by doubts, answered abstractly 'Not once did Dainius ask himself if it's love. Love can neither be written nor told. Love, like music, can only be felt.'[107]

By the end of the 1960s, 'true' love began to look like an almost impossible goal in the lives of ordinary people and an abstract concept with little significance. In 1972, according to a sociological study using public opinion surveys, newly-weds in Estonia listed love as the fifth reason for marrying one another. Their most important reasons for marrying were pragmatic everyday needs.[108] Less refined villagers described marriage relations pragmatically or extremely abstractly. Juzefa Aišmantienė (born in 1926) summarized her married life in practical terms: 'We lived together for twenty-three years … we bought a cow.'[109] For her part, Marytė Karpavičiūtė-Sadūnienė (b. 1934) in an interview said that she chose her husband based on spiritual attributes: 'I don't care what he looks like, whether he's attractive or rich. Externally, all that matters is that he's neat, not neglectful of his appearance. What I care about most is whether he's a good person. I watched how he respects his family and others.'[110] Calm affection and friendship became the ideal Soviet examples of 'true love', the principal attributes of which were respect for the beloved, a sense of responsibility, constancy and devotion.[111] Aldona Kvedarienė (b. 1955), married in the mid-1970s, similarly described the most romantic period of her life: 'In those days, we walked around, day after day in Vilnius; it was so nice, we held hands whenever we walked for two years. We got married 9 August, and hand in hand, joined together with this platonic feeling, we married. I thought that a spiritual bond was more important than any physical one.'[112] The communist newspaper *Komjaunimo tiesa* based on surveys of young people claimed that the majority of Soviet people already understood 'true love'. According to the authors, the surveys proved that the youth looked down on marriage based on passionate (untried) love and were outraged by the fact that marriages were still being formed for such unsuitable reasons. Survey participants demanded greater state assistance for families.[113]

At the end of the 1960s, Russian sociologist J. Riurikovas was likely the first to note the elimination of passionate romantic love and Soviet culture's terror of it. Timidly relying on his sources, Riurikovas argued that 'love is not always the family ideal [we imagine it to be] and it is often experienced with shock; [ultimately,] we are at our best when we love'.[114] Riurikovas did not bring up the question of why passionate romantic love cannot be the basis for marriage, but his work created a niche for the public discourse on sexual love.

The Soviet conception of love was formulated within the framework of Stalin's and Khrushchev's family policies. It sought to simplify sexual culture and to identify sexual experience with reproduction. In the late 1950s, a wide propaganda campaign was waged in the press against any manifestations of sex or gender. Sexuality was erased from clothing, language, images and self-expression. In 1959, there were no doubts about what would sexually stimulate a man: 'Not earrings, necklaces, rouged lips or painted nails, but a clean dress, well-fitting stockings, neatly combed hair and a clean neck.'[115]

At dances, young men were urged to dance with all women no matter what their age, because too much attention to one girl would be seen as churlish behaviour. However, the principles of 'true' Soviet love which had trained Soviet people to isolate passionate experience from marriage could not answer the questions raised by society, and in large part, led to the increasing number of unhappy marriages and divorces in Lithuania. In the opinion of sexologists, women's frigidity in the USSR was a huge problem, about which doctors, educators and other specialists were silent. According to Michail Stern's research, during the Stalin years, likely 80 per cent of Soviet women had never experienced orgasm. Starting in 1970, their numbers fell to approximately 45 per cent. Meanwhile doctors suggested to women complaining about their sex lives to take the waters at Soviet mineral water spas.[116]

In the early 1980s, the war on passion and sexuality began to give up its positions. No longer was passionate love seen as an immature period in the transition to marriage which must be overcome and forgotten as quickly as possible, but as one of the most important and most cherished human feelings. Lithuania took its first steps to officially deal with marriage problems beginning in the mid-1970s. The first family counselling and psychiatric clinics were established in 1969. Clinics operated on a voluntary social basis, but after 1974, they were financed with state funds. In 1984, there were family counselling offices in every major Lithuanian city, as well as two-year folk culture programmes for would-be newly-weds or those who had already started families.[117] In the 1970s, the first medical centres dedicated to the study of human sexual behaviour were established in Riga and Leningrad.

Increasingly, the idea that physical love and sexual satisfaction for men and women had been devalued gained currency in Lithuania. In the magazine *Tarybinė moteris* a male author wrote thus: 'This question was sometimes carefully broached in dry medical discourse and was often intimidating its goals, as described in some brochure lying around the polyclinic waiting room next to publications like "TB Is Curable" or "Beware of Dysentery." But you will definitely not find any advice there on how to better experience intimacy or meld into one another.'[118] Although the society was guided by conservative family policies and the puritanical Soviet concept of love, the absence of sexual education, lack of information about human sexuality and chronic shortages of contraceptives, in Lithuania as in all of the USSR, turned abortion into a legal means to regulate pregnancies. At the same time, the banning of sexual freedom led to a drastically decreasing marital age while it artificially increased the number of 'shotgun' marriages.

In 1978, public opinion surveys in Estonia revealed that approximately 82 per cent of young men and 71 per cent of young women had sexual relations before marriage.[119] In 1953, men had called their future bride's pregnancy a 'fault', but in 1984, in Lithuania, the number of pregnant brides with grooms who were barely adults was clearly increasing (see Table 2.2).

By percentage, men marrying under the age of 20 among the total number of grooms in 1980 were 6.8 per cent, and in 1990, their number was 8.8 per cent. Women marrying younger than 20 were 20 per cent, but in 1990, the number had increased to 27.7 per cent.[120] In response to these numbers, in 1983, educators established a course for secondary school students which was called 'The Ethics and Psychology of Family Life'.[121]

In the early years of Gorbachev's *perestroika*, sexual behaviour changed and became more liberal. In 1989, the magazine *Tarybinė moteris*, which had for decades propagated Soviet family policy, expressed shock about young women and their openly sexual clothing, hairstyles, make-up and provocative behaviour. The author of the article explained that most likely something had happened to the men and they were in need of supplemental 'dope'. The collapsing Soviet system attracted massive audiences wishing to learn more about the hitherto taboo topics of frigidity, impotence, homosexuality, orgasm and other sexual questions. After the collapse of the regime, young couples were no longer directly influenced by Soviet ideology and propaganda as they built their marriages. However, the idea of the family as an open collective promoted for decades

Table 2.2 Newlyweds under the Age 20 per 1,000 marriages, 1980–90

Year	Brides under the Age of 20, Per cent per 1,000	Grooms under the Age of 20 Per cent per 1,000
1980	55.3	17.8
1990	83.3	24

Source: Alina Zvinklienė, 'The State of Family Studies in Lithuania', *Marriage and Family Review* 22, no. 3 (1996).

had unavoidably moulded marital behaviour and relationships based on Soviet codes and communist morality, adapting them to the realities of Soviet everyday life. The most notable consequence of this was a drastic increase in the number of unhappy marriages and divorces.

Reasons for marrying

In Soviet society, the goal of 'true' love and choosing marriage for the appropriate reasons was to raise the next generation. One newspaper wrote thus:

> Some will say that love is all you need to find happiness in your life. This is a deeply flawed opinion. The Soviet person, in forming a marriage, should not be guided by this idea alone. It does not justify the principal purpose of family: to rear the next generation.[122]

Rearing the next generation in Soviet society was expected to be the basis of individual and family happiness. If passionate love was based in emotion and feeling, then family happiness could be achieved only by rationalizing intimate interpersonal relations. The official state newspaper *Tiesa* rhetorically asked: 'Is there a young person who doesn't seek a happy family life? However, in seeking that happiness, should one be motivated purely by emotion? Shouldn't one consider one's situation rationally?'[123] Ordinary Lithuanian men and women eventually began to conceive of their future marriages more pragmatically than emotionally and likely were not surprised by official reproductive wishes to Lithuanian women on New Year's Day 1961: 'A woman's strength is her heart. But to love, one must first have children.'[124]

In 1967, a survey revealed that 95 per cent of newly-weds in Lithuania formally explained that their motivation for marrying was love; however, in more detailed responses to the same question, love no longer came up, and respondents instead listed very practical reasons for marrying.[125] In 1973, in a survey of major universities in Lithuania, Vilnius University students did not mention love for their future spouse and instead listed reasons which years of propaganda had presented as appropriate for marriage and creating a good socialist family. Female students first expected intelligence and cultivation from their future spouse; second, they wanted him to be a good friend, and third, to be good with children; fourth, to be a good person; fifth, to be hard-working; sixth, to have a good sense of humour and to be physically attractive. In turn, for male students the most desirable attribute of their spouse-to-be was her ability to understand her husband, to mother him, be gentle, generous and have good housekeeping skills.[126] Some ten years later, in a 1984–5 survey in Vilnius of 220 newly-weds, respondents, when asked about their motivation for marriage, claimed that their decision was primarily based on the physical attractiveness of their future spouse, but they also listed practical motivations. Men saw in a successful marriage a woman's ability to be hardworking and tidy, and women looked for caring and dutiful men.[127] In the 1970s, Soviet sociological surveys revealed love and family as two separate and even contradictory notions: questionnaires posed the question which would they choose, family or love? In Estonia, only 11.8 per cent of men and 14.2 per cent of women said love was more important than marriage; 42.2 per cent of men and 53.4 per cent of women chose family as their priority. The remaining participants' choice between love and family was determined by their specific, concrete situations.[128]

As couples' motivations for marriage became more and more pragmatic, romantic relationships before marriage lost their meaning and naturally grew shorter. In 1966, questionnaire results showed that 33 per cent of newly-weds in Lithuania had courted for up to three months, and 45 per cent fewer than six months. In the 1970s, courtship became even shorter: 40 per cent of marriages occurred in fewer than twelve months. However, most commonly, couples married after one month, or at most, after three months of courtship. From 1984 to 1985, in Vilnius, 27 per cent of couples married after approximately three to six months of courtship, 8 per cent within one month of meeting and 22 per cent married within twelve months after they met.[129]

Khrushchev's propaganda formed young people's views on marriage. Parents were encouraged to cultivate in their children an 'appropriate' choice of marriage partner. They were advised to investigate their future son- or daughter-in-law's character, get a sense of their views on work and their elders, and to test their intellect by discussing books and films and analysing the behaviour of protagonists in plays with them.[130] Normative attributes for 'a good partner' inevitably stigmatized marriages that did not correspond to criteria determined by propaganda. Marriages with so-called former enemies of the people as well as their children undoubtedly belonged to this group. Appropriate and trustworthy motivations for marriage could be formed and approved by the work collective. Such marriages were presented by the press as especially enlightened and promising. An article 'Best Wishes, Nijolė and Alfredas!' describes the marriage of two members of a student song and dance ensemble; the couple's love, marriage and family are described as intrinsically linked to the collective ('happiness is working and being with others, and not closing one selves off within the family "fortress"'): not only did the couple meet as part of the collective, but they developed their feelings for each other with the help of the ensemble's members ('when Nijolė's and Alfredas's friendship began, the collective greeted it with happiness, they nurtured it, cared for it – they helped it flourish').[131] The active role played by the collective in confirming the couple's choice did not end with registry of the marriage. The work collective had great power and was responsible for solving problems within the marriage, and in case of divorce, even for dividing up of the couple's property.

Some publications encouraged looking not only a future spouse's moral qualities, but also their state of their physical health. The article 'Whom Shall I Marry?' advised evaluating the individual's biological characteristics because they were said to reflect the person's spiritual state. The recommendations were reminiscent of eugenics: 'We, psychiatrists have always based our work on the traditional prerequisite that the relationship between body and soul is proportionate.'[132] Specialists of various fields, including a surgeon, psychiatrist, hygienist, dermo-venereologist, physiologist and endocrinologist, advised noting physical defects such as asymmetrical eyes and face, uni-brows and cowlicks because these shortcomings were believed to be common among mentally challenged individuals. They also claimed that interethnic marriage improved the physical and mental health of future children.[133] There can be no doubt that the latter was meant to encourage the integration of the international Soviet nations.

Lawyers, educators and philosophers joined in the campaign for 'appropriate' motivations for marriage and the choice of marriage partners. In 1967, the journal *Jaunimo gretos* organized a roundtable discussion on the optimal age for marriage, preferable length of courtship and which state institution would best manage the future newly-weds' choices. One of the discussants offered the following vision: 'Perhaps someday I will be able to pick up my phone and dial 02, say "hello", describe my personal dilemma and be able to listen to advice on how to deal with it.'[134] In the 1970s, modern technology presented opportunities in the formalization of the quest for marriage partners with the assistance of information science specialists according to a pre-designed programme. After examining applicants' education, needs and preferences, it would create tables and 'electronic advisers'.[135] This formalized quest for marriage partners was not offered as practical assistance to those seeking a spouse, but rather as a universal state strategy.

The ideologues themselves admitted that marriage became a means for securing registration in a desirable city, and after completing university or specialized vocational studies, marriage was a way to get a good job together with one's beloved. Marriage and family status was also one of the conditions for improved material conditions for Soviet citizens, beginning with everyday household goods and ending with housing and a car. It is no accident that during divorce proceedings husbands accused their wives of ostensibly marrying only in order to change their last name. In 1972, a plaintiff in an application for divorce perhaps did not reveal the real reason for separating, but he revealed a stigma and stereotype about unmarried women: 'The main reason for the demise of our marriage is the following: in marrying me, the plaintiff was not thinking about a successful family life. She only cared about not remaining a spinster. She wanted to have a child and however possible to secure child support.'[136]

As the political thaw began, state family policy encouraged marriages that were not grounded in intimate and emotional ties between two individuals. Starting in the late 1970s, in Lithuania as in other Soviet republics, 'character irreconcilability' and 'lack of spiritual connection' became the most common reasons for divorce. Progressive sociologists of the time argued that love, indicated officially as the reason for marriage, actually hid the fact that in Soviet marriages there was increasingly less love and mutuality.[137] During the era of Gorbachev's *perestroika*, foreign scholars visiting the USSR found that Soviet couples treated their marriages very practically and pragmatically, and they were rarely construed as based on love, intimacy or mutual spiritual ties.[138] It is no accident that in 1988, official state data showed that, already before their wedding, 70 per cent of future grooms and 60 per cent of future wives could not immediately answer when the couple had last been together or how they had spent their time.[139] At the end of the 1990s, Lithuanian sociologists' studies also demonstrated that marriage partner choices were not spontaneous, and motivations for marrying were rather regular and predictable.[140]

Eventually, few in Soviet Lithuania believed in happy marriages. In 1984–5, barely half of marrying couples evaluated their family and marriage prospects optimistically, and on their wedding day only 49 per cent of brides and 60 per cent of grooms still believed that their marriage would be happy and that it would bring them personal satisfaction.[141] Married life and family began to be conceived of as hard work full of conflicts that would have to be suffered and resolved. This conception of marriage and family remained until the end of the 1990s. One of the most famous psychologists in the republic A. Alekseičikas wrote in the popular press that happily married couples understand family life first of all as 'complicated, difficult and full of responsibilities'. If the relationship is too easy and 'everything happens of its own accord', then the family is not performing its function.[142] The number of unhappy marriages increased throughout the USSR. In 1980, sexologist Michail Stern, generalizing the subject of his study, published results that showed 74 per cent of couples living in constant conflict. In 1977, a sociological questionnaire of fifty families in Russia also revealed that thirty-seven of the fifty families were experiencing constant conflict and scandal.[143] In Soviet society, in large part the very idea of family had degraded, and couples remained in unhappy marriages or got divorced.

Divorce

In 1566, the Lithuanian Statute, the second of three-principle law of the Grand Duchy of Lithuania, left marriage and divorce to the jurisdiction of the spiritual courts. Shortly after the elimination of the Polish-Lithuanian sovereign state and the so-called Third Partition, in 1840, tsarist Russian law was imposed and the statute was voided. Volume Ten of Part One of the Code of Laws of the Russian Empire and the tsar's decree of 1836 again left matrimonial questions to the spiritual courts.[144] Tsarist civil law continued to operate in the Independent Republic of Lithuania (1918–40), thus sanctioning only church marriages until the Second World War, which, in most cases, were entered into according to Roman Catholic canon law and did not offer a juridical basis for dissolving the marriage. If a church marriage was annulled, the couple's property disputes were handled by secular courts.[145]

After Lithuania's annexation to the USSR, the president of the republic on 15 August 1940 signed the *Marriage Law* which legalized the civil registry of marriages and regulated divorce proceedings. Divorce hearings would be held in the county courts, and couples could file for divorce in writing or verbally, by mutual agreement, or if one spouse expressed the desire to divorce. As the law did not require reasons for divorce, it was effectively authorizing 'no-fault' divorce. The county courts were required, however, to do everything possible to convince the couple seeking dissolution of their marriage to withdraw their petition and reconcile. Ultimately, if the judge was unsuccessful in restoring harmony, the marriage would be dissolved.[146] The *Marriage Law* remained in effect for only a few months because before long Soviet laws took effect on Lithuanian territory.

On 30 November 1940, the Presidium of the LSSR Supreme Soviet issued a decree regarding the application of the criminal and civil laws of the RSFSR to Lithuania (as well as Latvia and Estonia). The decree articulated that the laws would remain in effect in the Baltic republics until the respective republics implemented their own. The *RSFSR Marriage, Family and Guardianship Code* went into effect in the Lithuanian territory in December 1940; its complete official title was the *Marriage, Family and Guardianship Law Valid in the Territory of the LSSR* (henceforth referred to as the *RSFSR Marriage, Family and Guardianship Code*). A few years later, on 8 July 1944, the *RSFSR Marriage,*

Family and Guardianship Code was appended by decree of the Presidium of the USSR Supreme Soviet. Although it was expected that the *Code* and *8 July 1944 decree* would be temporary, they remained in effect with only a few minor revisions in Lithuania for the next twenty-nine years, until 1969.[147]

The *8 July 1944 decree* provided that either one of the parties or both parties through mutual agreement could file for divorce. The petitioner(s) had to lay out the reasons for the domestic strife and provide the names and addresses of potential witnesses. The court would assess a 100-rouble filing fee along with an additional 50 roubles to pay for an announcement in the local newspaper on the divorce proceedings. The information published in the newspaper was detailed and would include the surnames and address of the divorcing couple. One such 1944 newspaper announcement stated the following:

> The city of Vilnius District I People's Court announces that on 1 September of this year, petitioner Mečislovas Versockas, son of Juozas, residing in Vilnius, at Geležinė Str., Apt. 2, filed a civil case against respondent Ona Versockienė, daughter of Teofilė, born in 1912, and residing in Vilnius, at Geležinė Str., Apt. 2, regarding divorce case No. 2-11-44.[148]

Divorce proceedings were conducted as public hearings, unless the two parties requested otherwise and the court had consented that the case be heard behind closed doors. If the marriage was dissolved, one or both parties would be liable for 500 to 2,000 roubles in court costs. In the early post-war years, judges tended to assign smaller fines and extract more from the guilty party or the spouse with greater means. In 1945, the Supreme Court ruled in favour of Vladislova A., allowing her to divorce respondent Vladas A. due to his alcoholism, physical abuse and failure to care for their child. The petitioner was liable for 100 roubles, and the respondent for 200 roubles.[149]

Courts and judges

After the war, the Lithuanian court system was reorganized according to the Soviet model and divorce cases were heard twice by two different courts: the People's Court and the Supreme Court. The People's Courts did not handle divorce cases on their merits. The goal of the People's Courts was to try to reconcile the two parties and determine whether a life together henceforth was possible. For this reason, the findings of the People's Court were practically identical and would prepare the petitioners for the case to be brought to the Supreme Court. Most findings came to conclusions similar to the following: 'Because the two parties are unable to reconcile, the People's Court considers this case closed, and the petitioner hereby has the right to take their case to the LSSR Supreme Court.'[150] The People's Courts acted as formal mediators; this is why the judges' decisions followed the same formula for several decades. In 1965, the Švenčionys People's Court only formally confirmed that 'the divorce case of petitioner Genovefa K. against respondent Aleksas K. is considered closed by the People's Court due to the inability of the two sides to reconcile'.[151] During the course of the proceedings, the People's Courts would briefly present their findings on the circumstances of the divorce. The details however would have no effect on the court's decision and would be passed on to the Supreme Court. There were forty People's Courts in 1945 in Lithuania; by 1953, there were 112. This network of People's Courts remained unchanged until the 1960s.[152]

The Supreme Court heard divorce cases as the court of first instance and as the court of cassation. All divorce cases that came before the People's Court ended up there; the Supreme Court would in turn decide on the merits of these cases and establish the procedures for custody of the children and the division of marital property. Their rulings were not subject to appeal. Nonetheless, they were frequently reviewed under the supervision procedures initiated by the Presidium of the Supreme Court or by the chief justice of the Supreme Court of the LSSR. In such cases, the chief justice would write a letter of protest to the Presidium of the Supreme Court, requesting one or several of the decisions of the Civil Chamber of the Court be repealed. The Supreme Court's decisions could be reviewed and/or repealed by the petitioner's appeal to the party leadership or the LSSR Office of the prosecutor. At this point, one could expect the Supreme Court's ruling to be overturned along with the People's Court's findings regarding the grounds for divorce and their assignation of culpability for the domestic strife. One such petition for review was filed by an ex-wife and mother who petitioned the Lithuanian Communist Party Central Committee (LCP(b) CC) Secretary and LSSR Office of the Prosecutor over a ruling that assigned custody of her child to the child's father. The Ignalina People's Court's ruling was promptly overturned and passed on to the Supreme Court for a second review. The mother's suit was upheld.[153]

From 1951 to 1953, the courts of the Vilnius, Kaunas, Klaipėda and Šiauliai districts operated in Lithuania. The *5 August 1946 decree* of the Presidium of the LSSR Supreme Soviet allowed the district courts to also hear divorce cases on the merits. Like the Supreme Court, the district courts determined child custody, child support and division of marital property procedures.[154] After the administrative reforms of 1953, the district courts were eliminated.

Archival research on the practice of Soviet divorce conducted in this monograph for the first time has challenged statements in historiography that after the *8 July 1944 decree*, divorce proceedings became expensive, complicated and considerably stricter.[155] On the contrary, analysis of all Soviet divorce cases in the Lithuanian Central State Archive (LCSA) indicates that both courts, the People's Court and the Supreme Court, resolved divorce cases quickly and quite easily. The proceedings were brief, especially during the first decade after the war. From the date petitioners filed for divorce to the announcement of the Supreme Court's ruling, the entire process, including hearings in both the People's Court and the Supreme Court, took less than four months. In cases of the Supreme Court remanding the case for retrial, the proceedings before the People's Court and the Supreme Court in the first instance would usually last five to six months from the date the petitioner first filed a declaration of their desire to divorce to the People's Court. The Supreme Court did receive complaints about overly hasty rulings and superficial investigations into marital circumstances. In 1944, petitioner Vladas K. complained that the People's Court had not attempted to thoroughly investigate his case and that it hadn't even heard both sides of the argument. According to the petitioner, the judge had told him that if 'the Court were to delve into all the details, how would it ever conclude the proceedings?' The petitioner claimed that the judge was hearing several cases on the same day and for this reason did everything so hastily. He added, 'the courts are involved in soc. [socialist] competition'.[156]

Inadequate opportunities for professional education in the law and a shortage of judges hindered the effectiveness of the work of the People's Courts. Most of Lithuania's professional lawyers had fled to the West, while those who remained did their best to avoid the Soviet system and instead chose to practice law as attorneys. As a result, in 1946, of sixty-three lawyers working in Lithuania, forty-nine had university degrees, but only two judges in the People's Courts had actually graduated from university.[157] On the other hand, until the mid-1960s, divorce petitioners rarely sought help from attorneys and instead would file for divorce themselves, using every-day, colloquial language. In 1956, petitioner Kazimiera G., in her petition to the Joniškėlis People's Court of her intent to file for divorce, explained that she wanted a divorce from her husband Steponas G. because 'we just can't get along. He keeps hitting me and calling me every name under the sun.'[158]

The education of the judges of the People's Court often had nothing to do with legal studies. In 1946, only thirty-six judges out of the sixty-four in the entire People's Court system had completed secondary school. Judges of the

Supreme Court were better qualified: of the eleven judges, seven had studied the law but one had no legal education whatsoever. After the war, the process of studying to be a lawyer went slowly. In 1945, a two-year school of law was established and operated for ten years, and the first graduating class of lawyers from Vilnius University completed their studies in 1950.[159] Until 1950, only one out of two judges who headed the Civil Chamber of the Supreme Soviet of the LSSR was college-educated. The lack of professional competence led not only to slipshod divorce litigation, but often also to illogical and unfounded rulings. Often the very same arguments and identical conditions in various People's Court cases led to completely contrary conclusions. Because of their lack of professional training, judges would hear divorce cases based on their own discretion and life experiences. For this reason, among the first People's Court decisions, we find colourful language, rather than arguments presented in the legal idiom. For example, in 1946, a People's Court divorce agreement relies on the following testimony: 'The witnesses state that they know that the two parties can't get along, that the respondent is sick in the head and wets his bed in his sleep, and in general, whenever he gets angry, he stops working and calls the petitioner a whore.'[160]

On the other hand, some People's Court judges understood perfectly well that their role as assigned by Soviet law was to act as mediators, and therefore they did not delve too deeply into the substance of each case. Judges rejected accusations of slipshod work: since the couples had no intention of making up, a detailed analysis of their cases was unnecessary. If the People's Court had breached procedure, the Supreme Court could overturn the proceedings. In one case in 1956, because the Kėdainiai People's Court had not even called the two parties to the hearing, the Supreme Court returned the case to them for retrial. Judge Nutautas, furious, wrote the following explanation to the Supreme Court: 'I consider the case [in the Supreme Court] dismissed and [the People's Court] decision repealed without due cause. All the more because [the People's] Court did not decide the case on its merits but was only charged with trying to reconcile the two parties.'[161]

The two-instance divorce proceedings system was abolished in Lithuania on 10 December 1965 when the Presidium of the USSR Supreme Soviet announced court system reforms. Under their new jurisdiction, the People's Courts were authorized to continue performing their mediation function attempting to reconcile the partners. However, in the event that they were not successful, the court would consider cases on their merits. As before, petitioners were required to indicate their grounds for divorce, provide information on their children's place of residence, make suggestions for child custody, deciding which parent would be appointed guardian and indicating who would be paying child support and in what sum. Once the dual-instance divorce proceedings were discontinued, the stream of divorce cases brought to the Supreme Court by the People's Courts dried up. From then on, the Supreme Court heard only appeals of exceptional cases, primarily involving paternity disputes or complicated division of marital property cases. The reforms ended the requirement that announcements of the divorce proceedings be published in the newspaper. Once the decree of dissolution was issued, the former spouses were responsible for 50 to 200 roubles in court costs.[162]

On 16 July 1969, the LSSR Supreme Soviet ratified the *LSSR Marriage and Family Code*, which took effect in Lithuania on 1 January 1970.[163] The *LSSR Marriage and Family Code* replaced the *RSFSR Marriage, Family and Guardianship Code*, which had been in effect in Lithuania since 1940. Concurrently, the LSSR Council of Ministers ratified the new *LSSR Civil Registry Guidelines Law*, which also went into effect 1 January 1970.[164] Although officially the *RSFSR Marriage, Family and Guardianship Code*, which had been law in the Lithuanian territory since 1940 along with the *8 July 1944 decree*, had made the process of obtaining a divorce much stricter, in reality, the current practice of divorce proceedings was simple, fast and, in most cases, petitioners' requests for divorce were granted as long as there were no major disputes between the two parties. However, hearings of the case by the People's Court and the Supreme Court did not guarantee legal objectivity and the two jurisdictions did not concern themselves with the consequences of their rulings on the families in question, particularly the women and children. Indeed, whether the courts ruled in one way or another often depended on the direct influence of party leadership or trade union or work collective organizations.

Paragraph 87 of the new *Civil Registry Guidelines Law* simplified the legal procedure of divorce. From 1 January 1970, it became possible to obtain a divorce in the civil registry bureau if the couple did not have minor children, had no disputes over property and if both parties agreed to dissolve the marriage.

Statistics

The *RSFSR Marriage, Family and Guardianship Code* recognized only those marriages registered in the civil status registry or church marriages from before 1940. The latter marriages were treated as legitimate marriages registered according to the *RSFSR Marriage, Family and Guardianship Code* procedures, as long as couples had registered them in addition to the civil registry bureau. In reality, the Soviet government sought to separate the Catholic Church from the state and Lithuania's believers from the church as quickly and effectively as possible. However, marriage by religious ceremony, in existence in Lithuania for centuries as the only form of marriage, no longer satisfied the modernizing society's norms and desires. Some men and women inevitably faced failed marriages. Unable to divorce legally, Catholics had been forced to solve their personal problems illegally, for instance by abandoning their families or forming bigamous unions and marriages; their other option was an unbearable life together under one roof. Children born into bigamous families in Lithuania before 1940 were registered as bastards under their mothers' surnames and had no rights to their fathers' inheritance. It is believed that approximately 30,000 de facto marriages had not been consecrated in church in interwar Lithuania.[165] Thus Lithuanians, particularly those with failed marriages, greeted civil registry with relief and joy. In 1949, one would-be divorcee wrote the following free-form declaration of intent to divorce: 'I [have long] dreamed of divorce, but under the bourgeois system where everything was determined by the Church, divorce was impossible.'[166]

The society's need for divorce in the years immediately following the Second World War was obvious. And indeed an examination of summaries of divorce cases heard by the Supreme Court available in the archives shows that once civil registry was established, the number of divorces in Lithuania continued to increase. In 1947, there were 789 civil cases heard by the Supreme Soviet of the LSSR of which 750 were divorce cases.[167] The following year, from 25 February 1948 until 6 January 1949, 802 civil cases went before the Supreme Court in first instance; of these only sixty concerned matters other than divorce.[168] In 1957, the LSSR Supreme Court Chamber for Civil Cases heard 1,746 cases in all; of these 1,696 were divorce cases and only 50 were related to other matters.[169] As long as the LSSR Supreme Court heard all People's Court cases on first instance, divorce proceedings comprised the majority of cases heard by the Supreme Courts.

The first official statistics on divorce began to be collected in 1950 in Lithuania and the data confirm the consistent increase in the number of divorces. Divorce rates in the three Baltic Soviet republics surpassed those of the rest of the USSR. In 1950, of 100 registered marriages in Lithuania, there were 2.7 divorces; in 1960, the rate increased to 8.4 divorces; and in 1970, there were 23.1 divorces. In 1979, the number increased to 33.9 divorces per 100 marriages. In 1976 in Latvia, of 100 marriages, 52 ended in divorce, 1.4 times more than the Soviet average.[170]

In Lithuania's capital Vilnius, between 1972 and 1978, the number of divorces almost doubled. In 1972, the city of Vilnius registered 1,479 divorces, and in 1978, there were 2,037. That year, in Vilnius, there were 3.7 divorces for every 1,000 inhabitants, and in 1978, correspondingly, the number was 4.3. In Riga and Tallinn, the capitals of the other two Baltic republics, the divorce rates were even higher. In 1972, of 1,000 residents in Riga, there were 6.3 divorces, and in 1978, the number was 6.2. In Tallinn in 1972, of 1,000 residents, there were 5.0 divorces, and in 1978, the number remained the same: 5.0.[171]

Among the three Baltic republics, Lithuania's rate of divorce was the lowest. In Lithuania, over a period of thirty-eight years, from 1950 to 1988, the rate of divorce per 100 marriages grew from 2.7 to 33.5. At the same time, in 1988, the rate of divorce per 100 marriages in Estonia was 46.3, and in Latvia it was 43.6.[172]

The different dynamics playing out in the three republics could be explained by the demographics of each respective republic. A study done in 1987 determined that the most stable marriages in Lithuania were those of Polish and Lithuanian families: out of 100 marriages, these ethnic groups divorced at rates of 26.3 and 29.9, respectively. Meanwhile, the rates of divorce for Russian families were considerably higher. Of 100 Russian marriages in Lithuania, 61.3 ended in divorce.[173] Taking into account that the Russian community in Lithuania was considerably smaller (approximately 7 per cent) compared to that of Latvia or Estonia (approximately 30 per cent), the ethnic factor to a great extent explains the differences in divorce rates in the three Baltic republics. Although the divorce rates in Lithuania increased, they were still lower than the USSR average: in 1960, of 1,000 Soviet inhabitants, 1.3 divorced; in 1968, the number was 2.7. Meanwhile in Lithuania, out of 1,000 inhabitants, 0.9 divorced, and in 1970, the number was 2.2.[174]

During the first decade after the war, petitioners filing for divorce in Lithuania were exclusively men; however, from the mid-1950s, women joined their ranks. In 1954, 39 per cent of those filing for divorce in Lithuania were women and 61 were men. In the mid-1960s, rates reversed, and the number of women filing for divorce was somewhat greater than the number of men: in 1964, among those filing for divorce, 50.5 per cent were women and 49.5 were men.[175]

Some scholars claim that, from 1975 to 1980, divorce became fashionable or even prestigious in Soviet society.[176] Indeed, the divorce boom in the USSR paralleled the general tendency in modern societies, but on the other hand, in Soviet Lithuania, as in the other European republics of the USSR, divorces resulted from very particular reasons characteristic of the totalitarian regime.

Marital strife

Occupation and terror

In many cases, the occupation and crimes committed by the regime affected interpersonal relations. Until Stalin's death in March of 1953, a number of missing divorce petitioners and respondents never returned to the courtroom. They were exiled, imprisoned, persecuted and killed. On 23 April 1945, Otilija K. petitioned the Supreme Court for a divorce that both parties had agreed to. However, on 23 August, she did not appear at the hearing. After repeated summons to appear before the court, the case was dismissed on 7 January 1947 when the Volost of Ramygala Executive Committee Secretary Valdas Petrauskas informed the court that Otilija K. had been killed and her husband Vladas K. had been exiled.[177] Frequently, divorce cases were dismissed when the couple in question disappeared without a trace. In 1944, the divorce proceedings for M. V. and O. V. began in court, and in 1946, the case on first instance reached the Supreme Court. However, the public hearing never took place because neither the petitioner nor the respondent appeared in court. The court documents were returned with a stamp indicating that the petitioners had left no forwarding address.[178]

Marriages were not always able to withstand the regime, violence and chaos of the post-war era. Having one's spouse exiled or imprisoned often became an unbearable burden and grounds for divorce. In one case in 1953, the Supreme Court indicated on the divorce documents that the two parties had married in 1939; they had lived together until December of 1951 when the respondent was arrested and sentenced to three years in prison. A few years later, his wife filed for divorce because she wished to remarry. The Chamber of Civil Cases granted her divorce, arguing that the respondent was in prison and his wife was not willing 'to wait for him'. The same arguments were presented to the court by male petitioners whose wives were in prison or exile and who were likewise not interested in waiting for them.[179]

Not all prisoners returned to their families or to Lithuania after serving their prison terms or after being released from exile, and this ambiguous marital situation could persecute the couple for years. On 14 June 1965, a petitioner argued to the Šakiai District People's Court that in 1950 he had married Valentina Ž.-G., who, one year later was sent to prison. After serving her sentence, she left Lithuania. Only more than ten years later did her husband find out that she was living in Soviet Georgia under a different surname and was filing for divorce.[180]

Upon returning to Lithuania after long sentences in prison or exile, couples often did not find their homes or personal property. In 1963, one husband wrote in his petition for divorce to the Panevėžys People's Court that he had married in 1939, acquired a parcel of land, planted an orchard and purchased construction materials for building a home. But he did not manage to build his family home, because in January 1946, he was arrested and sentenced to ten years in prison. After returning to Lithuania from the labour camps in June 1954, his construction materials were nowhere to be found. His wife explained that she had sold them because she needed the money to live on.[181] The court had ruled favourably in similar divorce cases in the past. Post-war divorce case proceedings were formal and superficial and did not delve into details.

Church weddings and bigamy

On 5 August 1946, the LSSR Supreme Soviet issued a decree regarding revisions to the *RSFSR Marriage, Family and Guardianship Code*. First, regarding individuals who had been married by the church before the Second World War. The decree allowed these couples to register their marriages at the civil registry bureau, indicating the length of time they had lived together. In these cases, if the church marriage had been registered at the civil registry bureau, it was possible to dissolve it. But not all married couples had registered.[182] If the spouses had subsequently remarried, this time registering the union at the civil registry bureau, these men and women automatically became bigamists or polygamists, because their church marriages also remained valid. This phenomenon in Soviet Lithuania continued until the 1960s, when the number of church marriages that had taken place before the war naturally began to decline. If subsequent marriages also failed, the spouses would be forced to reveal their previously concealed bigamous marriages; they would often attempt to use them as grounds for divorce. In 1961, a petitioner told the court that her marriage was completely invalid. The woman explained that in 1954, shortly after registering her marriage at the Šiauliai registry bureau, she learnt that her husband had hidden from her his church marriage from before the war.[183] Therefore, according to the woman, they had illegally registered a bigamous marriage in 1954. Cases involving bigamy/polygamy became considerably more complicated when one of the spouses died. Then disputes would arise about inheritance. One such action was brought to the court by a woman married in church in 1916, whose husband subsequently registered a civil marriage with another woman in 1943. After the husband died in 1953, the widow from the first church marriage sued, arguing that the second civil marriage was invalid, and demanding that the court rule that the estate of the deceased along with the deceased officer's pension belonged to her.[184]

During the first ten to fifteen years after the war, most Lithuanian judges' ruling on divorce cases involving bigamy were more likely to recognize pre-war church marriages rather than civil marriages. A 1960 petitioner explained to the court that he had married in church in 1917, but later had remarried and was raising a child. The petitioner asked the Supreme Court to declare his church marriage invalid and to recognize the second. But as ordered by the Chamber of Civil Cases, the man's case was thrown out. The court found that the petitioner had been married with his church-marriage wife for more than thirty years, had a 36-year-old daughter and shared marital property with his wife. According to the judges, the years spent married by the church had 'tied' him and his wife. They also argued that the petitioner's life with the other woman was 'of a temporary nature' and could not be the basis for divorce. Nonetheless, once the petitioner had appealed the ruling to the chief judge of the Supreme Court, and this in turn to the Presidium of the Supreme Court, the Chamber of Civil Cases was forced to retry the case. The man's civil marriage was then recognized as valid and the church marriage was dissolved.[185] If petitioners managed to submit a complete record of the church wedding registration, judges would consider this solid evidence for recognizing church marriages. In 1957, one petitioner succeeded in recognizing her husband's civil marriage as invalid when she submitted to the court a church record inscription witnessing her marriage written by one of the most famous Lithuanian priests of the interwar era. The judges were undoubtedly impressed by the inscription made by Father Juozas Tumas, one of the most prominent figures in pre-war Lithuania: 'On 2 June 1923, at Vytautas Church, the Church Rector, Canon Juozas Tumas, married Jonas K., doctor, born in Seiniai on 1 August 1896, and Elena P., born in Petrapilis on 13 February 1900, both Catholics. Vytautas Church Rector, Canon J. Tumas.'[186]

The People's Court heard cases involving polygamy as well as bigamy. Unable to divorce, men and women in interwar Lithuania were forced to choose cohabitation or bigamy. After 1940, the Soviet People's Courts registered cases of polygamy married up until the war. In 1957, a petitioner asked the People's Court to dissolve her civil marriage due to her husband's many years of bigamy: two church marriages and one civil marriage. The basis for her petition was evidence that the respondent had illegally married in a church a second time before the war: the Samogitian Diocesan Curia had already punished the respondent in 1921 for bigamy.[187] During the Soviet years, trying to win bigamy cases and to validate new civil marriages, some lawyers would rely on the arguments of Soviet Russia's *1926 Marriage, Family and Guardianship Code*. At the time, the Bolshevik Code was famous around the world as an incredibly liberal law, the first to allow a single party to obtain a divorce without even notifying the other party. In 1926, the Russian law also validated de facto marriages; it was precisely this provision of the code that lawyers used in the Lithuanian People's Courts. In 1957, one lawyer argued in court that his client's church marriage had allegedly been automatically invalidated when he later remarried, registering his marriage in the civil registry bureau. He used the following complicated argument: 'According to the 24 October 1934 People's Commissariat of Justice interpretation, a factual marriage ... is the decisive factor and in every case, when an individual who is in a marriage to all intents and purposes dissolves it and to all intents and purposes remarries and later registers it, that [latter] record of the new marriage has complete validity.'[188] Of course, the lawyer's arguments did not work because even in Russia the code had not been in effect since 1936.

In the post-war era, bigamy and polygamy proliferated not only because of interwar period church marriages that were never officially registered at the registry bureaus. The mass emigration to the West, the partisan uprising and Soviet deportations of Lithuanian civilians to Central Asia and Siberia had torn the majority of families apart and quite often men and women had been forced to hide their true marital status. New romantic relations often began with one party not knowing or unsuspecting of the true marital status of their beloved. The truth would be revealed only when they would attempt to officially register their marriage. In 1953, a petitioner in a divorce case asked the court to allow her husband's live-in girlfriend as witness. The witness explained to the court that she had met the petitioner's husband M. and had 'believed him to be a good person'. The man had asked her to marry him, admitting he was 'a grass widower', whose church marriage had never been officially registered at the civil registry. The witness asked the court the opposite of what the petitioner was asking: to dissolve the husband's first church marriage and allow him to officially register his de facto marriage. The woman also admitted that she 'felt that she was pregnant and that was an even stronger tie to her *de facto* husband'.[189]

Violence, alcoholism and infidelity

Repression, constant material shortages and everyday fears inevitably inflamed aggression, alcoholism and violence in the family. It was no accident that from the end of the war until the early 1960s, the most common grounds for divorce were violence, alcoholism and marital infidelity. Alcoholism proliferated among both men and women in Lithuania; however, violence in the family in the absolute majority of cases was directed against women and children.

As in most countries up until the very end of the 1980s, violence in Soviet Lithuanian families was regarded as a private matter and rarely garnered social or governmental attention. Courts treated violence no differently from any other grounds for divorce, such as infidelity or irreconcilable character differences. And as men did not consider violence worthy of prosecution, they did not even deny it when it came up during divorce proceedings. When in 1944, petitioner V. K. filed for divorce in the People's Court, her husband admitted without any hesitation that he beat his wife and 'that was why their life together was unbearable'.[190] Women could also be the perpetrators of violence. In 1956, a petitioner accused his wife, assistant to the director of a law school, of physical and psychological violence. The man claimed that his wife had whacked him in the head with an iron rod and he had to go to hospital. He also presented evidence that his wife had allegedly forced him to serve in the Soviet Army which he had successfully avoided to that point because at the time there was no draft.[191]

Everyday domestic violence was not punishable or even particularly disparaged, and married couples' angry outbursts were a common sight in public. In 1954, at a People's Court hearing, neighbours were providing testimony regarding their neighbour L. who was constantly beating his wife and daughter. The neighbours stated that, in 1952, the man had almost beaten his wife and daughter to death and that he had cut off one of his daughter's braids. The man was sentenced to three years. However, in the same year, he was offered amnesty, and he avoided prison altogether.[192] The perpetrator could be prosecuted only if there was evidence that the violence had been systemic and life-threatening. In 1959, a ruling by the Biržai District People's Court, claiming that 'in order to be considered brutal torture, the actions must involve systematic beating. The actions of P. meet the requirement of systemic beating of his wife Elena P.'[193] Some district central committees would intercede in the People's Court proceedings, demanding rulings to protect the victims of violence. At times, party functionaries would take personal initiative to provide temporary security measures: they would order the violent offender moved out of the flat and leaving it for the mother and children, charging the *militsiya* to provide protection for the mother and children against the perpetrator.[194]

The LSSR penal code did not provide for liability in cases of domestic violence. Likewise, the government of the republic did not authorize any all-encompassing preventative programmes in the battle with violence and did not administer systematic assistance to victims. However one can find pledges written by perpetrators of domestic violence already in the early 1960s. One man wrote to the Biržai District People's Court: 'Pledge: I, Stasys P., hereby solemnly swear in the presence of the court, that, in the home I share with my wife, I will not brawl with her or beat her, and I will refrain from drink and I will provide her with my wages.'[195] This oath had no legal power to restrain or punish the perpetrators, however the government could note the existence of such written documents and apply regime-sanctioned methods, such as discussing inappropriate behaviour and condemning it at their work collective. Violence in the home of a Communist Party member could lead to party sanctions. Inappropriate sexual behaviour beyond the home, however, could lead to more significant consequences. In 1965, a school principal had initiated romantic relations with a 16-year-old pupil V., for which he was investigated and fined by the party.[196] The physical abuse of women as a large-scale social problem only began to appear in the press in the advent of Gorbachev's *perestroika*. Women's magazines were the first to ask the questions: Why are they beating us? And when will they stop?

After the Soviet annexation in 1940, every inhabitant of Lithuania experienced significant upheaval, personal tragedy, and for many, alcohol effectively became their only available safe harbour. Alcoholism proliferated in every social demographic. Monika Jonynaitė-Makūnienė (b. 1920) told of starting to use alcohol immediately after the occupation when she could no longer control the deprivation, hopelessness, pain and unknowingness. She remembered:

> I – I probably haven't told this to anyone – but while working at the dairy, I was a heavy drinker, because life seemed so meaningless. There was no future, no hope; we didn't know how to improve things. I didn't see any future: My brothers were murdered, my home was dismantled; we'd lost our foundation, perhaps even our self-respect and ability to feel shame. Maybe that's why we stopped appreciating life.[197]

Even those who were in part protected from direct repression because their spouses worked for the regime did not escape self-destructive drinking. In 1950, the Jurbarkas People's Court received a letter from the Comsomol organization which claimed that Antosė O., who is married to an ethnic Russian member of the Communist Party, denigrates the authority of the party because she passes out drunk by the fence, sleeps around with other men, and because of her drunkenness, she has already been fired from her position as director of the library. The letter added that Antosė was also sullying the reputation of the Comsomol organization in that she has a brother and sister who had been arrested by the secret police.[198]

Alcoholic married couples sought help and tried to cope with addiction. In 1957, a petitioner explained to the People's Court that his wife A. M. (b. 1915) tried to overcome her need to drink in various ways: by writing pledges to him and the children and getting treatment at special dispensaries, but nothing worked. Finally, in an attempt to stop the divorce, the respondent presented documentation to the Supreme Court that she was indeed in rehabilitation trying to get over her addiction at the Vilnius Psychoneurological Dispensary.[199] Others tried to keep track of their individual alcohol use habits, including how much drink was consumed. Leaving his family in the countryside when he left for Vilnius to study, a young man kept a diary to track his addiction. Later, his diary became evidence used in court during the divorce hearings because his wife had sent him money to live on in Vilnius. He wrote in his diary:

> I'm trying to get a handle on the number of benders I've had during the last four months. August: 3 benders, September: 3, October: 2, November: 10, and December: 8. So, in four months, 22 benders. And now for the money that I drank away: 4 roubles in September, 4 roubles in October, 70 roubles in November and 40 roubles in December. In four months, 120 roubles wasted on alcohol.[200]

In the 400 divorce cases studied that came before the Supreme Court from 1954 to 1964, the majority involved excessive drinking.[201] By the early 1960s, it was obvious that alcoholism was affecting consistently larger demographics and had become a social problem. Drunk people's behaviour more and more often led to aggressive actions towards their families. In 1963, a woman came before the Plungė People's Court describing her husband M., the director of the town's school of music:

> Martinkus would tell me that he had always drunk and would continue to do so. One time, in broad daylight, he smashed out all the windows of our apartment, threw all our plants and dishes out the window, and a crowd of people gathered outside our house … That evening, he threatened to kill me; he caught up to me on the street, choked me, and when I fell on the ground, he ran away.[202]

The woman gave many other examples of violence. But her case was dismissed because according to the judges, 'the husband and wife are educated people and can make amends'.[203]

Likely the first step taken by the Soviet Lithuanian government to respond to the alcoholism problem was the 1 February 1959 resolution made by the LCP(b) CC and the LSSR Council of Ministers on reducing the use of hard alcohol. The resolution confirmed the scale of consumption of alcoholic beverages in Lithuania and the extensive network of the commerce of alcohol. The resolution made it illegal to sell hard alcohol in food stores, district industrial product and department stores, as well as bistros, snack bars, cafeterias, cafes and sandwich shops. The sale of hard liquor was banned in train and bus stations and ferry terminals as well as near hospitals, schools and kindergartens. The resolution made the sale of hard alcohol to minors illegal; alcohol could not be sold before 10 am and the maximum amount that could be served in a restaurant was limited to 100 ml. The Soviet government adopted similar resolutions every few years, stressing the destructive effects of alcohol on family life. In 1961, the government provided for mandatory treatment for regular drinkers, especially those whose behaviour created intolerable conditions for their family. The *1966 resolution* intensified the battle with alcoholics and drug abusers. The *1972 decree* was a rather comprehensive document on the battle with alcoholism in the republic.[204]

The unsuccessful battle with alcoholism continued during the entire history of Soviet Lithuania because the laws and resolutions did not manage to change the traditions surrounding alcohol use that had formed in the society. On the other hand, the government's attempts were *pro forma*, because alcohol was entrenched as an integral part of public culture in the USSR. Regardless of the fact that the regime acknowledged the destructive influence of systemic drunkenness on the family, in the courts, alcoholism was not treated as grounds for divorce. Judges evaluated the situation by applying patriarchal stereotypes and blaming women for their inability to get along with their alcoholic husbands. In 1956, petitioner Elena M., who had married composer Nikodemas M. in 1921 when she was 17 years old, asked the court to grant her a divorce because of her husband's drinking problem. The petitioner presented the court with notes on her husband's inability to hold a job. She explained that her husband drank every day, and during the last seven years, he had been returning home beaten, bloody and muddy. Although the petitioner wrote to the court that her husband's alcoholism had erased her respect for him and had made any kind of trust between them impossible, the court threw out her request for divorce. The judges ruled that

> it has been determined that the respondent often uses alcoholic beverages, and this negatively impacts their common marital and family life. However it has also

been determined that the couple lived together as husband and wife for a long time, thirty-five years, and at this time still live together in the same apartment. Besides, it has been determined that the couple is not young (the petitioner is fifty-two, and the respondent is sixty-eight) and after such a long life together, the court considers that the petitioner is not serious about her marriage if she is bringing such a case before the court.[205]

In the late 1970s, alcohol abuse became the second most common reason for divorce among the families of professionals in the USSR; the first was 'character incompatibility'.[206] Meanwhile, in Russia, during the two-year period 1976–8, alcoholism and drunkenness was the most common reason for divorce, causing 44.6 per cent of all divorce cases. In Russia, 12.2 per cent of divorcing couples indicated character incompatibility, 10.8 per cent blamed infidelity and 9.2 per cent of respondents were divorcing because of endless arguments and disagreements.[207]

The third most common reason for divorce in Lithuania was infidelity. Until the mid-1950s, female petitioners most often indicated alcoholism and physical violence as their reason for seeking dissolution, and male petitioners most often indicated their wives' psychological instability, sexual promiscuity or inappropriate behaviour. In 1955, a petitioner told the Vilkaviškis People's Court that he had calculated the length of his wife's pregnancy and had realized that she was three months pregnant on their wedding day. He proved that he was not the child's father and that he did not intend to raise a 'stranger' and thus was asking for a divorce. The respondent tried to show that his wife had 'damaged her own dignity as well as that of the family' by being unfaithful and moving in with the director of their *kolkhoz*. And in 1944, petitioner Mečislovas V. who was filing for divorce wrote that he feels no love for his wife because she doesn't want to live with him and 'has gotten herself another man'.[208] Undoubtedly, some petitioner husbands accused their wives of infidelity and psychological problems in order to hide their own infidelities and thus obtain a divorce. In 1954, during divorce proceedings in Ukmergė, a husband accused his wife of promiscuity and drunkenness. The accused explained to the People's Court that she was neither promiscuous nor compromised. She explained that if it were so, she would not have been able to be a teacher at the local middle school where everything about everyone was widely known. Another petitioner claimed that his wife was particularly nervous and nit-picky, which got in the way of his creative work. This was why he had found himself another woman and was asking the court to allow him to divorce his wife.[209]

Not all accusations of sexual promiscuity on both parts were without grounds. The courts would register the divorce cases involving infidelity while at the same time sexually transmitted diseases were spreading throughout the society. In 1953, the Kaunas District Court summoned the venereal disease dispensary of Kazlų Rūda, asking for clarification on whether Algirdas P., born in 1927, or Juzė P., born in 1930, had contracted any venereal diseases, and if they had, the court asked the clinic to show who had contracted the venereal disease first.[210] The government battled the spread of venereal diseases as can be seen in the *19 February 1967 resolution of the LSSR Council of Ministers* on further methods for intensifying the battle against venereal disease. The resolution provided for methods for identifying infected individuals and their involuntary treatment.[211]

Ideological motives for divorce

Some petitioners used ideological arguments to justify their divorce and presented them to the court as factual evidence allegedly proving their spouses' hostility towards the Soviet government. Such grounds for divorce and the court's new practice of incorporating the Communist Party and various workers' organizations into the divorce proceedings speak to the publicization of family life and the increasingly diminishing distinction between public and private space in Soviet Lithuania more generally. It is not insignificant that in the absolute majority of cases in which these tactics were used, the petitioners were all men.

Complaints of an ideological nature against spouses are distinguishable by their rather artificial and overly formal articulation of damages. Typically, the events in question occurred several years prior. In 1955, a man asked the court for a divorce and complained that in 1951 his wife had allegedly been very hostile towards him for wanting to join a collective farm.[212] The strongest ideological weapon in the obtaining a divorce was the attempt to show that the spouse had ties to the Lithuanian resistance (partisan) movement. One petitioner to the Alytus People's Court was arguing that his wife's female friend was Citizen K., the sister of resistance fighters in the forest who had supposedly committed massacres against peaceful civilians. The petitioner claimed that the partisans' sister maintained close ties with his wife and wife's brothers who were reportedly also partisans fighting against the Soviet government.[213]

Some petitioners did indeed believe in the new Soviet system and their spouses certainly interfered with their new ideals and career goals. These types of declarations of intent to divorce were most common immediately after the installation of the Soviet government, from 1944 to 1945. High-ranking Lithuanian Communist Party (LCP) activist Motiejus Š. in his action for divorce wrote thus:

> During the Great Patriotic War, I was living in the city of Penza, my wife was well taken care of there, but nonetheless she continually compromised me with her anti-Soviet behaviour and her conversations with acquaintances in public spaces wherein she would express her dissatisfaction with her life and the current system in general. After the LSSR was liberated … she never stopped compromising me.[214]

The average Communist Party member could use their party membership as an opportunity to obtain a divorce. On 19 October 1944, one petitioner wrote to the court that early in the war, as the Germans occupied Vilnius and the Soviets retreated, his wife started persecuting him, calling him a communist and threatening to notify the Gestapo about him.[215]

Petitioners also used arguments of a moral nature through which they attempted to show their spouses' inability to conform to Soviet values and norms. Spouses were accused of resisting the atheist world-view, for their predilection for bourgeois lifestyles and for speculation. Because the divorce hearings were public and until 1965 were announced in the press, newspapers published feuilletons satirizing real-life individuals in the process of obtaining a divorce. The publications were written in the style of Soviet propaganda and were didactic in tone. The Šiauliai newspaper *Spalio vėliava* (October Flag) described an entire divorce case in detail and came to their own conclusions about the two spouses. The article was appended to the divorce documents as evidence for the respondent's immoral behaviour. The author wrote thus: 'and this two-legged cat cosied up to Irena, who was of the same character. Candies, sweet words, wine, long nights of drinking and lustful caresses cast them both … into the rubbish bin of life'.[216]

In 1957, the Raseiniai People's Court in its ruling on a divorce case based its decision on the petitioner's submitted documents about his wife's behaviour which was antithetical to Soviet society. The court noted that 'the submitted documents make clear that K. had been charged twice for acts of petty hooliganism'. The husband argued that his wife engaged in speculation, fraternized with men and was rowdy. She was often manipulated by her idealistic world-views and religious practices. In 1947, the petitioner wrote to the court that while he was on a business trip to Utena, his wife christened their baby boy without his knowledge. The petitioner alleged that as a member of the Communist Party, it was difficult for him to come to terms with this and this was when disputes began in their family life.[217] In 1949, ideological differences brought another couple to the People's Court. In his suit, the husband argued that he had reoriented himself and now embraced a materialist world-view because he was a university lecturer. Meanwhile, his wife was 'conservative with strong religious convictions'. In his declaration of intent to divorce, the husband wrote, '[W]e are fighting about our beliefs. It has become impossible for me to reconcile my life's materialist orientation with my wife's conservative religious views. Our common life together is becoming unbearable and there is no other option but divorce.'[218]

Mothers-in-law

Urbanization and post-war land reclamation projects changed the face of Lithuania. The children of villagers studied and worked in the cities as their parents left their declining homesteads and moved to collective farms or into tiny rooms belonging to their urban sons and daughters. Young families who had not gotten spots for their small children at local nurseries and kindergartens were also forced to live with one of their mothers-in-law. In most cases, parents' assistance was inescapable, especially when the children were little or not yet in school. On the other hand, the first generation arriving from the villages to the cities had strong connections between the two generations. A good number of adult children thus retained strong ties with their parents and interacted with them often. Active parental, especially maternal, participation in their adult children's family lives was quite common. This is evident in numerous divorce cases in which meddling mothers-in-law are presented as the primary cause of marital discord.

In 1956, a young woman in her declaration submitted to the court for divorce wrote,

> My husband decided to go live in Telšiai with his parents. I did not want to, but he picked us up from the birthing centre and took us there. Our in-laws greeted us with a smile. However when my husband stopped coming home, his mother began to explain to me that divorce was in style and that he was too young to worry about small children.[219]

Mothers feeling responsible for their adult children's well-being played the role of arbiter and judge in their marital relations. There were instances of mothers bringing divorce cases to court, evaluating their sons' or daughters' marital situations and providing the court with reasons and circumstances for divorce. In 1964, one petitioner's mother sent a letter to the Supreme Court, dictating to the judges what the course of the divorce proceedings ought to be:

> I guarantee that there would be no need for a divorce to be brought forth if not for that interloper [her daughter's lover]. Obviously, I might not write or say anything if that interloper was a better catch than her husband ... Most esteemed Supreme Court, I am sixty-four years old; my health is poor and I have no way of going there to have a serious talk with them, to advise them. I do not know when my daughter Stanislava P.'s case for divorce will be brought to the courts, but I beg of you, please do not grant her the divorce.[220]

In most cases in which mothers-in-law were the reason for the divorce, the daughters-in-law spoke of emotional abuse and admitted to crying all the time over their husband's mother's attacks. In the meantime, husband-petitioners associated their wives with their mothers: their wives were 'bad persons' and their mothers-in-law had 'a negative influence on their family life'. The husbands claimed that for these reasons their marital life was unsalvageable.[221] In some cases, arguments and disagreements with mothers-in-law could escalate into physical violence. Petitioner Asta G.-K. explained to the Vilkaviškis People's Court that they live with her mother, whom her husband despised and whom he even beat. She tried telling her mother to stop meddling in their marriage; however, this did not help their relationship and her husband continued to drink and beat his mother-in-law.[222]

Clashes between married couples and their parents could arise due to the chronic shortage of living space. In Soviet Lithuania as in the rest of the USSR, residents were obliged to be registered at their place of residence. When a newly-wed couple moved in with one of their parents, they would be registered there as their permanent residence. But if the marriage failed and the wife and children were forced to move out from their in-law's apartment, the courts were unlikely to safeguard for them the most precious treasure in Soviet society, the right to a place of residence and permanent registration. One daughter-in-law, who in 1979 had moved into her husband's parents' home in Klaipėda after their wedding, left her husband due to violent abuse and took refuge with her children at her mother's. A year later, she filed for divorce and asked the court to grant her 21.64 metres of her in-laws' apartment because that was where she was registered. The court refused to grant her request, arguing that the woman had lost her registration because she had not lived in the apartment during the last twelve months.[223] Ultimately, however, the influence of mothers-in-law diminished when Lithuania began building massive housing developments and expanding the network of preschool institutions.

Paternity tests

After the two-instance divorce proceedings had been abolished, only complicated or complex cases were sent on to be tried in the Supreme Courts. Until the final days of the Soviet regime, quite frequently these were paternity cases. Historically, biological paternity had always been an important and sensitive issue in Lithuanian society. In the traditional nineteenth-century village, babies born to single mothers had very little chance of surviving. The so-called bastards (*benkartai*) were not accepted by their families or by Lithuanian society as a whole. Even if the illegitimate child's mother would manage to get married, the child would be welcomed by the family only until he was old enough to be useful like any other hired hand: shepherding or working in the fields.[224] The notion of 'bastard' child lost its meaning under the Soviets and the state provided single mothers with certain privileges. However, the question of biological fatherhood remained relevant and important to the society. In essence, it was understood as essential to mutual respect, love and trust on the part of both spouses for one another. Damage to the first led to the demise of the marriage.

Biological fatherhood was important to women as well as to men. Even if a wife managed to hide the fact that her husband was not the biological father of her child, the deceit would be a difficult burden for her to bear. In 1973, Rima L. told the court that a few years prior she had an extramarital love affair and became pregnant. She admitted that she had convinced her husband that she was expecting his child and that she had the newborn registered under her husband's surname. The woman claimed that 'for some time I felt very clever for having put one over on him; however, my conscience eventually forced me to speak up and tell my husband everything'.[225] When he found out the truth, the husband denied paternity of his daughter Sandra and the court satisfied his request.

Determining paternity in the courts was a complicated process and took several stages. First, the petitioner had to request a test to be done by the court's medical expert. The test examined blood groups and was not accurate. In the absolute majority of cases, the experts' conclusions did not help the court make a ruling or the petitioners to make up their minds regarding paternity. In 1975, in a case in which an applicant requested revocation of his obligations as a father, the court obtained the following medical report on the blood groups: 'Citizen M. L.'s blood is type B alpha-III, M, P1, Rh-, Hp 1-1 groups ... We have determined that the above-named individuals all have this blood type. For this reason, according to the results, we can say that any one of these men (including the petitioner) can be the father of M. G. Thus, paternity cannot be revoked as a result of the tests that were conducted."[226] Upon receipt of expert conclusions and in the absence of any other evidence, the court would typically throw out cases requesting acknowledgment or rejection of paternity. When the court's medical experts neither confirmed nor denied paternity, the court would be forced to base its rulings on witness testimonies. The judges had to be persuaded about sexual relations between the petitioner and respondent, their commonly run household until the birth of the child and child support.

Recognition of paternity after accidental romantic encounters or clandestine love affairs was practically impossible in Soviet Lithuanian courts. In 1979, the Klaipėda People's Court threw out a petitioner's request for recognition of paternity for her newborn baby. The court determined that the petitioner, the father, indicated that he had no relationship with her and did not run a household with her because he had his own wife and children. The respondent also insisted that he could not be the father of the child because his only relationship with the petitioner was as a co-worker. Without additional evidence about their clandestine workplace romance, the woman claimed that the man had sent her juice and flowers to the birthing hospital through a friend. The friend refused to corroborate this fact, and the paternity suit was dropped.[227] The courts only recognized obvious and witness-verified sexual relations between the petitioner and the respondent and a commonly run household. In 1976, a different petitioner, seeking to prove paternity and win child support, presented the court with a chronological sequence of the romantic relationship. The woman explained that she had met the child's father in 1973 in Veisiejai and that they had begun a serious relationship on 1 January 1975. The respondent, according to the petitioner, would come to her house in the village of Varviškė in the evening and leave in the morning. At times, the couple would not part for weeks and would stay together in her home. The woman claimed that they hoped to start a family and that's why they had begun a sexual relationship. Nonetheless, after several months, when the woman became pregnant, the man abandoned her.[228]

It was not difficult for men to prove to the Soviet courts that they did not run a household with the petitioners, did not support them financially and that their relationships were purely of a sexual nature. In patriarchal Lithuanian society, judges trying divorce cases typically tried to determine which party was to blame and this would affect the process of the case. Because of well-established sexist stereotypes, most judges were certain that pregnancy was the responsibility and fault of the woman and the result of inappropriate behaviour. Quite frequently, the evidence women brought to the court was used against them. In a paternity case in 1968, the respondent denied moving in with the petitioner, buying household items, clothing and giving the petitioner his wages. He also denied having serious intentions and explained that he viewed the respondent as a girl with loose morals, suitable only for a short-term sexual affair. He told the court: '[W]e met at a dance in 1968, and for some time we were close. We would go see movies and go dancing. I came over to her house a few times. She invited me to her drinking parties. We did not run a household together. I never gave her a kopeck.'[229]

Paternity case proceedings and rulings often were affected by judges' assumptions on gender stereotypes. In 1974, Lina M., married, gave birth to a third child; however, the father denied paternity and asked the court to remove his name from the birth certificate. He claimed that he had not run a household with his wife since 1971, and since 1973 he had been living with another woman. The court recognized his paternity and argued that the respondent's extra-marital relationship with another woman did not refute the fact that he maintained close ties with his legal wife.[230] The courts tended to recognize paternity to children born into the family when husbands filed suits against their wives.

From the 1980s, the Supreme Court would also often recognize paternity if both parties were young and unmarried. Judges' rulings were influenced by rapidly changing sexual mores in Soviet Lithuania and the new, almost universally tolerated, liberal outlook on sexual relations before marriage. Sociological data from 1984 indicates that approximately 20 per cent of brides in Lithuania were pregnant. Few were shocked by this, especially since contraceptives were not readily available to most citizens.[231] Romantic and sexual relationships before marriage were seen as substantially strong evidence of paternity even if the marriage never took place and the man married another woman. The court believed and understood the petitioner when she said that the relationship she had with the respondent lasted until she was 'visibly' pregnant. As the petitioner claimed, she had no worries because the respondent had promised that 'the wedding would take place at the same time as the christening.'[232]

Women would present the various types of factual evidence in paternity cases, some of which could only be analysed by forensic experts. In 1971, the experts of the LSSR Court Forensics Research Institute were given fragments of a letter written in Russian and asked to do a handwriting analysis. The fragments were supposed to prove that the child's father had written love letters and had a romantic relationship with the petitioner. The court asked the handwriting experts whether the opening words 'Dima Byl' and ending with 'obiazatelno' were written by the same individual V. D.[233]

In the 1950s, the most persuasive way to deny paternity was with clinical evidence of the father's infertility. In 1952, a respondent avoided paternity and child support by providing forensic evidence regarding his infertility. The documents showed that the respondent had been injured in 1938 and his testicles removed. Doctors testified that from 1940 the man's sexual potency had completely disappeared, and for this reason citizen J. V. could not perform the sexual act and fertilize any ova due to the fact that he had no testicles.[234] In the early 1970s, expertise on infertility became somewhat more complicated. Proof of infertility was provided by clinical tests. They were critical and could sway the court's decision when the forensics experts' determinations regarding blood group were ambiguous or witnesses had not provided significant evidence. In 1970, a man's infertility was verified by a commission which consisted of the head of the Legal Department of the Kaunas Institute of Medicine, the City of Kaunas Court Medical Expert, the City of Kaunas Medical Expert-Biologist, and the City of Kaunas I Soviet Hospitals Surgeon-Urologist. According to the commission, the sperm analysis verified that the respondent was infertile.[235]

In a patriarchal society, paternity cases were especially important for married couples hoping to save their marriages and maintain harmonious interpersonal relations and their marital status. For young, pregnant women, this could be the chance to marry the child's father or get the court to grant child support. Proof of paternity cases also had significant impact on relationships between parents and children because paternity and biological paternity were identical notions in socialist society. Unquestioned biological paternity affected the existence of the family and the relationships between family members. Another important aspect of recognition or rejection of paternity was material: it affected the awarding of alimony and child support.

Life after divorce

Changing surnames

After their divorces, most women asked the court to allow them to use their maiden names once again. This opportunity was provided for in all marriage and family codes in the Lithuanian territory until independence in 1990. The *LSSR Marriage and Family Code* signed into law in 1969 discussed in detail the process for changing married names after dissolution of marriage. The process was simple, and the women's requests were not met with opposition from the court or from their former spouses. The society treated the family name as a moral or even material value, and for this reason, most men tried to 'protect' their surname and thus distance themselves from their ex-wives. One important reason was the men's fear that their ex-wives might register children born after divorce under their names. They were not only afraid of paternity, but also of the potential child support the court would order them to pay. For this reason, they were the ones who approached the court to ask that their former wives' surnames be changed back to their maiden names. One such petitioner in 1964 appealed to the Supreme Court after the Joniškis People's Court had granted his divorce. He wrote: 'I will not allow my wife to keep my last name … The reason for this is so that my wife doesn't do what her sister Lionė did. Lionė also divorced her husband, and then had other men's children yet wrote his name on their birth certificates.'[236] Women of every age requested to change their surnames after divorce: young women who could expect to marry again, as well as considerably older women. The question however remains: to what extent were women who lived in socialist society seeking to marry ('to change their last name') in order to gain married status, which, according to Lithuanian surname traditions, was indicated by the suffix of the woman's surname?

Financial obligations

The *RSFSR Marriage, Family and Guardianship Code* and the *LSSR Marriage and Family Code* provided for financial hardship through material assistance in the form of spousal support after divorce. In 1966, the *RSFSR Marriage, Family and Guardianship Code* was revised and financial assistance could be limited if the spouse requesting spousal support was to blame for the divorce.[237] However most divorcees tried to avoid this obligation. The Lithuanian courts were not likely to support ex-spouses seeking assistance and typically ruled in favour of petitioners asking to be released from financial support. This tendency was notable. In 1956, a petitioner filed with the Tytuvėnai District People's Court asking his obligation to pay alimony to his handicapped ex-wife be revoked. He explained to the court that he now was 61 years old and was retired. The People's Court granted the man's request and although his ex-wife appealed to the Supreme Court, the decision stood. The Supreme Court ruling was based on the age difference between the two former spouses. The court argued that the husband had been born in 1895, but the respondent was born in 1911. According to the court, although the woman was handicapped, as she was much younger than her husband, she could support herself.[238] Similarly, in an alimony case in

Kazlų Rūda District People's Court, the court significantly reduced the alimony granted to a woman, incapacitated and older than her ex-husband. Instead of her requested sum of 200 roubles, the court ordered her ex-husband to pay her 30 roubles per month.[239]

The *1969 LSSR Marriage and Family Code* provided situations in which spouses had the right to spousal support after divorce. Paragraphs 27 and 28 of the code provided support if the spouse became unable to work within one year after the divorce, and alimony if the divorce proceedings took a long time and the spouse reached retirement age within five years after the divorce. The right to financial assistance was available to the wife while she was pregnant or until eighteen months after giving birth. But in actual Soviet life, these rights were rarely guaranteed because divorced fathers avidly avoided alimony, even for their own minor children.

Dividing up property

Soviet laws guaranteed that both spouses' shares of marital property were equal; however, until the mid-1950s, disputes over division of property rarely reached the Supreme Court at first instance. Until 1964, there was not a single divorce registered that was motivated by family property disputes. In the early years after the war, most Lithuanian inhabitants did not have much significant income or material wealth. Real estate and moveable property had been nationalized, appropriated by neighbours, subsumed by collective farms, destroyed and razed during the war, confiscated and never returned or compensated under chaotic conditions. Thus, couples divorcing after the war had only a few common household items or furniture to divide up. In 1948, in the Ukmergė District Court, Bronislovas and Adelė S. were dividing up their commonly acquired property: 'a table, sewing machine, sleeper sofa, bookcase and two ordinary chairs'.[240]

Because the Soviet *Marriage and Family Codes* recognized only civil registry, cohabitating couples dividing up property found the most unfavourable outcomes. In 1946, Vilnius resident M. explained to the court that for fourteen years she lived unmarried with K. in the house that belonged to him and his sister. When K. died, M. asked the court for the half of the house that belonged to the couple along with the movable property inside the house. Witnesses testified in support of M.'s case, arguing that the man and woman had lived 'like husband and wife' and that the petitioner had taken care of the house and nursed the sick man. Nevertheless, the court ruled that the sister was to inherit the entire property, including 5,500 roubles for the couple's things that had already been sold.[241] During the first decade after the war, the judges of the People's Courts ruled on property division cases according to their own understanding and discretion. At times, their rulings were grounded in the socialist principle of 'each according to his needs'. In 1951, a widow appealed to the Jonava People's Court regarding her rights to the house that had belonged to her deceased husband and his brother. Regardless of the fact that the house had been divided up according to a 1938 will, the brother-in-law was requesting the larger part of the house (70 metres) which belonged to the widow and her four children. The petitioner explained that according to the will, only the smaller part of the house, 25 metres, belonged to him, but he had married and now needed the larger section. The People's Court ruled in favour of the man and gave him the widow's part of the house. Only after four years of appeals did the Supreme Court return to the widow her part of the property.[242]

During the final decade of Soviet rule in Lithuania, the division of marital property became increasingly complicated and fierce, involving an ever larger bureaucracy. These property disputes provide insight into Soviet Lithuanian gender stereotypes. Judges based their rulings on the conviction that men are the heads of the household and the rightful owners of mutually acquired property. In the view of the court, men were better workers, more talented artists, and for this reason, naturally, the greater portion of common property belonged to them. In 1987, in the division of property of two artists, the petitioner argued that he alone should be given the couple's commonly owned artist studio. He explained that his former wife was merely a craftswoman and that her works were lesser in size than his creative work. Accordingly, her work 'could easily fit inside a normal-sized apartment'. The judges found this argument convincing and ruled in his favour. Moreover, it seemed to the court that the two former spouses were malevolently disposed to one another and would not be able to work together in rebuilding their studio in order to build two separate workspaces with two separate entrances.[243]

After the divorce, husbands were typically awarded the second most precious piece of Soviet property, the family automobile. The judges' rulings were based on the fact that the husbands were the drivers of the cars, and their wives did not have driver's licenses. Ex-wives would receive financial compensation; however, as often the cars would have been acquired on the black market or through bribes, the compensation rarely corresponded to the actual amount the couple had paid for it. Perhaps this is why during divorce proceedings women would ask out of hopelessness that they be returned or compensated for even the most minor household items: 'a tent: 70 roubles; sandals: 35 roubles; three pairs of sandals: 85 roubles; two dresses and a robe: 80 roubles; an umbrella: 35 roubles; a sweater: 48 roubles; and a makeup kit: 40 roubles'.[244]

The most disheartening consequence of divorce was the couple's prospect of having to live in the same apartment together for many long years, or in some cases, for the rest of their lives. If the family had a private house or a larger apartment, the court would agree to divide up the space. Such rulings would determine precisely how to build two separate entrances. In 1958, in the case of one couple that was dividing up a four-room flat, the court ruled that 'it's possible to divide up the flat because two rooms are connected to two remaining rooms with a door, which, when closed, leaves the two spaces isolated ... The rooms are 10.82 metres and 11.69 metres, respectively.'[245]

The shortage of living space in Soviet Lithuania was acute until the mass production of housing developments began at the end of the 1960s, and petitioners would sometimes ask the court to divide up little more than 1 metre in hopes of improving their living conditions even slightly. In 1953, such a ruling was given by the Supreme Court in a division of property case: 'The petitioner seeks to move the respondent Jonas R., his entire family and all their possessions from a room which is 12.4 metres plus a kitchen into a room of 13.64 metres in the same apartment, while N. is moved from a room 13.64 metres in size into a room that is 12.4 metres, plus a kitchen.'[246]

Unfortunately, the mass production of homes in Lithuania did little to improve people's living situations because they were not allowed to sell the communal apartments received from the state in order to solve their housing problems. Communal apartments could only be traded; however, usually because they were so small, this was difficult to do. Exchanging tiny single apartments for two separate living spaces inevitably worsened people's conditions. Thus, former spouses often remained in the same apartment even after they'd married a second time or were cohabiting with someone else. The common space shared by former husbands and wives created endless misunderstandings and arguments. Sometimes after the divorce, the furniture awarded with great difficulty simply wouldn't fit into the room awarded them. The situation would become even more complex and complicated if both former spouses were on their second marriage. In such cases, after the divorce, the two former spouses would move into their assigned rooms together their children from their previous marriages. Such a situation was recorded by a respondent in 1981 when he told the court about the flat he was sharing with his second ex-wife:

> The flat has three rooms totalling 43.8 metres in size. Four of us live in the apartment: the petitioner, her daughter from her first marriage, and my son from my first marriage and myself. There is one closed off room in the apartment (13.9 metres) where my son and I have been living since the end of 1980 ...

> Moreover, in 1971, I purchased a Czechoslovakian living room set in Jurbarkas for 1200 roubles. This set is my property, but the petitioner has not let me use it since our divorce.[247]

Discordant family life would begin well before the divorce proceedings and the estranged spouses would be forced to live under the same roof for many years after the divorce. However, if the court would throw out the divorce case, the situation of the warring spouses living in the same apartment would remain unresolved and complicated. In 1964, Jurgis S. wrote to the Lenin District People's Court in Vilnius: 'Stefa S. and I have been unofficially separated since 1962. We share an apartment but live in separate rooms. I have been paying alimony since 1962 … I'm in a new relationship now.'[248] The court threw out this request for divorce, arguing that the hostile environment was the petitioner's own fault and that a new, unregistered marriage was not grounds for a divorce.

The problem of securing living space after divorce was much less complicated if one of the spouses was a member of the party *nomenklatura*. Then, their original apartment would be left to the spouse as assigned by the court, while the state would automatically provide the other spouse with a new one. After his divorce which he initiated due to his wife's infidelity, Albertas B., who lived on Akmenų Street in Vilnius, avoided having to divide up their apartment. Because he belonged to the party *nomenklatura*, he asked the court to grant him their current apartment and assured the court that he would personally provide his ex-wife with living quarters. In his petition, Albertas B. wrote, 'I promise to provide Vanda B. with a self-contained communal apartment, no smaller than our current one.'[249] The Supreme Court decided this case within one month, ruling in the petitioner's favour.

Spouses' trade unions and other workers' organizations actively got involved in the dividing up of apartments in divorce cases. In 1980, during court proceedings, the Klaipėda refrigerated fleet base union committee provided their opinion to the Supreme Court in writing on how the apartment belonging to their employee and his wife ought to be divided up. The union claimed that

> the petitioner's proposed plan for dividing up the flat exceeds the norms provided by law for herself and her daughter. In addition, the union believes that it will be difficult for the respondent, who is not at fault in the divorce, to use a common kitchen and to live in a common apartment with his former wife. For this reason, the depot asks the court to rule on the involuntary dividing up of their flat into two apartments.[250]

It appears that the union's words were decisive. The court ruled that two of the three rooms could not be given to the ex-wife and her daughter because one of the rooms had an enclosed balcony. If the enclosed balcony went to the wife and daughter, then, according to the union, it would become additional living space and would infringe on equal division of marital property. It was calculated that the petitioner and her daughter were receiving 1.65 metres more space. Therefore, the judges decided not to divide up the rooms in their common flat but force them to trade it for two separate individual spaces.[251]

The spouses' work collectives also could petition the court to postpone their decision until the union's local committee initiated a friendly trial and formed an opinion on the motives and reasons for the divorce, determined which of the parties was at fault and decided on the substance of the case. In divorce cases involving a third individual, his or her workplace could and would be required to express their opinion. In 1961, the local committee of the republic's Institute of Water Management Design requested that the Supreme Court postpone their decision on the divorce case of Aleksandra B. until after a textile plants had conducted a friendly trial considering Aleksandra and Jonas Ž.'s behaviour.[252]

Civil registry was established in Lithuania in 1940 and provided an opportunity for strained and discordant marital relations to be dissolved by divorce; this undoubtedly met the needs and desires of modern society. Divorce proceedings in the Soviet People's Courts and the Supreme Courts were conducted quite cursorily, especially during the early post-war years. Moreover, the party leadership and various workers' organizations held considerable sway over the courts' rulings. For this reason, the judges' decisions were often affected by party bureaucracy and by patriarchal stereotypes prevalent in the society. The decisions were often partial and unfavourable to women and children.

3

Parents and their children

The state and childcare

Ideal families

Authorized by Soviet experts from a variety of disciplines, Khrushchev's family policies offered models for marital behaviour, cohesive motives for marriage and a Soviet version of romantic love adapted from nineteenth-century romantic ideals. As these policies were being implemented, a stereotype about the ideal size of a family was forming in Lithuania composed of two parents and one or two children. Pre-war demographic trends still predominated in post-war Lithuania: from 1936 to 1939, there were 22.9 newborns for every 1,000 inhabitants, and this statistic remained nearly unchanged for the next two decades. In 1950, there were still 23.6 births per 1,000; in 1960, there were 22.5. In the 1960s, however, the population growth began to slow demonstrably. In 1970, for every 1,000 inhabitants, there were 17.6 births, and in 1980, the rate decreased to 15.1. From then on, trends in birth rates, entrenched during the Khrushchev years, remained unchanged until the final years of Soviet Lithuania (see Table 3.1)

The stereotypical family with two parents and two children was desired by the majority of the Soviet population across all the republics. A centralized survey of 33,000 inhabitants throughout the USSR, including the Central Asian republics with traditionally larger families, was conducted in 1974. In response to questions about ideal family size, at the time of the survey, 1.5 per cent of respondents were planning on having one child. 42 per cent of couples wanted two children and 39.4 per cent desired a family with three children.[1] Regardless of the fact that officially Soviet demographic policies aimed to increase birth rates, domestic reality had solidified the small-family model. The ideal family with one or two children certainly corresponded to the demographic situation in Lithuania: in 1971, 34.4 per cent of professional families and 26.2 per cent

Table 3.1 Birth rates in Lithuania, 1950–88

Births per 1,000 Inhabitants	1950	60	70	80	81	82	83	84	85	86	87	88
	23.6	22.5	17.6	15.1	15.1	15.2	16.3	16.2	16.3	16.5	16.2	15.4

Source: V. Gaidys, 'Demografinės situacijos Lietuvoje bruožai: Šeimos ir santuokos aspektai' (Characteristics of the Demographic Situation in Lithuania: Features of Marriage and Family), *Žvilgnsis į šeimą* (A Look at the Family) (Vilnius: Lietuvos mokslų akademija, 1990), 151.

of workers' families were raising two children.[2] In 1979, in Lithuania, families corresponding to the socially accepted, normative family size made up the majority: 42.8 per cent of families were raising one child and 37.3 per cent of all families had two children. In 1989, the number of small families increased even more: families with only one child made up 50.4 per cent and those with two children made up 39.7 per cent of all families.[3]

Legally, families with three or more children in Soviet Lithuania were considered large families and on average made up approximately 8 per cent of the population. Large families, however, were treated as non-standard by the culture; they were stigmatized by those around them and ignored by the state. Soviet society was under the mistaken impression that large families received more government benefits and social services, including the right to shop at special stores and priority for obtaining housing and automobiles. But on the contrary, a study conducted during the 1979–89 period shows that barely 10 per cent of families with three or more children in Lithuania had any special access to material goods or social benefits. The study in fact finds that large families were living at the edge of poverty and only 62 per cent had their own separate living space. Fifty-six per cent of parents surveyed claimed that they and their children were treated with contempt by those around them because their families were larger than the cultural norm. It is no accident that the number of families with three or more children was on the decrease in Lithuania: in 1979, they made up 8.9 per cent of the population. By 1989, they comprised only 7.0 per cent of all families.[4]

Coordinating work and family

After the war, the government integrated Lithuanian women into Soviet society by incorporating them into the public sphere; women's financial independence was ostensibly guaranteed through state-paid jobs. The unprecedented and compulsory participation of women in work and social activity as well as Soviet propaganda regarding motherhood provided women with three primary roles: worker, mother and wife.[5] From the very first days of the Soviet Union, Lithuanian newspapers argued that women were obliged to live up to all three roles proscribed to them by the state: they had to succeed in their professional careers while caring for home and family.[6] These stereotypical roles established in the Stalin era remained unchanged until Gorbachev's *perestroika*.

The *8 July 1944 decree* and subsequent resolutions on maternity leave and preschool institutions as well as expanding the network of boarding schools for the needy were supposed to help women coordinate their family life and mandatory state jobs. However, the meagre assistance provided by the 1944 decree was not appropriated universally, but only to single mothers, mothers of large families and widows. The state most aggressively supported single mothers to whom lump sum or monthly childcare benefits were paid out on the birth of each child. Mothers of large families and widows could only expect a one-time, lump sum payment upon the birth of their third child whereas monthly assistance kicked in only after child number four turned 2 and this benefit expired at age 5. Mothers of large families were also honoured with state medals of various orders.

The *8 July 1944 decree* authorized maternity leave of up to seventy-seven calendar days for expectant mothers working in state jobs. On 1 April 1956, the Presidium of the USSR Supreme Soviet extended pregnancy and birth leave to 112 calendar days: all women (except for *kolkhoz* workers) were provided with eight weeks fully paid maternity leave before the birth and an equal number of weeks afterwards. For the first time on 1 June 1970, the Soviet government acknowledged both parents as a child's guardians and hence beneficiaries of partial social assistance. The Lithuanian Soviet Socialist Republic (LSSR) Council of Ministers' ordinance *On Reductions in Child Support for Fathers While Their Child Is Not Attending Childcare Institutions during the Father's Annual Holiday* was a revision of the 1948 law which provided for an exemption only during the mother's annual vacation.[7] The resolution *Methods for Increasing State Support to Families with Children and Improving the Demographic Situation in the Republic* which was adopted on 11 March 1981 authorized partially paid family leave until the child turned 1, paying a monthly 35 roubles, and unpaid leave until the child turned 18 months.[8] Starting in 1985, this resolution was applied to single fathers raising more than one child under the age of 12. In 1987, for the first time, a resolution was adopted which provided improved flexibility for mothers in the workplace: mothers of children under the age of 8 could take advantage of the opportunity to work part-time. On 22 March 1989 by decree of the Lithuanian SSR (LSSR) Supreme Soviet, maternity leave was once again extended until the child turned 1.5, allowing unpaid leave until age 3 with guaranteed job status. During the first twelve months of caring for a child, monthly benefits for mothers were increased to 50 roubles, and 35 roubles until the child turned 18 months. The resolution also increased benefits – 70 roubles per month – for disabled children until they turned 16.

Financial benefits paid by the state were insufficient and mothers could only make use of the maternity leave granted by the 1981 and 1989 resolutions, which provided partially paid or unpaid childcare if they could demonstrate that they had supplementary financial funds. For this reason, a majority of Lithuanian families inevitably ran up against the problem created by the Soviet system: how to reconcile childcare when both parents were obliged to work? The solution proposed by the post-war press was for the state to assume the childcare function and to establish so-called children's villages. Indeed, the official newspaper *Komjaunimo tiesa* in 1951 asked when the republic's government would begin implementing the *LSSR Council of Ministers' 7 July resolution* to establish the promised children's village in Vilnius? The newspaper was referring to the village, serving as a place of residence and school for the children, which had planned to open at the Vilnius Jaunimo sodas (Youth Garden) by 25 July.[9] After Stalin's death, however, the government refused to seize childcare from families and limited itself to providing assistance to families with the primary goal of fully developing day schools and a network of residential childcare facilities.

Boarding schools for the needy, orphanages and residential kindergartens

Boarding schools for the needy, orphanages and residential kindergartens were supposed to be accessible to all and should have completely solved the problem of reconciling work and family. Children received room and board at the residential kindergartens and boarding schools. Orphanages were also part of the plan as single mothers were advised by the state to surrender their children temporarily and to resume their parental responsibilities at a later date.[10] In the early 1960s, Soviet educators began extolling the educational and material possibilities of boarding schools. As the Soviet press claimed, half a million children were living in the boarding schools in 1960 and there were plans to accommodate 2.5 million children by 1965. Soviet ideologues encouraged the establishment of the children's villages, symbolically comparing them to major cities of the world like Rome or Rio de Janeiro.[11] In 1959, the USSR Central Committee and the Council of Ministers adopted the resolution *On Methods for Developing the Boarding Schools for the Needy from 1959 to 1965*; the goal of the resolution was to expand the network of boarding schools for the needy. Lithuanian journalists discussed the resolution, insisting that the boarding schools were one of the best ways to raise children and create a communist society and that an increasing number of parents were eager to send their children there.[12]

In 1978, there were thirty-one boarding schools and four orphanages in Lithuania. They were isolated and closed-off institutions where minor children, separated from their families, spent the greater part of the year while they completed their elementary or secondary education. These were children of needy families or families that lived far from local schools; they were orphans, children of parents who had lost their parental rights and children left there on temporary custody.[13] Parents paid a fee of 8 roubles per month for food and boarding at the school's dormitory, but even this modest fee was beyond some parents' means. In 1971, a student wrote in her diary:

> We have no money at home again. This happens a lot because my dad's pension is so small. And my sister is studying at the technicum and does not receive a stipend for her tuition or dorm. On top of that, they must pay 8 roubles for my boarding school. What can they do? After vacation, the girls show off all the pretty things they bought, but I have nothing.[14]

In order to provide parents with financial assistance, on 30 October 1973, the LSSR Council of Ministers issued the ordinance *On Overhauling Fee Assessment for Room and Board at Boarding Schools of the Needy*. Fees were waived if the child missed five days in a row due to illness or vacation.[15]

The boarding schools ran on military-style discipline. In 1962, the LSSR Ministry of Education published the following guidelines for the children's behaviour at the schools: if the children wanted to go home on weekends, they had to show they had a serious reason and family members could only visit at specified times. The rules forbade the children from speaking to one another in the bathrooms, and they were only allowed to use the showers according to a confirmed schedule. In the mornings, the children were not allowed to get up until they had received a signal from the guardian on call, and in the evenings, they would have a sponge bath, wash their feet and brush their teeth.[16]

The boarding schools and orphanages were an ideal instrument for instilling propaganda. Teachers and guardians had precise instructions regarding the children's ideological upbringing and education, which, for example, can be seen in the methodological guidelines for helping students understand political events happening in the republic and around the world 'in light of communist principles', as presented by the educators of the Panevėžys Boarding School in 1966. The teachers and guardians shared innovative educational methods for analysing Soviet conventions and Central Committee plenary materials, and they were pleased that, during class, the children 'denounced the exploiters of our people and delighted in our country's achievements'.[17] Another experimental method for disciplining the students flouted by Soviet education specialists was observation. But before observing a particular child, teachers were advised to carefully study the child's individual file and read their teacher's notes on the child's daily diary entries. According to the specialists, the ultimate goal of observing the student was to form their personality, to eliminate negative attributes and to develop the ones necessary for socialist society. Aside from teacher observations, the children practiced self-observation, which allowed quicker identification of attributes that needed to be changed.[18] To promote active self-education, the children were encouraged to keep journals; the teachers controlled, analysed and used the students' entries as educational tools for auto-suggestion. Self-observation as a form of propaganda was widely applied by educators in the 1970s. In 1971, a teacher shared her experiences: 'As we concluded our lesson, we all agreed to obtain thick notebooks and to make entries three or four times a week on the more interesting facts about life, our thoughts and dreams ... These entries provide substantial material that can help to understand the student. One needs only to know how to make use of it.'[19]

Most children in the boarding schools and orphanages suffered strict discipline, isolation, homesickness and longing for family. A programme allowing the children to spend time with female factory worker volunteers was an organized attempt to fill their emotional emptiness. The meetings were part of the children's ideological and vocational education programme, but they speak to the children's desperate need for home and family. The educators admitted that the youngest girls at the boarding schools would refuse to leave the workers' sides and in tears would try to hug them, or at least touch them.[20] In due course, detractors began to warn that the boarding schools and residential kindergartens were alienating the children from their parents and that they were a dangerous means of raising and educating children. In 1977, Soviet scholars wrote that the experience of the past ten to fifteen years had showed that these institutions must be replaced with expanded after-school activities and preschool day schools, but their warnings were not heeded: a 11 March 1981 resolution *On*

Methods for Increasing Assistance to Families with Children and Improving the Overall Demographic Situation in the Republic provided for further expansion of the network of residential childcare institutions as a form of support for families and orphans. For some mothers, residential kindergartens and boarding schools were their only access to social assistance and their only option for childcare. For Rūta Skatikaitė (b. 1952), weeklong kindergarten became unavoidable as she tried to reconcile her work and studies with caring for her three children. She explained thus:

> In such situations with no close friends or relatives who could help care for the kids, it was still possible in Lithuania to study and pursue a career. Of course, the children suffered for it, as mine did. I birthed all three of my children while completing my degree at university as a correspondence student. Twice a year, I had to appear in person for exams, and I was working at the time. This is why I often had to leave my children at the residential kindergarten.[21]

Children living at the orphanages were extremely isolated from the rest of society and could not acquire the practical skills necessary for real life beyond the walls of the orphanage. Former orphanage resident Aneta Šlegel (b. approx. 1940) remembered:

> Nobody did anything for us and they certainly didn't pamper us or attend to us. From the first grade you had to know how to wash the floor, peel potatoes, and clean the kitchen. I remember we were tenth-graders when a supervisor came to check on whether we were ready 'for life'. She asked: 'How much is a kilo of sugar at the grocery store?' We didn't know. She asked again: 'How much does bread cost?' We didn't know that either. Then in our presence she started to scold our tutor Tatarlienė. I remember as if it had happened today. All of us girls stood up for the tutor. We said that it wasn't her fault that there was always sugar in our tea, the bread was sliced and served on the table, and that we didn't need to buy cereal because it was delivered by someone else in the orphanage. Was our tutor supposed to take us out to the grocery stores? Anyway, after this happened, our tutor Aldona made up a game to help us learn about shopping in the city. At around 8 o'clock after dinner she'd write an address and divide us into groups of five or six and we'd start searching all over the city. Those who were first to find the right street and building were rewarded with candy. We ran around the city, asking everyone for directions, and it was really interesting. That's how we got to know the city and life outside the orphanage. But I only stopped being afraid of going shopping in my third year at the Academy.[22]

Creches and nursery schools

There were 253 nursery schools operating in independent Lithuania before the Second World War and they were attended by 13,500 children.[23] After the pre-war network of preschool institutions had been destroyed, rebuilding was slow. It was only during the final decade of the Soviet Union that it was even partially realized. Creches and kindergartens particularly were in short supply in the first years after the war. For example, in Kaunas, the second largest city in Lithuania, in 1947, there were five creches operating with 260 beds, but that same year there were 2,349 single mothers and mothers of large families registered in Kaunas who had priority for state assistance.[24] For this reason, in 1959, the USSR Central Committee and the USSR Council of Ministers adopted the resolution *On Methods for Further Developing Pre-school Institutions for Children and Improving the Education of Pre-school Children*. The directive contained a grandiose promise to build the nursery and kindergarten network in size previously unseen, building pre-school institutions closer to city housing developments throughout the republic 1965. The resolution noted that when a mother brought her child to a preschool facility, the time she could devote to housework increased by two to three hours. It also added that the state spent approximately 300 roubles to maintain a child in a preschool facility, but parents paid only 70 roubles per month.[25] The LSSR government proposed increasing funding directed towards the construction of preschool institutions in the sum of 7 million roubles in 1960, and 25 million roubles in 1965. Between 1959 to 1965, the government anticipated creating 25,125 spots for children in the creches and kindergartens.[26] However, these plans were never realized and a majority of parents never benefited from the kindergartens or reductions in fees. In 1960, 2,500 Vilnius residents applied to send their children to day school creches and kindergartens, but in actuality, only 500 applications could be filled.[27] In the 1950s, 80 per cent of working age women in the USSR held state-paid jobs, but only 13 per cent of children under the age of 6 were enrolled in preschool facilities. The number of preschools did increase in 1965, but still only 22.5 per cent of city dwellers and 12 per cent of residents of rural districts were able to enrol their preschool-aged children in day schools or seasonal preschool institutions.[28]

The worst situation was in the rural areas because the collective farms were sluggish to establish seasonal kindergartens. In 1954, even the newspaper *Tiesa* had to admit that there were almost no creches/nursery schools available there at all. Women complained that the *kolkhoz* administrations were adopting fabricated resolutions to establish childcare facilities and simply filing them away. These fictional nursery schools would be assigned space, children's furniture would be bought and even staff would be paid, but the seasonal nursery school would never actually begin operations.[29] In 1973, the resolution *On Methods for Further Expanding Pre-school Institutions at Collective Farms* was adopted. The Ministry of Agriculture, district executive committees and their agriculture boards were charged with enacting it to improve the material and hygienic conditions of the nurseries. In 1960, only forty-two small creches and nursery schools were operating in the rural districts; by 1980, their number had increased to 432.[30]

In 1958, the LSSR Council of Ministers adopted a resolution on workplace kindergartens, establishing them for the children of employees of institutions and factories.[31] However at larger textile factories like Mastis or Kauno audiniai or in the milk and food industries where 75 per cent of workers were women, the creches and nursery schools never met demand. Of course, exceptions could always be made for husbands or wives holding positions with more clout. Natalija J. (b. 1937), who in the mid-1960s worked for a military production factory in Vilnius and was the factory director of the women's council, was able to benefit from her position. She explained,

> In 1960, I returned to work three months after my son Ričardas was born. My husband and I worked alternating shifts. One of us would run home and we would trade places because the factory was quite close to home. I enrolled Ričardas at nursery school when he was two and a half, and I sent my daughter Margarita to daycare when she was one. The nursery school was very good – our factory nursery school. I was the director of the women's council and used my connections. We were very lucky, very lucky indeed, because it was a huge problem at the time. I scoured all of Vilnius to find daycare for the other women at our factory. Daycare was hard to find, yet the demand for it was enormous. Mothers sometimes were on waiting lists so long that their child would begin first grade without a spot at a pre-school ever opening up.[32]

In 1980 in Lithuania, there were 1,116 kindergartens enrolling 152,100 children in all.[33] Census data from 1989 show that there were 408,536 children in Lithuania under the age of 6.[34] The birth rate in Lithuania remained practically unchanged from 1980, and thus it is possible to conclude that in 1980 in Lithuania, approximately 40 per cent of children under the age of 6 were enrolled in creche-kindergartens. The same year, approximately 3 million children throughout the

USSR were still on waiting lists for preschool facilities.[35] Some data from the 1980s suggest that approximately 70 per cent of children under the age of 7 were enrolled in preschool facilities in the USSR.[36] A sociological study conducted during the final decade of the USSR in neighbouring Latvia showed that 55 per cent of women aged 55–9, 40 per cent of women over the age of 60 and 30 per cent of men over the age of 60 contributed significantly to helping raise their grandchildren.[37] Although statistics on the availability of preschool institutions in the USSR in the mid-1980s may vary, families that placed themselves on waiting lists for creches/kindergartens before their child was born could expect to get a spot for their child in preschool facilities.

Being a mother: Private strategies

Children who were unable to enrol in preschool facilities or for other reasons remained at home were the responsibility of their mothers or other family members. Unable to send their children to a creche-kindergarten or residential kindergarten, mothers had to turn to close friends and relatives for help. Their help was also necessary when mothers worked long, irregular hours, or were forced to take several jobs due to extremely low salaries. The annual salary increase from 1950 to 1964 in the USSR was barely 3 per cent, and women's salaries were approximately 40 per cent of men's.[38] Burdened by the constant shortage of material goods, women searched for jobs offering the best possible earning potential.

For women in the countryside, the job of milkmaid at the dairy farm was the best paid position at the *kolkhoz*. The physically demanding work began between four and five in the morning and ended between six and seven at night or even later. As long-time milkmaid Apolonija Birutė Paliulienė described her work in the following words:

> That's how it was: I left one child with my mother, about two kilometres away, and I raised the other one at my aunt's place, even though I had to start my trip to the farm at 3 o'clock in the morning. Those women who didn't work looked after their children themselves, but I wanted to work. I was afraid of losing my job. It was essential to me, a vital issue, because I had to earn money somewhere. I was very thrifty and I strived for a better future.[39]

Women forced to work irregular hours and unable or unwilling to send their child to weekly residential kindergarten often sought help from several relatives, dividing up the childcare among them. Long-time Soviet Lithuanian Deputy Premier of the Council of Ministers and Minister of Foreign Affairs Leokadija Diržinskaitė (b. 1921) was always leaving her children with her mother or mother-in-law; later her second husband cared for them. In 1948, when Diržinskaitė moved to work in Šiauliai, her children stayed with her mother. Her third child was cared for by Diržinskaitė's mother-in-law. When she moved to Vilnius to study at the Higher Party school, her children stayed with a relative. 'That's how we shared the kids', Diržinskaitė explained.[40]

Rūta Skatikaitė and her future husband were both raised by their grandmothers. In an interview, Skatikaitė explained that most mothers spent time with their children only intermittently and their constant work responsibilities outside the home led to emphatically respectful but emotionally cold relationships with their children. Skatikaitė remembered,

> [M]y ex-husband's mother (b. 1926) was a teacher at the village school. When heading out to work, she would feed her son and leave him with her mother. She'd run home during her lunch break and feed him again. Then, on her next break, she'd run home again … Her mother was with her child the rest of the day. The thought never occurred to me to ask my parents to spend time with me. I can't even imagine saying to my mum: 'Mama, I want you to spend more time with me.' That would be blasphemous, egotistical. It's something that you're not expected to want. It's even worse than, let's say, asking for a bike.[41]

Women who did shift work found it difficult to find time to spend with their children. In 1970, the magazine *Tarybinė moteris* surveyed readers on how they reconciled the responsibilities of work and home. The 1,291 women who responded wrote that the third shift, that is unpaid work at home, was the most exhausting because it drained them of all their energy. They wrote: 'I'm as tired on Friday when I get home from work as I am on Monday when I leave for work.'[42] G. M., who worked at the fuel hardware factory in Vilnius in 1960 described the efforts she made trying to manage both shift work and childcare:

> I worked in the afternoons; my husband worked nights. After lunch, I'd put the kids down for a nap and leave them in our locked apartment, hiding the key in the mailbox. When the factory would schedule three shifts, I would work on Saturdays. Then I'd come home after working the night shift and the kids would be awake already, shouting, "Mummy, we're hungry!" Then I'd make them breakfast, do the laundry, wash the dishes – I did everything. When my husband came home from work, he'd take the kids outside and I would get some sleep. And at 11 p.m., I'd leave for work again. That's how we worked week to week.

One week on the night shift; the next week, it was the afternoon shift; the third week the morning shift. But, eventually, I couldn't take any more and began looking for another job.[43]

Latchkey kids

Children, whose mothers worked irregular hours and didn't have close friends or family to help out, inevitably spent some of their time alone, without adult supervision. These kids were easily identifiable on the streets or in the courtyards of every Soviet republic by the latchkey hung around their necks. As parents would leave for work, they would remind their children of the most important rules of safety using gas stoves or electricity because their young children heated up their own food, did their own homework and left for school on their own. Even Soviet journalists wrote that the latchkeys hanging around the kids' necks made it difficult for mothers to work with any kind of peace of mind. One journalist, writing for a Lithuanian weekly, wrote thus:

> Women sacrifice a greater part of their leisure time for their family. They are always uneasy, especially if they have small children. The lucky ones have a grandmother living at home or after-school activities for the child. The unlucky ones hang a key around their child's neck, providing him with myriad directions on how to behave with natural gas, matches, electricity – and then it's off to work! Those keys weigh on mums' hearts like thousand kilogram weights. Back home, there's dinner, dishes, laundry, shopping, etc. Women's workdays are often fourteen to fifteen hours long.[44]

No matter their age, the latchkey children were subject to discipline and the demand of unconditional obedience. Mothers who left their children alone and were eternally concerned about their safety often berated themselves for their rigid and often severe behaviour with their small children. Natalija J. would leave her school-aged son at home alone. Although her privileged position at the factory allowed other opportunities for dealing with her son left alone at home, her fear of potential dangers caused her to be very strict with her son:

> When I worked at the trade union, I had the opportunity to take leave from work. All I had to do was ask my supervisor and I could take some time off. I would run home during my lunch break and find [my son] Ričardas outside. I'd bring him inside, check his homework and send him off to school. And then I'd run back to work again. This was our routine! But I was too rough on him. I was

very strict with my kids, extremely strict. At the time, the TV did a show on us, depicting us as an exemplary family.⁴⁵

Children caring for children

Without other alternatives, parents used the tried and tested traditional method, namely, assigning childcare to their elder sons and daughters. In such cases, the children became responsible for their younger siblings' care and safety. As a kid (she must have been 7–8 years of age), Janina Žižienė (b. 1946) helped her mother raise her two younger brothers:

> I got along well with my brothers. I would see to them and then go to school. I was obliged to cook and care for my younger brothers. Mum worked really hard on the farm. Back then, farmwork was not mechanized and she would get very tired. She worked every day, no exceptions, from morning until night. Her health eventually deteriorated. When I was eleven, mum was diagnosed with cancer.⁴⁶

Adults' overly complicated duties and responsibilities not only dampened their children's childhoods, but they also potentially complicated siblings' relationships. Elena Steponavičienė (b. 1928) remembered her elder daughter's childhood:

> in 1961, my eldest daughter Ona began her first year at the Vievis Middle School. At the time, I was working as a seamstress. My little one, Gražina, grew up a latchkey kid. At first we had a caregiver, but when Gražina turned six, I would lock her inside the apartment on my way to work until my eldest daughter would return from school. You see, I worked two shifts. Well, my eldest daughter would come home from school, unlock the door and feed her sister. That's how we lived ... But my two daughters did not get along. The kids would invite the elder one to play outside. And I'd tell her 'put Gražina down, and then you can go outside to play'. So Ona would rock Gražina's crib and order her sister to close her eyes. The little one would close her eyes, but as soon as Ona tried to run out the door, she would start hollering. I would tell her again, 'Ona, come back!' She would get angry and say 'You little brat. You won't let me go outside and play!' The elder daughter was like our caregiver. My parents raised me like that too. I worked a lot and didn't have much time for other kids.'⁴⁷

Some young mothers would choose their mothers' help, but that often meant leaving their husbands and going to another city or to the countryside. This practice of raising children became particularly popular in Lithuania in the

1980s when maternity leave was considerably longer and young families did not have their own space for raising children under the age of three. Young families didn't have enough money to pay rent because public benefits to mothers were not generous. Petronėlė-Aldona Adomonienė (b. 1929), shortly after giving birth, went to her mother's:

> We lived in an extremely tiny, one-room apartment. After our daughter was born, I moved to my mother's. Later, I returned to my husband but left our child with my mum. Eventually, we got a bigger apartment and brought our child home. But we had to hire a caregiver because the waiting lists for getting into kindergarten were very long.[48]

Working homemakers

Soviet census data from 1959 show a comparatively large number of people not working outside the home. That year, the population of working age adults in the USSR was 119,821,618, among whom 27 million did not hold state-paid positions.[49] Although the data do not indicate the precise percentage of women among the officially unemployed, one can find mentions in the press that for many families, financially, the work women did in the home was more valuable than the wages they received working at their jobs.[50] However in order to be able to remain at home and survive financially without a job, women were forced to engage in illegal home businesses.

Angelika Grikšienė's (b. 1958) mother cared for her children herself and sewed piecemeal for private clients. Grikšienė explained:

> My father worked at the dairy six days a week. He earned sixty roubles per month. I know that on Saturdays he would work until 3. After paying taxes, he would have fifty-eight roubles left over. I remember this sum very well. Because my brother and I were little, my mum wanted to spend more time with us and didn't want to leave us in an empty house. So she didn't go to work at the farm, because then she'd have to leave by dark and come home by dark. Work would have stolen all her time, and mum was afraid of this because she wanted to be with us. She was a good seamstress and sewed secretly. But it was very dangerous because everyone spied on one another and could inform on her any time. Even those who brought fabric and asked her to sew them some article of clothing could inform on her.

> Mum was always afraid. If someone brought her a larger piece of fabric, she would hide it in the attic. If someone would come over while she was sewing, she would try the article of clothing on and say that she was sewing something

for herself. One time, someone came to check on us, and looking for fabrics, they turned everything upside down. But mum kept on sewing. Normally, she sewed early mornings because she was worried that neighbours would hear her sewing machine humming. My dad regularly lubricated the machine so it would make less noise. Everything was done out of paralysing fear and we kids felt it. Mum kept sewing and would tell us: 'Go outside and make sure a stranger isn't coming. We were constantly on the lookout, and we internalised that fear.'[51]

Mothers who cared for their own children at home but wanted to earn a state salary could expect only the most basic physical and unqualified work, regardless of their education. After her daughters were born, Viktorija Varganienė (b. 1931) became a custodian. She remembers:

In 1955, my first daughter Marytė was born, in 1958, my second daughter Eugenija, and in 1963, my son Romanas. My life was difficult. I couldn't get them into kindergarten because we had just moved to Klaipėda. We hired a caregiver, but the children began to get sick. I changed the caregiver, but they were still getting sick. At the time, I began working as a custodian so that I could take care of my kids. I'd get up at four in the morning and sweep the sidewalk and street. Then I'd return home and watch the kids. When they were a bit bigger, I brought them with me to work.[52]

Mothers raising disabled children had no choice but to stay home. Mothers of children with psychological disabilities in particular could not work because, until late 1960s, the state did not provide any special assistance to disabled children or financial assistance to their parents. Monika Jonynaitė-Makūnienė (b. 1920), whose son required constant care, stayed at home for almost two decades. Her efforts to integrate herself and her son into society were met with resistance from Soviet officials. The following is her account:

At the time, in 1961, he was nine years old. Until then, I'd lived with him and nobody had helped us. Nobody. Absolutely nobody. There was a woman named Fainbliuvienė; she was the head of the social welfare division. I asked her to admit Genutis to the childcare center. I begged her with tears in my eyes, and she said, 'So what? You want the state to support your child?' She refused, and that was it. And thus I lived on with three children and two parents, and in 1962 I started thinking about sending him to a nursing home. I thought it would be easier for my family; I'd get a job. At that time, my second son, Jonas, was already eight, my daughter Nijolė was three. Because the head of the division refused to speak to me, I used my connections and paid a visit to the chairman of the Executive Committee. He gave me a letter of resolution, and I got a letter of reference for the Kaunas nursing home for the handicapped. I gave Genutis a bath, put some clean clothes on him, and took the child there. Eleven days later, I paid him a visit only to realise he didn't even have his underwear on; he was soiled. Who would look after him when there were twenty-three children in the group, and only one supervisor? The kids threw cereal into each other's hair. In those days, social matters were totally neglected; nobody cared! So those Communists really shouldn't boast.[53]

The first time the question of caring for special needs children appeared in the Soviet newspapers was in 1968 when the state adopted a resolution on providing basic financial assistance for children and adults born with disabilities. Jonynaitė-Makūnienė was able to benefit from this assistance only for a few months: 'In 1968, when Genutis turned 16, I got 16 roubles of social benefits for him. I received them for two years because he passed away at the age of 18. He lived for 18 years and four months. I almost wanted him to die; it may sound cruel, but … I knew he wouldn't be able to live.'[54] School-aged children with physical disabilities could be enrolled in one of seven special assistance schools operating in Lithuania. Children with minor psychological disabilities lived and studied at one of thirty-four special needs boarding schools.[55] However, these schools were not outfitted for serving children with severe physical or psychological disabilities.

Extraordinary strategies

In addition to their official jobs and childcare responsibilities, women were also expected to do the lion's share of housework. Urbanization which had begun in the post-war era changed the lifestyle of the majority of the Lithuanian population. The rapid pace of relocation to the larger cities of the Soviet republic meant that people were adapting to new conditions and leaving behind the way of life to which traditional interwar families were accustomed. This was indeed a challenge for the sons of former farming families, who now found themselves working in Soviet plants and factories. Raised in patriarchal families, they found it hard to adopt the more egalitarian role of husband as partner. Bronė Sopienė (b. 1941) spoke about her husband: 'My husband had a difficult childhood. His father was a forest ranger. That's why he was skilled at manly tasks which were necessary on the farm. But we were living in the city and there were no jobs there requiring manly work, yet all the tasks associated with women's work remained … This burden fell on me alone.'[56]

Husbands who were born and raised on traditional interwar farms and who were now urban rarely or never helped with housework or childcare. In 1960, the

LSSR press acknowledged that in the Soviet family, women were the busiest of all family members. A few years later, in 1966, sociologists found that urban women who were married and raising children on average spent five hours per day on housework and only the rare husband contributed two hours on average.[57] These statistics are borne out by later studies. According to Vladimir Shlapentokh, in 1980 in the Baltic republics, among young husbands aged 19–24, 63 per cent actively contributed to housework; that same year, among husbands aged 30–9, 40 per cent, and among 50-year-olds, only 36 per cent actively helped their wives with housework.[58] According to sociologists, women in the Hungarian People's Republic in the 1960s worked for nine hours outside the home in paid work, slept for seven hours and spent seven hours on housework and childcare. They devoted only one hour to rest and relaxation.[59]

In Soviet Lithuania, women didn't expect their husbands to voluntarily help with housework or childcare, but neither did they believe they had the right to rest or entertainment. Even after completing their daily housework tasks and having taken care of the children, young women were unable to get away from concerns of home and family even for a short time because men were not keen on caring for children during their free time on evenings or weekends. Women sometimes employed drastic, non-traditional strategies that were harmful to the family. Elena Steponavičienė (b. 1928) explained how she managed to enjoy cultural events:

> My husband had golden fingers and was expert at repairing motors. He worked for the Vievis truck dispatching company but had a drinking problem. I married young and really wanted to go out and have a good time. There was a House of Culture in the town of Vievis that screened films and hosted theatrical productions. My husband had no use for cultural events. So, my husband's cousin's wife Liucija and I would buy him a bottle of wine in order to get him to watch the kids and feed them. That's how we managed to go out to the movies, theatre and dancing.[60]

Practically all women living in the European part of the USSR worked a full eight-hour day beyond the confines of the home and insisted that they valued their right to work. In the early 1970s, most Soviet women said that working outside the home was their personal choice, not a financial necessity and not something they were coerced into doing. A sociological study from 1972 to 1974 asked 470 married women living in Moscow which goal in life was more important to them: work or family? Eighty-six per cent of respondents said 'both'; however, they explained that work was their priority.[61] These results are confirmed by other sources. Anastasia Posadskaya-Vanderbeck and Marianne Liljeström, using women's biographical accounts, found that, during interviews, women tried to focus on their professional activities and avoided talking about family and children.[62] Work and social activities became emotionally important to women's sense of identity and came to be understood not only as the norm of Soviet life but as a woman's self-expression, her inner necessity. Although in almost every interview conducted in Lithuania (1989–2005), women stressed that family and children were their most important concern and life goal, only a very few of those women were not working in an official job and devoting all their time to their families.[63] Interviews with the women of Lithuania testify to the fact that women often worked for their children and family under very unfavourable conditions. Of course, most families faced difficult financial situations which could be eased only through the wages of both parents. But women's decisions were not always determined by deprivations and material necessities. Quite often their decisions coincided with personal interests: career goals, the desire to be valued and important as well as their needs as consumers.

At the end of the 1990s, during the Gorbachev *perestroika* era, women who had spent their adult years in Soviet society reacted to the new images of motherhood quite emotionally, longing again for the status of unemployed homemaker and mum. Sometimes this unfulfilled longing would manifest in an envious retort directed at those who, even under Soviet societal conditions, managed to create a different, more sensitive and more favourable environment for their children. In the 1990s, after Lithuania regained independence, hundreds of thousands of young women of Lithuania left their paid jobs or simply did not look for a job outside the home, opting instead for the role of homemaker and mum.

Children caught between fighting parents

Divorcing parents

The People's Courts in Soviet Lithuania applied the practice of hearing out what minor children had to say about their parents' reasons for divorcing in order to help determine child custody after the divorce. Children's written affidavits could be used as evidence in the case; for this reason, divorcing parents would use their children's testimonies to manipulate the proceedings. In one of the letters to a court, an 8-year old girl wrote to the court that she will not live with her mother because her father loves her and she wants to live with him. She asked her mother to return her brother because she thought the mother does not love him. An older school-aged girl wrote to the Superior Court explaining the circumstances for her father's extramarital affairs and asked the court not to allow him to divorce her mum because 'Daddy will come home and our family will live together again.' In her letter, she explained that their current family situation was inhibiting her and her brother's studies and asked the Chief Justice of the Superior Court to hurry his ruling. In 1961, a third-grade student from the Šiauliai Music Conservatory appealed to the Druskininkai Comsomol[64] organization asking to sanction the music teacher who had seduced her father, the director of the school. The daughter's appeal gained some attention and the teacher was discussed at several meetings: at the Varėna chapter of the Comsomol organization, the primary party organization of the boarding school and the Varėna District Central Committee.[65] It is not clear the extent to which their decisions were influenced by the evidence brought by the minor children, but their testimonies were indeed considered by the party and social organizations and they were examined and discussed parallel to the court proceedings. More prominent divorce and child custody cases were taken up by trade union meetings of companies and institutions as well as newspaper editorial offices.

Until the court reforms in 1965, child custody matters in divorce cases were heard by the Superior Court, but afterwards, they were handled by the People's Courts and by the Superior Court in cassation. Born and raised in interwar Lithuania, most sons of the interwar farming community considered themselves to be the head of the household; in their mind, the duty of women was to have babies and do housework. As they divorced, such husbands did not discuss their cases with their children's mothers and would dictate custody arrangements to the court. For example, in 1948, Povilas M. wrote to the court:

> I assume custody of my son Povilas, born in 1942, and I grant custody of my daughter Genovaitė, born in 1946 to the defendant.' During the early years of the postwar era, most husbands in their declaration of intent to divorce would indicate the conditions under which the divorce should take place. In 1953, a petitioner argued to the court that 'I wish to raise my son M. Rūstenis, born 1939, because I have better means to provide for him. After the divorce, I want my wife to use her first husband's last name.[66]

Biased rulings and demands to the court regarding child custody would be submitted by ordinary civilian husbands as well as by Communist Party members holding high positions. In 1945, while divorcing his wife, one party functionary demanded that the court 'recognise our common-law children Birutė and Danutė as mine and to grant me custody … because she [his wife] is not suited for bringing up children'.⁶⁷ The Civil Court Chamber of the Supreme Court generally granted the requests of the party *nomenklatura*. In the early post-war years, if respondents appealed court decisions to the Prosecutor General of the USSR, the cases could be reviewed even if the petitioners were party functionaries. However, starting in the 1960s when the *nomenklatura* was assuming increasingly more prestigious positions, high-ranking individuals' divorce and child custody cases were ruled in their favour with very quick turnaround times without even hearing the other side's arguments. In 1969, a party functionary asked the court to question his 12.5-year-old son, asking for full custody. In court, the boy testified: 'I am thirteen years old. I have completed five grades and am now in sixth grade ... If daddy divorces mummy, I would like to live with daddy in his apartment because that's where my older brother lives.'⁶⁸

The decisions of the court did not always grant both parents the right to regularly meet with and interact with their children after the divorce. This practice encouraged divorcing couples to take personal initiative and ensure their participation in the child's upbringing.

In one particular case in 1956, after the court had granted custody to the mother, the woman's ex-husband demanded that she write the following affidavit and to present it to the court: 'Affidavit. I, Danutė P. Ž., do hereby promise to provide Romualdas P. the opportunity to see his daughter Jolanta P. whenever circumstances permit as well as to inform Romualdas P. about the state of her health.'⁶⁹ In more complicated cases, before ruling on child custody, the court could request to examine the situation and enforce the *Act of Inspection of Material and Sanitary Conditions* regarding the child's living environment. These inspections were conducted by workplace women's boards and other social organizations. Their representatives would visit the home of one of the parents or grandparents where the children were living and evaluate the situation. In one instance of the act being enforced in 1968, the child in question was described as found in a puddle, wet up to his waist and wearing tattered and patched pants and no gloves. The inspectors stressed that the living space was connected to the barn under one roof and there was no electricity.⁷⁰ In some post-war divorce cases, the court would independently evaluate the family's material conditions and rule based not just on the interest of the couple, but also of the children. In a 1950 case, both spouses were seeking divorce, but the judges denied their request, instead ordering the husband to pay 50 per cent of all his wages for child support of the couple's three children until they ceased to be minors.⁷¹

Under Khrushchev, rulings on divorce cases were heavily influenced by the active participation of the Communist Party, various workplaces as well as trade union organizations. Their representatives would provide the opinion of the collective in deciding child custody arrangements, providing supplementary testimonies and the personal characteristics of petitioners and respondents, acting as go-betweens between the two parties and offering decisions in actual cases. In 1963, the Vilnius Vincas Kapsukas University (now Vilnius University) Library Board formed a committee to assess their employee E. D.'s 'abnormal family relations'. The committee was composed of the library's director, party organization secretary and the president of the university trade union. The committee testified to the Superior Court that E. D.'s wife was regularly coming to the university library, being disorderly, harassing the other employees and making it difficult for her husband to work. In a similar case, the Vilnius Trolleybus Park Commission evaluated the extramarital relations of one of their trolleybus drivers with another driver from the same collective and asked the People's Court to grant custody of their son to the woman's husband, ordering her to pay him child support. Meanwhile, in 1962, the Jurbarkas kindergarten collective asked the court to grant custody of their employee's 3-year-old son, Edmundas, to the boy's father, because his mother was 'pregnant with another man's child'. And representatives from the trade union executive committee and school board from the Švenčionys School of Agriculture Technology party organization No. 4, in a divorce case regarding their employee Bronė R., persuaded the Supreme Court that they had not seen any blemishes in the woman's behaviour and vouched for her as active reader of books on foreign affairs and literature and asked the court to grant her custody of her daughter.[72]

Husbands with the help of their work collective would ask the court to grant them custody, in hopes of avoiding child support. But if custody was granted to their children's mothers, the men rarely appealed the decision, because after the divorce they would often stop participating in their child's life and supporting them financially. Avoidance of child support by deadbeat dads was prevalent and became a social problem.

Recovery of child support

All family and criminal codes in effect in the LSSR provided for the payment and recovery of child support, allocating one-quarter of the responsible parent's salary for the maintenance of one child, one-third salary for two children, and one-half salary for three children. At times post-war courts would require partial payment of child support in kind. In 1948, at the Second People's Court of the city of Panevėžys, the father of two children explained that he allotted 90 litres of milk, 1.5 kilograms of butter, 16 kilograms of rye, 16 kilograms of barley and 25 kilograms of potatoes per month for the maintenance of his children. The ex-spouses agreed in court that because the husband's earnings had decreased and his obligations to his children had increased, he would pay child support in kind by providing smaller quantities of food products.[73] During the first decade after the war, the courts hearing divorce cases decided child custody and child support only in exceptional situations. The children would automatically remain with their mothers, and they rarely expected material assistance from their children's fathers. For this reason, in 1950, the Plenary of the LSSR Supreme Court (the Highest Instance of the Supreme Court) adopted the resolution *On Judicial Practice in Recovering Funds for Child Support* and authorized the People's Courts to hear civil cases regarding child support speedily and justly. The judges however did not abide by the regulations and decided cases haphazardly. Almost 40 per cent of cases were decided without the participation of the respondents, who at times were not even notified about the hearings that would determine the child support they would be obligated to pay. In such cases, the hearings should not have proceeded or they should have been postponed; however, the judges did not heed the regulations and made formal rulings regardless.[74]

Once the ban on marriages with foreign nationals was lifted on 26 November 1953 and marriages with foreign nationals were subsequently allowed as long as they were registered in the territory of the USSR, and following the decree of 12 September 1958 which provided legal assistance in civil, family and criminal cases in countries with which the Soviet Union had signed an agreement, the Superior Court began to receive cases involving the recovery of child support after the dissolution of mixed marriages of individuals with different citizenships.[75] Most of these requests came from Poland as its citizens were repatriated from Lithuania during two periods: between 12 October 1944 and 1 November 1947 as well as between 1956 and 1959. During the first wave of repatriations of 1944–7, Lithuanians and other ethnic groups from Lithuania were banned from going to Poland. Thus, unless spouses of different citizenships forged their identification papers, they were forced to separate. In some cases, child support requests would come to Lithuania a significant number of years after the child's birth. In 1970, the Legnica District Court of the Polish People's Republic by its own ruling demanded from LSSR citizen Vaclovas Z. child support for his sons Stanislavas, born 1953, and Rišardas, born 1959. The petitioner asked the court to order her ex-husband to pay her 400 zloty per month. The Lithuanian Supreme Court only partially granted her request by awarding child support in the amount of 29 roubles, 43 kopecks for one child.[76]

From the mid-1950s in Lithuania, child support became an integral part of divorce case decisions and, along with the division of property, the principal dispute to be litigated. However, during the entire history of the USSR, a good number of divorced fathers managed to avoid paying child support for their children. The men's behaviour was determined by several factors: Soviet family policy not only encouraged spouses to each develop their own separate space within the marriage, but it also tried to limit interactions between parents and their children. In the Soviet family, parents and their children spent the greater part of their days apart: extracurricular activities in school, vacationing with only one of the parents because spouses would receive separate and different trade union travel vouchers, and at Young Pioneers summer camps. In 1961, the LSSR Council of Ministers approved regulations regarding preschool institution/creche-kindergarten time schedules, which took into account fathers' as well as mothers' work schedules. Children would attend creche-kindergartens after maternity/paternity leave had ended, from age 2 months to 7 years spending up to twelve hours there a day.[77] Soviet Lithuanian experts themselves acknowledged the fraying emotional ties between family members. In 1977, they stated that in cases of divorce, 80 per cent of fathers' involvement in their children's lives was to do with only providing child support.[78] However, the majority of divorced men avoided contributing to the financial maintenance of their children.

Lithuanian court practices testify to the fact that from 1958 to 1967, the number of child support recovery cases increased two-fold, while 88.8 per cent of respondents did not pay the child support they were ordered to pay. In 1968, after hearing 5,998 child support recovery cases involving malicious avoidance to provide support for their children, Lithuania's judges declared an epidemic of child support obligations avoidance in the republic.[79] In 1967, the resolution *On Paying Child Support and Improving Recovery Procedures* was adopted, which tightened the recovery of child support.[80] Workplace administrators were henceforth required to check their workers' identification documents for potential child support obligations and to inform the court. Social organizations were also required to participate in the recovery of child support. Malicious avoidance of child support could be punishable by prison.

There were no legal obstacles to awarding child support for children born in wedlock, but the state was nonetheless incapable of enforcing child support payments or fathers' participation on their children's lives after divorce. Awarding child support to children born out of wedlock, within unregistered partnerships or to single mothers was a different story altogether. On 14 March 1945, the resolution *On the Application of the 8 July decree Issued by the USSR*

Supreme Soviet Presidium to Children of Parents in Unregistered Marriages amended the *RSFSR Marriage, Family and Guardianship Code*. According to the resolution, mothers, whose children were born in a church marriage before 8 July 1944, could petition in court for child support if the respondent was listed on the child's birth certificate as the father.[81] However, children born after the *8 July 1944 decree* could not be registered under their father's surname (even if the father did not object) if the marriage was not registered at the civil registry bureau. In such cases, the child would be registered under the mother's surname and the line for the father's name would be left blank. Thus, the right for single mothers or mothers who lived as cohabitating partners to petition for child support in court was denied because legally the father remained anonymous.

Some men took advantage of this legal gap and renounced their paternity, in this way avoiding the obligation of paying child support. In 1957, a petitioner came to court with a paternity suit even though his son was 12 years old. He wrote to the court:

> On 12 June 1945, I registered my marriage to citizen Janina M. at the Raseiniai civil registry bureau; she is the respondent in this case. Before our marriage, on 24 May 1945, the respondent had given birth to a son who I registered under my surname 'Alfonsas K.' even though the civil registry bureau did not have the right to register the child under my name as he was born after the *8 July 1944 decree* was issued. This child is not mine and I refuse to pay his child support.[82]

After the *8 July 1944 decree* came into effect, the fathers of children born out of wedlock had no legal options for recognizing their children and registering them under their surnames. In these cases, the state would recommend the only possible legal avenue available to the parents: adoption. In 1964, the director of the Mažeikiai Executive Committee sent a similar official explanation to a man in response to his questions about having his child born out of wedlock recognized and registered under his surname. The official wrote in the letter that, absent any legal courses of action for registering the child in his name, his best option was to adopt the baby. There were no obstacles to adoption if his legal wife gave her permission.[83]

From 1 October 1968, paternity was again based on the father's voluntary decision to recognize the baby and register him or her under the father's surname. At the same time, however, starting in 1968, the child's mother could require paternity to be recognized and sue for child support through the courts. Unfortunately, verifying biological paternity was very complicated and depended on multiple circumstances: medical expertise, witness testimony and evidence of a commonly managed household. A single mother who could not provide for the court sufficient evidence that she was cohabiting with the child's father had no realistic possibility of being awarded child support. In 1962, a petitioner, who was living with the respondent in an unregistered partnership, had a baby daughter. The man was drafted into military service and did not return to his daughter and cohabiting partner. In 1963, the woman sent the girl to an orphanage. In 1967, she took her back and petitioned the court to verify paternity so she could obtain child support. But the court did not recognize paternity because the woman was unable to show that the man had contributed to the household or helped raise the child.[84]

The number of single mothers and children born out of wedlock in Lithuania was increasing. In 1980, the percentage among all newborn children born out of wedlock in Lithuania was 6.3 per cent; it was 6.7 per cent in 1989, and by 1992, it had grown to 7.9 per cent. The percentage of children born out of wedlock in Lithuania was lower, however, than the USSR average and lower compared to the other two Baltic republics. In 1980, Latvia's babies born out of wedlock numbered 12.5 per cent, and in 1989, it was 15.9 per cent. In Estonia, the numbers were, respectively, 18.3 per cent and 25.2 per cent. In 1980, the average number of children born out of wedlock in the entire USSR was 8.8 per cent, and in 1989, it was 10.7 per cent. The number of children living with only their mother or her parents also increased. In 1979, in Lithuania, there were 94,500, and in 1989, the number was greater than 100,000 (100,600). Children living with only their father or his parents that year was respectively 7,600 or 8,100.[85] Nonetheless, the number of single-parent households in Lithuania remained smaller than in the neighbouring republics. In 1979, single-parent households in Lithuania made up 11.9 per cent of all families. In Latvia, the number was 14.9 per cent, and in Estonia, it was 15.6 per cent.[86]

4

Household

Housing

Political prisoner Stefanija Kučinskienė spent five years in Stalin's prisons and Siberian labour camps and returned to Lithuania on 29 May 1952. She reached her birthplace Kelmė at dawn, but standing in the rubble of what had been her town, she couldn't recognize a thing. Many years later Stefanija remembered:

> They left me in the very centre of town. I looked around and felt dizzy. I couldn't tell where I was – nothing but ruins. So I kept walking around like that – and I saw the church. The church hadn't been demolished! Its bell struck at eight. God, this was our church! Then I recognized the place: the marketplace – ruins, nothing else. I found the ruins just as I had left them. 'God', I thought to myself, 'I spent five years in prison, and we re-built an entire town [Ukhta], but not a single house had been re-built in Lithuania during these years.' I left my bags with someone I knew. I found my street and walked five kilometres until I reached home.[1]

In 1944, as the war was ending in Lithuania, Kelmė, Raseiniai and Šiauliai saw one of the fiercest battles of the entire war. Clashes between the German and Russian armies left barely 15 per cent of Kelmė's buildings standing, and several kilometres away, in Raseiniai, there was barely a building that had not been damaged. In Lithuania's largest cities, Vilnius and Kaunas, 4,612 buildings were destroyed; every structure in the city centre of Šiauliai was demolished. According to witnesses, some buildings in Vilnius were ravaged by Russian soldiers: 'If the Russian Soviet Army soldiers found a building that had been bombed, damaged, its roof caved in or windows smashed, they would set fire to the whole thing with their ... flamethrowers to make sure that anyone hiding out there would be killed.'[2]

It wasn't just military actions that damaged buildings. Prisoners returning from the GULAG camps and places of exile were unable to reclaim their property or they would find their family homes had been destroyed by strangers and even neighbours. One deportee reported thus:

> my parents' homestead was empty and the abandoned house was scheduled to be demolished. The homestead was so run down that the house had no roof, windows, or doors – just the walls standing, waiting to be torn down and burned up. The stable was also roofless, it had no doors, and the barn was entirely destroyed. Only the shed was left intact.[3]

After the war, every half-metre of living space was important as families of three or more were being accommodated in spaces as tiny as 7–12 square metres. As centralized plans for the distribution of living space were being enacted in post-war Lithuania, the Soviet government made sure that no single person would be allotted any more space than the norms allowed. The courts by their own discretion could confiscate living space that exceeded norms even if it was owned by right of inheritance. In 1948, a daughter asked the court to award her a portion of a private home as part of her deceased mother's estate, but the court first determined whether, according to state norms, the inherited property was 'needed' by the heirs.[4] Moving residents out of communal apartments was easier because the space belonged to the state: in 1958, the city of Kaunas VI People's Court confiscated a plaintiff's right to rent a 7-square metre room with a kitchen and transferred it to another renter.[5] In 1966, the republic's dormitory rules indicated that every worker or service sector employee must be appropriated no less than 4.5 square metres, and pupils were to be allotted 6 square metres. As these requirements were imposed, four to six people would be moved into dormitory rooms of 18–24 square metres.[6] As mass urbanization began in Lithuania, the problem of housing became acute: the population of the capital Vilnius in 1945 was 145,000 inhabitants; by 1959, it was 236,000, and in 1979, it was nearly half a million.[7] From 1951 to 1976, approximately 700,000 inhabitants moved from Lithuania's countryside into the cities. In 1945, Lithuania's urban dwellers made up 15 per cent of the population; by 1989, they made up 70 per cent.[8]

In 1948, a construction trust was established in Vilnius and construction organizations and building material production plants were established in other cities as well. The first prefabricated concrete-panelled buildings were produced at the Vilnius Home Manufacturing plant in 1959, and the first mass-produced housing development, the micro-district of Žirmūnai, was built in 1962 in the capital.[9] A little over ten years later, in 1974, the Lazdynai micro-district was completed in Vilnius with four different shopping centres, cultural centres and kindergartens. As some critics contend, the first Soviet bloc apartment buildings, *Khrushchiovki* as they were referred to, were of poor quality and only partially completed when they were handed over to residents.[10] At the same time, however, Lithuania's so-called prefabricated bedroom communities were evaluated highly by professionals and residents. In 1968, the Žirmūnai micro-district was awarded the Lithuanian Soviet Socialist Republic (LSSR) of Ministers' Prize and in 1974, Lazdynai became the first micro-district to be awarded the highest recognition in the Soviet Union, the Lenin Prize. Young families appreciated Lazdynai in particular: in 1975, 91.6 per cent of Lazdynai residents claimed that they would stay there even if offered a chance to move to a place of their choice in any other part of the capital.[11] The construction of prefabricated block buildings was underway throughout the republic. In the tiny town of Gargždai, between the years 1960and 1990, a total of 115 apartment buildings were built, comprising two-thirds of the town's buildings. Mass-produced micro-districts were being constructed throughout the USSR on a massive scale; between 1956 and 1965, 108 million young families moved into the new apartment complexes.[12] But housing continued to be a problem throughout the country and in the republic.

The shortage of living space in Lithuania was partially addressed through the construction of private homes, *dachas* (also called collective farm cottages), and private cooperative apartments. The latter had to abide by established norms governing total area: in the 1950s, the combined total area of all the rooms in the cooperative apartment could not exceed 60 square metres. Owning a cooperative apartment could be risky in case of divorce, because the second spouse did not have a right to the space itself, but only to a portion of the monetary share that had been paid off. According to regulation no. 31 of the Residential Construction Cooperative, a flat could only be divided among former spouses if the space was large enough to be separated into two isolated, individual premises. Still, sharing the same apartment after divorce was preferable to being given the paid-in share and losing the right to the treasure most dear in Soviet life, housing.[13]

On 26 August 1948, the Presidium of the USSR Supreme Soviet granted every Soviet citizen the legal right to build a house of no more than five rooms. On 18 July 1958, the decree was amended regarding living space norms: the total area of all the rooms added together in a private house could not exceed 60 square metres. It was also forbidden in the republic to build wooden homes, with the exception of collective farm workers who were transporting wooden cottages from their old homesteads to the new collective farm settlements. The state made loans available for the construction of private homes, but these loans were accessible only to certain social groups: demobilized military officers, generals, teachers working in rural districts, doctors and engineers. Regulations also curtailed the acquisition of construction materials: roof tiles, bricks, cement and other building materials were available only to those holding executive committee registered accounts. The rules also required that the homes be completed within three years – although it was possible to extend by one more year.[14] In 1974, the regulations regarding the construction of private homes were amended yet again, and lot size was limited to 0.06 hectares. The rules also limited ownership to one home or part of one home per family and did not allow construction permits if one or both spouses had received another permit during the past ten years, or if one or both spouses had already built an individual, private home.[15] Lots for private home construction were not given out in the capital, the city of Kaunas or the Palanga coastline resort area. In the early 1970s, individual, prefabricated, private and departmental homes began to be promoted and built. There were several standard projects for homes of various sizes: the three-room (two bedroom) model, the four-room (three bedroom) model and the five-room (four bedroom) model, all with central heating. Considering the average salary of the time, very few Soviet citizens could afford the prefabricated private homes as their price was high: a three-room 85.43-square metre home cost 15,690 roubles; a four-room 103.72-square metre home cost 18,070 roubles; and a five-room 119.9-square metre home cost 20,130 roubles.[16] If one was not issued a communal apartment, a private cottage at a collective garden could also become the family's primary residence and, quite often, an alternative to Soviet apartment buildings.

Lithuanian architects' projects for typical single-family homes were not designed according to Soviet standards alone; they also incorporated urban planning project ideas from abroad, which the architects kept track of through unofficial channels. In 1956, a book from Lithuania on home design received by a Boston architect testifies to the fact that the professional perspective of Soviet architects did not rely exclusively on formal Soviet rules of construction.[17] However, regardless of the mass construction of residential properties, for most people in Lithuania, an apartment of their own was a dream that remained difficult to realize. In 1970, approximately 70 per cent of newly-weds began their new lives living in the parental home of one of the spouses.[18] Regardless of where young couples made their homes, they tried to run their household according to the modern aesthetic propagated by Soviet magazines and newspapers.

The turn to everyday life and the desire for aesthetics during the Khrushchev Thaw

Material conditions

Not only did post-war Lithuania experience a housing shortage, but the most essential necessities and food products were also in short supply. In the winter of 1945, 1 litre of milk cost 10 roubles, and 1 kilogram of butter was 150 roubles at the city market in Panevėžys. But it was impossible to find wheat anywhere because farmers were forbidden from selling it.[19] Most of the population during the post-war period could barely afford to shop at the local market because the average family lived at poverty level. In a 1944 divorce case, a couple from Vilnius asked the court to equally divide the family property that remained after the war: two rugs, four curtains, four tablecloths, three tables, six chairs and two beds.[20] Men and women returning from forced exile would bring back with them nothing more than a small satchel or suitcase. Sometimes, divorce cases of deportees would include the reminder that 'my wife left the camps without even one decent dress to her name'. Some women married to former Red Army soldiers would improve on their miserable domestic situations with war trophies from Germany for things they never had before like radio receivers, porcelain tea sets or beautiful rugs. But any property acquired before the war could be subject to state confiscation. In 1947, as family members fought in court over their deceased relative's estate, the Civil Chamber of the Superior Court adopted a resolution that the property belonged not to the heirs, but to the state, and that it had to be handed over to the Finance Ministry.[21]

Currency reforms removed the so-called *chervoncy* from circulation on 14 December 1947 and replaced the old roubles with a new currency with the same name but different design, exchanging at the rate of 10:1. After these reforms, basic food products sold by farmers became four to ten times cheaper; however, from 1947 to 1950, state grain collections from farmers were increased two-to-five-fold.[22] In 1947, with the beginning of mass collectivization, farming families were reduced to poverty: when they joined a *kolkhoz*, the property they brought in became collective property and their wages were miniscule. In 1953, almost half of Lithuania's collective farms did not pay wages to their workers; for one workday, the administration would provide up to 1 kilogram of grain and 6 kopecks, and 10 kopecks in 1954. In 1955, the earnings paid to a family employed by a collective farm made up only 15.2 per cent of what they needed to live on; 74.5 per cent came from their small private plot of land. In

1968, the government approved a fixed minimum monthly wage of 60 roubles for collective farm workers, but meanwhile, ideological propaganda trumpeted the ever-improving lives of collective farmers and their perpetually increasing buying power.[23] The Trade Ministry proclaimed Stalin era-type percentage increases of supposed purchases of silk fabrics (146 per cent), turntables (230 per cent) and cameras (120 per cent) by collective farm workers, comparing 1950 to 1948.[24] In 1956, the Twentieth Congress of the Communist Party of the Soviet Union denounced the Stalin cult, and in 1958, the First Secretary of the Lithuanian Communist Party Central Committee (LCP(b) CC) Antanas Sniečkus, at the Tenth Lithuanian Communist Party Congress, acknowledged that the state of the republic's agricultural sector from 1951 to 1956 was dire.[25] The material conditions of people in the villages of Lithuania began to improve somewhat only in the latter half of the 1960s.[26]

In 1963, a woman wrote in a letter to her husband that fish oil and vitamins were very hard to find in the stores in Kaunas, and she was always feeling weak. And yet, from 1953 to 1964, Lithuania's urban grocery stores were better supplied than Russia's and were selling basic food items and consumer goods. Urban dwellers holding certain positions could enjoy a substantially comfortable standard of living.[27] In 1957, the last will and testament of Vilnius University Department of Medicine Professor Jonas K. reveals a relatively stable material situation for his family: the professor left his wife their flat in the centre of Vilnius, a Znamya television, a Riga radio receiver, a Dnepr refrigerator, a turntable and a collection of two hundred vinyl records, a huge rug, a clock, the *Great Soviet Encyclopaedia*, and a Moskvič automobile. The will also listed additional items of value, which after the professor's death would be inherited by his son and daughter.[28] Given the post-war economic situation, the professor's estate was likely not accumulated exclusively through his official salary but was augmented by his offering medical services privately. Nevertheless, most ordinary families in Lithuania walked a tightrope between deprivation and the daily needs that were difficult to satisfy. It is no coincidence that in 1962 a rise in prices of food items led to street protests and demonstrations in some parts of Russia.[29]

Salaries for work in various sectors of Soviet society differed greatly by amount and in the availability of bonuses. In 1958, the monthly salary of the director of political education of the Lithuanian Communist Party (LCP) Executive Committee in the city of Mažeikiai was 975 roubles, plus 125 roubles for business trip expenses. But it was not just party functionaries who received even higher salaries. In 1954, the salary of the director of store no. 5 of the consumer cooperative Talka was different every month, varying from the lowest of 326 roubles to one that was several times larger: in summer, the director's salary was as high as 1,761, 1,247 and 1,789 roubles. During the same period, the shift forewoman of a beauty salon earned an average of 200 roubles per month, and the monthly salary of a seamstress at the Kaunas state fur factory Raudonoji Vėliava (the Red Flag) was 505 roubles. The currency reforms in 1961 devalued the rouble ten-fold, although differences between salaries remained considerable. Thus in 1968, the average factory worker's monthly salary was between 100 and 120 roubles, and, in 1972, the assistant director of the Kaunas Medical Institute made nearly twice as much, or 220 roubles.[30]

Couples earning higher salaries or who worked in the unofficial economic sector could acquire the basic material wealth typical for a Soviet family. In 1981, a well-to-do couple from Klaipėda asked the court to dissolve their twenty-two-year marriage and divide up their mutually acquired estate: a living room furniture suite (800 roubles), stereo equipment (800 roubles), kitchen furniture (100 roubles), a Zil refrigerator (200 roubles), a radio (100 roubles), an old television set (50 roubles), a flashlight (50 roubles), an old bedroom furniture suite (50 roubles), a VAZ-2103 automobile (8,600 roubles), a garage (1,000 roubles) and a collective garden (1,857 roubles).[31] By far, one of the most precious and most difficult to obtain of all material items was the automobile, which, until the final years of the Soviet Union, remained a deficit item. In the 1970s, there were twenty-six cars for every 1,000 inhabitants of the USSR. In the Baltic republics, including Lithuania, the population had twice as many cars compared with other Soviet republics, but the numbers remained considerably lower than those of the United States, where at the time there were 426 cars for every 1,000 inhabitants (see Table 4.1).

Table 4.1 Cars in the Soviet republics, 1977 and 1985

	1977	1985
USSR	26	45
Estonia	61	96
Lithuania	50	93
Latvia	45	81
Russia	21	44
Moldova	14	33

Source: Lewis H. Siegelbaum, 'Cars, Cars, and More Cars: The Faustian Bargain of the Brezhnev Era', in *Borders of Socialism: Private Spheres of Soviet Russia*, ed. Lewis H. Siegelbaum (New York: Palgrave Macmillan, 2006), 90.

In search of a comfortable and beautiful home

During the Khrushchev Thaw, not only did the government expect to fully satisfy the Soviet people's everyday needs for consumer goods, but it also sought to create a 'cultivated, beautiful, and aesthetic lifestyle'. This campaign in Lithuania, as in the rest of the USSR, began after Stalin's death as it sought to distance itself as quickly as possible from pre-war bourgeois culture as well as from the Stalinist past. The creation of a new lifestyle and aesthetic thus became no less important a task in the building of communism than the cultivation of a communist morality. A carefully cultivated culture of proper etiquette was also part of the 'cultivated, beautiful, and aesthetic lifestyle' project. Newspapers and magazines were full of articles about proper table etiquette for adults and children, the placement of tableware and the proper ways of using them. The first advice columns appeared at this time, showing how to create a formal holiday table menu, set the table and entertain guests appropriately. The Lithuanian newspapers and magazines all offered similarly titled articles: 'Your Child's Table Manners', 'Let's Be Sophisticated, 'Holiday Table Preparations' and the like. Like most Soviet campaigns for an aesthetic lifestyle, this one too reflected the gigantic gap between the ideological propaganda and real everyday life, the Soviet people's financial abilities and the production capacity of light industry. Given the universal shortages, these ambitions by the Soviet government became an unrealizable project, and to the society exhausted by deprivations, the vision of life according to Western standards as presented by the propaganda did little more than intensify their unsatisfied hunger for consumption.

Even before the resolutions of the Twenty-first Congress of the Communist Party of the Soviet Union on improving everyday life and transferring beauty from 'the privileged salons into people's homes' in 1959, in Lithuania they were attempting to expand the network that produced home appliances. In 1954, an industrial trade show highlighting more than a thousand samples of widely used products from across the Soviet Union was held at the Vilnius Exhibition and Convention Centre. The purpose of the exhibition was to encourage and oblige state companies to begin production of modern and various consumer products: from wind-up children's toys and wooden kitchen sets to women's purses and enamel cookware in the newest styles. The government was nonetheless annoyed with some Lithuanian companies which hadn't found the appropriate tone and exhibited banal products like slippers, reusable shopping bags, and basic traditional children's toys.[32] In 1957, there was talk in Lithuania about door-to-door food delivery with newspapers publishing propagandistic photos of happy women receiving products delivered by courier. In the early 1960s, journalists began to publish ideological propaganda reports about high-end Soviet designer fashion; local and Soviet Bloc furniture makers' modern furniture; and fancy holidays celebrated in new apartments. The newspapers discussed the benefits of 'smorgasbord' buffet tables and the importance of Western-style women's clothing at social events. But the ideal of 'a beautiful and aesthetic lifestyle' clashed with the rudimentary capabilities of Soviet light industry because at the time, the Lithuanian population – both children and adults – did not have shoes. And so light industry producers were given orders by the government: by 1965 they were to produce three pairs of shoes for every inhabitant of the USSR. But in response, the shoe factory administrators argued that before they could produce that many shoes, the leather industry would have to be expanded and the shoe production factories would all have to be rebuilt.[33]

At the same Congress of the Communist Party, Nikita Khruschev also announced that socialism as a system had been realized and the next step was to build communism. Shortly afterwards, the United States and the USSR organized a series of trade shows to brandish the two countries' achievements in everyday consumer products and home appliances. In Moscow, President Richard Nixon presented a lemon-yellow kitchen built by the American company General Electric, and the Soviets displayed fashion, home technology and dishes at the Soviet National Exhibit in New York City. At the time, Khrushchev publicly promised that by 1970, the USSR would match and even exceed the United States in the per capita production of widely used consumer products.[34] In 1961, Khrushchev personally corrected the party platform which was approved that year at the Twenty-first Congress and announced that during the forthcoming ten years, every single citizen would be fully provided for materially, especially with regard to everyday consumer goods, including household appliances.[35]

The reforms for the socialist home were underway and Western standards of what was considered modern were being applied. For this reason, in building post-Stalin material culture, for the first time, the Soviet government sanctioned and encouraged exploiting foreign experience and technological advances.[36] In wanting to ensure that the republic's consumer goods industry met international norms and standards, the LSSR government in 1962 published a resolution on technical standards, which in essence legalized the plagiarizing of product samples of consumer goods from other countries and authorized the production of their replicas in the republic's factories.[37] Aušra Dilienė worked at one of these organizations:

When I got married in 1958, I changed my job and started working at the Vilnius branch of the Moscow Chamber of Commerce.[38] For a young specialist, this was a very interesting position. Teams from the Moscow Chamber of Commerce travelled abroad and bought samples of the latest models of clothes and household appliances, tricot, haberdashery, foodstuffs, and food for children and babies from various foreign countries and tried to introduce similar production in Soviet enterprises. You could say this was a kind of international thievery. Our Vilnius branch also received some of the best foreign fashion magazines: *In Vogue*, *Kobieta i Zycie*, and *Femine*.[39]

The Twenty-second Congress of the Communist Party platform, promising to improve the lives of all Soviet citizens by 1970, remained unrealized. In 1966, only 16 per cent of families in Leningrad or Kostroma had refrigerators, 30 per cent had vacuum cleaners, 38 per cent home sewing machines and 77 per cent had basic mechanical washing machines. The quality of Soviet-manufactured home appliances remained shoddy, and meagre family budgets did not allow for people to eat in cafes or restaurants. In 1973, of 1,343 Moscow residents who were asked how often they visited cafes on holidays and weekends, barely 0.6 per cent responded 'Often and very often'; 12 per cent responded 'Rarely or very rarely'; 15.5 per cent said 'Sometimes'; and 73 per cent of respondents said they never went to cafes on any occasion. Expensive eating establishments and food shortages in the stores were reflected in household time schedules: in the Soviet household, 30 per cent of time dedicated to domestic chores involved meal preparation.[40] In 1962, Lithuanian cities and rural district centres saw the opening of 750 new stores, 300 cafeterias and 36 household service companies offering home vacuum cleaner and mechanical washing machine rentals. But the very same year, the state found that the established home appliance companies were not being used for their intended purposes and what was needed in the republic instead were hygiene-promoting facilities such as public shower/Russian sauna facilities and hairdresser shops.[41]

In the end, the plan to improve home life and make it beautiful remained unfulfilled: in 1971, ten years after the Twenty-first Congress of the Communist Party of the Soviet Union, the government was still proposing the same initiatives for improving production of consumer goods.[42] In the early 1960s, the government had planned on creating a network of home services in order to liberate women from household chores; however, throughout the country, women continued to accept their double burden. Women and men working in state-paid jobs in Lithuania worked six days a week until the five-day work week was introduced on 11 December 1967. The workday would begin at 9:00 and end at 18:00, with forty-five minutes for lunch; the last day of the work week was one hour shorter.[43] On 9 December 1971, the newly ratified *Work Code* created a forty-one-hour work week, and this norm was enforced by the 1977 Constitution of the USSR. Starting on 1 January 1968, in Lithuania like in the rest of the USSR, blue- and white-collar workers' vacations were extended to an annual fifteen workdays in place of the previous twelve.[44]

In 1980, women accounted for 51 per cent of the country's work force; alongside their male counterparts, they worked a full workday, every day, with a brief annual summer holiday until they reached retirement age. Yet in the public discourse, women were nevertheless referred to as 'homemakers', despite the fact that they were entirely responsible for the care of the household.[45] In a 1972 study, women in Lithuania were asked how their husbands' attitudes about sharing domestic chores had changed: 4.6 per cent of respondents said that their husbands' contribution had increased significantly, 24.3 per cent said somewhat, 55.4 per cent said that housework remained their own exclusive responsibility and 10.3 per cent of respondents said that their husbands' help with the housework had in fact decreased. Of the women in Lithuania, 98 per cent washed all of their families' laundry by hand or used a mechanical washing machine, and 87.2 per cent of them were solely responsible for meal preparation in their home. Men's contributions to domestic work were somewhat more significant with respect to child-rearing: 17.8 per cent of men attended parent meetings at their children's schools and 18.84 per cent helped their children with homework. In 1977, on an average, women spent 34 hours and 45 minutes per week on domestic work. A third of this time was spent on meal preparation, 20–25 per cent on housecleaning and 15–20 per cent on buying groceries and overall time spent in stores.[46] Without any significant help from their husbands, mothers, especially in the villages, were forced to make their children lend a hand. An ethnographic study determined that upwards of 76 per cent of children under the age of seven in the Lithuanian villages helped with domestic work in the home. Once they were attending school, between the ages of 12 and 17, children's responsibilities in the home decreased somewhat to 18 per cent; 60 per cent of girl respondents knew how to knit and thus contributed to domestic chores.[47]

A full workday, two weeks of vacation annually, low wages, unaffordable eating establishments, poor selections of home appliances and neo-patriarchal gender roles forced women to accept a double burden: in a normal workday, women's time was divided between work outside the home and household work. They managed the home, and all the while also attempted to improve their living conditions and material well-being in whatever unofficial means they had access to.

Informal solutions to chronic shortages

Citizens' complaints

After the war, the Soviet government introduced the practice of lodging complaints, but this had nothing to do with citizens informing on one another to security structures on political/ideological matters. Citizens lodging complaints were not seeking to inform on anyone or to get them punished. By complaining, they hoped to solve the problems of everyday life and alleviate the deprivations of their family's material conditions. In the process, the authors of the complaints became subjects in the system of informal economic relations, not unlike the patrons and clients of the Soviet *blat* tradition. The *blat* as an informal shadow activity was accessible only to privileged members of Soviet society, as its participants exchanged deficit products and services that they were privy to. Complaints and requests became a legal surrogate of the *blat* system to be used by ordinary members of Soviet Lithuanian society (i.e. those without privileged social connections). After experiencing material hardships in the post-war era, the Lithuanian population had actively and enthusiastically embraced the cultivated and aesthetic lifestyle being propagated by Khrushchevian ideology. But without any realistic means for providing materially for their families according to publicly advertised Western standards, most Lithuanian citizens were forced to use informal initiatives like the *blat* or lodging complaints and making requests.

If they observed poor quality services, citizens were encouraged to communicate their dissatisfaction to authorities in situ by writing in the book of complaints. The official newspaper *Tiesa* was regularly reminding readers about their right and duty to demand the book of complaints in public establishments. In a 27 April 1950 article entitled 'Daugiau dėmesio skundų knygoms' (Pay More Attention to the Book of Complaints), *Tiesa* informed readers that the books would help improve customer service at stores and teahouses. The newspaper provided advice on how to properly point out and criticize deficiencies, arguing that the government would improve:

> The Soviet consumer cannot tolerate it when the rules of Soviet commerce are broken, when a store has a poor selection of goods and its products are of poor quality. The consumer, seeking to correct these problems, writes his observations

down in the book of complaints and suggestions, which must be present at every organization doing commerce and every public eating establishment. Indeed all directors of stores and cafeterias must take their books of complaints very seriously. They must acquaint themselves with their clients' comments and respond promptly, taking action to eliminate the deficiencies that clients call attention to.[48]

On 2 August 1958, the lodging of complaints about the deficiencies of socialist life was legally authorized by the Communist Party of the Soviet Union resolution *On Serious Shortages, Analysing Workers' Letters, Complaints, and Suggestions*. The principal institution charged with ensuring the people's trust in complaints-writing was the LCP(b) CC and LSSR Council of Ministers' Party State Control Committee. In 1965, the Committee Director Albertas Barauskas, in an article entitled 'Signalas, laiškas, žmogus' (Signal, Letter, Person), wrote how important it was to not discourage people seeking justice and to help them. He wrote thus:

> Unfortunately, there are still occasions when employees analyze the workers' complaints and requests formally, dither in resolving the issues they raise, or provide irrelevant responses, and some choose bureaucratic and irresponsible ways of addressing the problems: they forward the workers' letters to subordinate organizations, and sometimes to the individuals being complained about … City party committees, district committees, party-state control committees must do a better job leading support groups and posts and 'Comsomol Spotlight' units, so that they can more actively help party organizations develop their employees' sensitivity and attentiveness to the letters and needs of working people, seeking out the procrastinators and exposing them.[49]

Such encouragement to voice concerns about problems at stores and companies that provided services led people to trust the practice of lodging complaints. And the 1966 *Provisions for Handling Residents' Letters, Complaints and Applications* provided guidelines for the process.[50] In their letters to the government, party structures and newspaper editorial boards, the Soviet people not only expressed their anger regarding inappropriate behaviour of officials and salespersons, but also regarding injustice overall. Propaganda campaigns created an ever greater trust by Lithuanian citizens in complaints as an effective means of solving problems. In the mid-1950s, particularly pragmatic complaints and requests began to proliferate. These complaints about living conditions had one and only one goal: to obtain the home appliances and consumer goods that they were lacking.

Complaints and the *blat* as informal initiatives

Liuba D., a young resident of Kaunas, sent her first complaint to the *Tiesa* newspaper correspondent Jūra Baužytė in 1964. The 19-year-old woman, was hoping, with the correspondent's help, to realize her dream of studying at one of the republic's conservatories of music. The doors of these institutions were locked and barred to her due her disability since birth. The physically disabled, socially unconnected and financially challenged young woman was hoping that the newspaper correspondent and the major official newspaper she was working for would be her window of opportunity, which, under more fortunate circumstances, money, well-connected friends and the appropriate social situation of her parents – or in other words the *blat* – would provide her. Liuba D. and the correspondent communicated for ten years and their correspondence perfectly illustrates the informal, government-sanctioned method for surviving the socialist system, namely the practice of lodging complaints.

Liuba D.'s dream to study music came true after the correspondent wrote her article. On 20 February 1964, the young woman wrote a thank you letter to the correspondent and told her how effective her article had been:

> Dear Correspondent, ... when your article appeared in *Komjaunimo tiesa*, my friends, guardians and teachers were quite moved. We were overcome with joy and hope. Well, I must admit that I secretly believed that something had to change for the better. The article was beautifully written. I reread it ten times, crying. I saw my life and my dreams in it. The article was published on Sunday 19 April, and on Monday I received a call from J. Gruodis from the Musical Conservatory. He asked for my given name, family name, patronymic and date of birth. Although he ultimately did not admit this mobility-challenged student, the J. Tallat-Kelpša Conservatory in Vilnius did enroll me as a correspondence student to study choir conducting.[51]

In 1966, after graduating with a degree in choir conducting, Liuba D. again wrote to correspondent Jūra Baužytė. This time, the young woman asked Baužytė to write an article that would help her get a job at an orphanage. The article proved successful and Liuba D. wrote another thank you letter: 'Your article was marvelous, so profound, moving and beautifully written. It was effective because it got them moving as if they'd been jolted with a hot wire.'[52] But this time, the author of the request experienced not only happiness, but also negative emotions. Even though the article had achieved its desired goal and Liuba D. had gotten the job she wanted, her new colleagues did not approve of the methods the young woman had employed. In her letter, Liuba D. consoled herself:

It's hard for me to say this openly, but truly, I could not contain myself. First of all, I never believed that the article 'would so terribly harm' the orphanage staff and teachers. Sure, I believed that it would offend them a little, but I thought that 'the pain' would affect only the hearts of the director and his assistant. It was a shock to me when the director invited me to his office and began pouring out an endless array of accusations. In other words, I was a terrible person. Despite how much I insisted that I was defending my human rights, fighting for them, he did not change his position. Of course, after all this (I mean, the article), he will keep me, I mean, employ me, but… after such an article no one else would dare work at this collective!!![53]

The penning of complaints and their publication in the republic's newspapers could potentially pit colleagues, responsible officials, neighbours and relatives mentioned in the article against the author. But the authors of the complaints and the government officials and newspaper staff dealing with their problems frequently were sympathetic towards one another. In her letter to correspondent Jūra Baužytė, Liuba D. expressed her affection for her:

Jūratė, It's impossible. I cannot find the right words to fully express my gratitude to you. I feel bolder than ever before. I stand upon the *strong backs of good people*. My prior belief that wonderful, good people still do exist is now more firm. When the article appeared, I truly thought that it wasn't the right time. But shortly afterwards, I spoke with my teacher and became convinced that it was indeed the perfect time, and for them, it is simply an excuse for harassment.[54]

As the years passed, this sympathetic understanding grew into relatively friendly relations between the two women once both parties, the petitioner and the benefactor, understood each other's character traits and abilities. Unavoidably, the complaints and the requests accompanying them came to reflect the particularities of the *blat* and formed a patron-client relationship. As she began to receive tangible help, Liuba D. finally felt that she had a patron, and she felt safe. In her letter, she wrote 'My Esteemed Jūratė, I offer my sincerest gratitude to you for your concern about me and my fate. It's so good to live knowing that good people support me with the warmth of their hearts, their kind words and generous help.'[55]

Patronage can be treated either as a certain kind of friendship or sympathy, in the name of which kind deeds and pleasantries are done. Patronage can also be thought of as a type of feudal system, wherein help is provided by one and the same patron, and a voluntary change of patron does not go unpunished.[56] After the correspondence lasting several years, Liuda D. sincerely believed in the mutuality of her friendly feelings towards Jūra Baužytė and felt it appropriate to address the correspondent informally. As her letters show, Liuba D. demonstrated trust in Baužytė, opened herself up to her and was quite bold in her plans for future complaints and requests. In 1966, she wrote thus:

> Dear Jūrate (if I may), You were so helpful to me… Back in March, I supplied the required documents: my application, copy of my diploma, personal statement. They promised a response by June. But I have yet to receive one. I spoke to my teacher and decided to wait until August 1. If they do not accept me, I will appeal 'further' and 'higher up'. But, I've been thinking, how long might it take for someone from 'higher up' to help me? I never imagined that your concern for me would help settle everything so quickly.[57]

In one's relationship with one's patron, however, it was important not to overstep the boundaries of familiarity because, as in the case of Liuda D. and Jūra Baužytė, their correspondence created only the illusion of friendship. The petitioner, having lost his or her dignified distance once they started treating the patron as someone from his or her circle of friends, could lose their trust and assistance.[58]

The patron's role in itself was not enough for ensuring goods or services for the client-petitioner. Because the Soviet planned economy experienced constant shortages, the patrons inevitably became go-betweens between government institutions, powerful individual officials and the client-petitioner. In other words, the patron either had to hold a solid position in the socialist hierarchy, or he (or she) had to have the authority to approach officials holding the power to distribute goods and services.[59] As in the case of the *blat*, the official, professional employee or correspondent receiving the complaint would examine the petitioner's problems in detail and in time themselves initiate a solution without any particular requests. It was enough for the petitioner to just mention one or another problem and the complaint would become an appeal for assistance. Often, these requests would involve housing. In 1966, Liuba D. wrote to Jūra Baužytė again. She asked her to intervene regarding a small living space that was being granted to her. But a few years later, Liuba D. was making clear she expected the correspondent's help simply by describing her miserable everyday living conditions. She told Jūra Baužytė that she had recently married, given birth to a daughter (whom she named Jūratė in the correspondent's honour) and then she detailed her miserable living conditions. In her letter, Liuba D. wrote the following:

But, Jūratė, my troubles are endless. I will describe them here. When someone has problems and misfortunes, they remember those who helped them in the past. I have been absolutely crushed by misfortune. I could not study at the conservatory due to my worsened health. I work at a boarding school as a teacher. I got married, and this year, gave birth via C-section to my little daughter Jūratė. My husband Romualdas D. is an orphan and grew up in an orphanage. After returning from the Army in November of this year, he has been working at the Pergalė factory as an electro-welder. We live at the dormitory for the speech and hearing impaired. Two families – six people in all – live in our 12-metre room. The room is small, narrow, damp and stuffy. This is where we sleep and store Jūratė's stroller. There is no storage space. We keep potatoes and our meagre food supplies in the same room. As I already said, this is where we eat and dry our diapers. Stuffy, damp and cold. My husband has applied at his factory for better accommodations, but he is 204th in line; we have no chance of getting anything any quicker. The factory gave us a response in writing, stating that anything sooner than three-to-four years is impossible.[60]

Liuba D.'s 'apartment' complaints reveal the manipulative nature of her requests. The woman figured out the distribution system for obtaining goods and services in the Soviet Union as well as the privileges granted by patronage and attempted to use her experience to her advantage in her complaints. Eventually, her letters to her patron did more than ask for help solving one problem or another; she was starting to instruct the correspondent on how she ought to be performing the role of go-between. In one of her letters, she wrote the following:

Jūratė, I just hope I don't get the boarding school director and all the personnel angry at me again. I beg of you, Jūratė, just don't tell them any of this. I so desperately want peace. I'm afraid of getting them angry. All I want is to work and raise my little Jūratė. By the way, I recently found out that the staff all chipped in some money and got me a little something. When I was in hospital, the cashiers, my friends, were asking about me, to find out how I was feeling. Anyway, it made me so happy to know that despite everything, they care… Narkevičiūtė was pleasant when we came to see her. She said that Comrade Baužytė told her everything, and that they wrote and called Romas's factory director, and so on… They say we should write to Baužytė and ask her to write to the factory management.[61]

Permanent patrons understood the insinuated needs of their client and would arrange for government assistance using their own discretion. On the other hand, in long-term 'patron-client' relationships, the client risked crossing permitted boundaries if they started to direct their patron's actions. In one of her letters, Liuba D. boldly pointed out:

> Jūratė, It's funny: I just finished one letter and now I'm hurriedly writing another. Jūratė, I beg of you, just don't ask them for anything on our behalf. We know that you are very good to us. You do so much more you need to. But in this case, really, don't do anything. I wrote that it's hard for Romas to get off from work, but please don't interpret this as: ask in his name. No, no! All we want is to find out precisely where and when Kairys or Maniušis receive visitors, and Romas can definitely arrange a day off if he talks with his boss.[62]

The *blat* relationship was based on mutual obligations and their realization, but in the case of complaints, the person writing the complaint believed she was fighting for her rights and did not feel obligated to the patron. Still, the long-term patron-client relationship created a system of relations similar to that of the *blat*. At the end of the 1970s in Lithuania, as protectionism and corruption became increasingly entrenched, the delivery of any deficit service or product automatically came with a price tag. Most clients were well aware of this attribute of Soviet society. Liuba D. too began to feel like she owed something to the correspondent for the help she consistently provided. And so she wrote to the correspondent who had 'taken care of her' for so many years:

> To be honest, Jūratė, I cannot say that things – myself, my family, my apartment – are going well. But first, a few words on the issue you are concerned with. I always thought that after you 'took care of' my apartment issues, I would have to pay you back. And this always worried me. To return the favour is impossible, but to refuse is even more so. What can I do? … Now do you understand my silence? I've been hesitating, thinking: How shall I respond? What can I do so that I don't seem ungrateful? But I just can't. That's just how it is: I definitely must repay you for your assistance with something tangible. Forgive me for the irony. I do not fault you for this. No, never. But that's how it is, and people have accustomed themselves to this.[63]

In 1968, with her patron's help, the Soviet government provided Liuba D.'s family with an apartment. The woman was sincerely happy that her battle for securing better living conditions was over and she shared her enthusiastic gratitude:

> Jūratė, Call me sentimental, but I cannot but write this sentimentally. I want to get on my knees (if I only could) before you. I don't know what to say. Shall I thank you, or cry in happiness? Again, for the second time in my life, if not for

you, we would not be celebrating like this today. We would never be moving out of this cramped room.[64]

However, in the same letter the woman was already dreaming about exchanging the apartment for a better one and was already plotting her next complaint and request. She complained to her patron:

> We got our apartment. As we were waiting, we were counting the days, the hours, when we could leave this cave. Our happiness was boundless when they told us to come get our documents. But when they told us to get our keys, I was overcome with tears. They stuck us in the middle of nowhere. The bus stops 300–400 metres away. In spring and fall, the mud is impassable. Three transfers to get there by bus, three times farther away from work. I'm sitting here crying and all I can think about it just how miserable my life is, and it's all their fault. We're not moving… I've gone to the office, begged… Nobody wants to help me exchange this apartment. They tell me: 'Write to Moscow all you want.' I wrote a doleful declaration, but I don't have a glimmer of hope.'[65]

Informal initiatives with the purpose of obtaining goods or services like Liuba D's were integrally related, according to Julie Hessler, not only to existential needs, but also to the increasing reach of consumerism and consumer society.[66]

When obtaining goods or services through informal initiatives like the complaint or the *blat*, the client's sense of moderation was extremely important. Using the *blat* for humble or essential needs seemed acceptable. But requests for goods and services obviously in surplus could be interpreted as borderline thievery or corruption. In other words, the request had to be morally justifiable in the eyes of both the patron and the petitioner-client.[67]

In 1973, almost ten years after her first letter to Jūra Baužytė, Liuba D. tried again to convince her patron of the worthiness of her next request. Describing the inconvenience of public transportation, the woman asked Jūra Baužytė for the perhaps the greatest Soviet luxury, a car. On this occasion, in her letter, Liuba D. Lamented and to a certain extent even frightened the correspondent stating that she was thinking about retiring as she had no way to get to work. Liuba D. explained:

> I don't know. I may regret it some day, but now all I can think is that the sooner I get my pension, the sooner I can say 'Bye, work!' Besides, if you think about it, it makes no sense for me to work. From where I live, there's no bus to get me there. It's too far to walk and so I have to take a taxi every time. In a month, that's 25–27 roubles in expenses. I wrote to the Ministry of Social Welfare regarding getting a car for a reduced price, but the answer I received was that the disabled

from birth must pay full price. Now I wrote to the Ministry of Transportation asking them to let me buy a used taxi. I doubt they'll agree either.[68]

Soon, in another letter, without beating around the bush, Liuba D. clearly stated her request:

> This time, although I feel very uncomfortable about this, just for a minute I want to drag you away from your work and ask for a small favour. I'd prefer not to bother you. If only we had some acquaintances in Vilnius … But other than you, we don't have anyone else. The issue is as follows: we want to buy a car. A Volga from the Kaunas taxi park.[69]

In her letter, Liuba D. demonstrated her masterful command of the logic and mechanism of informal relations. She showed her patron how to play her role as go-between more effectively: 'Another thing – and this is most important. They will say that they won't install hand controls in a Volga. Tell them my husband will do the driving.'[70] Liuba ended her letter with concrete instructions: 'I hope this is not a great inconvenience for you. If not, we ask for this favour and thank you in advance. When you find out when and where he will see us, please write or call.'[71]

Complaints and requests became everyday practice for most in Soviet Lithuania. Although neighbours and colleagues were mistrustful of the usual and best-known authors of complaints, but the number of 'complainers' grew by the day. Nonetheless, Liuba D. bemoaned to Jūra Baužytė that her colleagues at work considered her the only one among them writing complaints to the government. In a letter written in 1971, she commiserated:

> I found out quite by coincidence that Šumskas will be stepping down as director. I don't know if it's his choice or if he's being transferred elsewhere, or if, yet again (like everyone who came before him – all directors get thrown out as ineffective) someone wrote a complaint about him. I'm a little uneasy: if they're throwing him out against his will, I hope I didn't have anything to do with it. I certainly never wrote a complaint about Belkevičius. I didn't even know anything about it, and yet they told me straight to my face that I was the one who complained, or if not, then I went straight to Vilnius … Anyway, I wouldn't want to be a tattler, to be hated and criticized by all.[72]

Although the acquisition of goods and services with the help of complaints was less conspicuous than the *blat*, complaints as a means of solving problems inevitably proliferated. In 1969, Liuba D's teacher P. G. wrote a thank you letter to Jūra Baužytė for her help to Liuba and lamented the fact that she hadn't started writing complaints ten years earlier, in 1956. Describing Liuba D.'s childhood and the insensitivity with which directors of orphanages and middle schools viewed the physically disabled girl, P. G. was convinced that only complaints would have helped: 'Seeing this [the ambivalence of the directors], I suffered with my teeth clenched, holding my fists tight (together with Liuba), but I was helpless to change our fate … I'm sure that if it were today, you would make it right. But it's too late now, and I didn't know you back then.'[73]

Informal economic initiatives were tolerated in Soviet everyday life. The *blat* and complaint writing were understood as unavoidable Soviet practices as well as a form of resistance against the system and a way of influencing the bureaucracy. Such practices are sometimes called cooperative because they sought to affect the barriers created by the system. The *blat* and complaint writing are also considered to be unifying practices in that they required substantially close, mutually trusting relations among members of Soviet society, of friends and acquaintances. On the other hand, the writing of complaints solely for consumerist goals formed the egotistical aspects of Soviet Lithuanian society. After they had mastered Soviet demagoguery and figured out its meaning in everyday life as well as understood the utility of the patron-client relationship, the writers of complaints took on the role of abused victims within the patron-petitioner environment they created.[74] Ordinary women without useful social connections, well-paying jobs or husbands holding important positions in society inevitably made up the greater part of this group. Writing complaints with pragmatic and exceptionally consumerist aims fostered egotistic individualism in Soviet Lithuania. Having perfectly mastered principles of Soviet demagogy and being fully aware of its importance in everyday life, knowing the advantages given by equilibristic patron-client relationships, authors of complaints identified themselves with constantly suffering victims, thus creating a milieu of professional petitioners.

Conclusions

Soviet type gender equality was without exception geared exclusively towards women's situation and their changing role in family and public life. It did not foresee, nor did it strive for, equal rights for men and women or for the elimination of discrimination against women. The extreme gender equality policies of the post-war period were enacted under economic and political turmoil and Lithuanian women's activism was exploited for difficult and often dangerous work. In the name of gender equality and women's rights, women worked the most disparate jobs: they went to the villages in brigades helping mothers of large families and widows of Soviet Army soldiers who had perished in the war with the harvest. They not only worked in the *kolkhoz* fields, but they also organized the so-called red carts, the mandatory delivery of grain to the state. The number of women actively engaging in the new Soviet reality increased by the day. With time, women were not only driven by fear and duty, but an inner need to be active citizens and to work outside the confines of the home. In 1959, in Soviet Lithuania, 66.3 per cent of all adult women were working outside the confines of the family home, while in 1979, the number of women working full-time had increased to 83.3 per cent.

Despite women's active participation in public life and labour market, the regime never attempted to change the foundations of patriarchal stereotypes about men's and women's roles both in public and private spheres. Opportunities for women to participate in decision-making were frozen in a formal quota system. The number of women deputed to the Lithuanian SSR (LSSR) Supreme Soviet never changed: In 1967, women comprised 32.4 per cent; in 1971, 32.33 per cent; in 1975, the number was 34 per cent; and in 1980, 35 per cent.

The Stalinist notion of gender equality was integrated to the Soviet family policy which held women solely responsible for the household and family.

In December 1940, the legal rule the *Marriage, Family and Guardianship Law Valid in the Territory of the LSSR* was adopted. The new *LSSR Marriage and Family Code* went into effect only on 1 January 1970. Along with the new *Metrics Instructions*, it remained in effect until Lithuania regained independence in 1990. The 1970 *Metrics Instructions* required couples to publicly announce their intention to marry and to notify their employers or, if they were students, their educational institutions, of this fact. The couple's passports were stamped with the surname of their respective spouse along with information on prior divorces, if applicable. Lithuanian men and women were forced to decide certain family issues in public. As the Soviet courts, work collectives and party organizations were involved in more and more issues related to family life, the regime's institutions came to be considered capable of and even required to respond to Soviet people's personal problems and to provide suitable solutions. Couples who solemnized their marriages in church could expect negative consequences if they held professional positions of any importance. In 1958, more than ten years after the war had ended, even after the Soviets had closed the majority of churches in Lithuania, over 60 per cent of civilly registered marriages were still being performed in church. Another ten years later, in 1968, however, due to propaganda and persecution, this number had been reduced by half: 30 per cent of all registered marriages were solemnized in a religious ceremony.

Still the state's educational and family policy encouraged a drastic reduction in marital age. In 1960, men in Lithuania typically married between the ages of 26 and 30, and women, between 21 and 25; in 1980, men were marrying at barely 22–3 and women at 20–1. In 1980, 48.5 per cent of marrying couples in Lithuania were between 20 and 24 years of age, and 20 per cent of them married before age 20. In the villages, marriages occurred somewhat later. In 1970, men in the villages married at 26–30 years of age, and women at 21–5. As the marital age fell and housing became scarce, inevitably a new form of family life in Soviet society was encouraged: two generations living under one roof. Such a neo-extended family was useful to the state as it instilled the concept of the family as a collective; this became yet another norm of married life. Most newly-weds' first home was a room in the apartment of one of their parents. According to data from 1970, on average, 70 per cent of new families in the USSR lived in the home of their parents right after marriage.

From its early years, the Soviet regime strove to model interpersonal relationships of citizens and inculcated which type of family and love was acceptable. The love being propagated in post-war Lithuania was different from that of the western romantic tradition but also contrary to revolutionary

Bolshevik 'free love'. The knowledge that a happy family life and passionate romantic love were not identical concepts entered into currency together with the Soviet regime. Although the political thaw in the 1960s opened up greater opportunities for cultural, artistic and scholarly expression, the sexual education of Soviet citizens was ignored. Calm affection and friendship became the ideal Soviet examples of 'true love', the principal attributes of which were respect for the beloved, a sense of responsibility, constancy and devotion. In 1967, a survey revealed that 95 per cent of newly-weds in Lithuania formally explained that their motivation for marrying was love; however, in more detailed responses to the same question, love no longer came up, and respondents instead listed very practical reasons for marrying.

In the early 1980s, the war on passion and sexuality began to give up its positions. No longer was passionate love seen as an immature period in the transition to marriage which must be overcome and forgotten as quickly as possible, but as one of the most important and most cherished human feelings. Lithuania took its first steps to openly deal with marriage problems beginning in the mid-1970s. The first family counselling and psychiatric clinics were established in 1969. In 1978, public opinion surveys in Estonia revealed that approximately 82 per cent of young men and 71 per cent of young women had sexual relations before marriage. In the early years of Gorbachev's *perestroika*, sexual behaviour became even more liberal. The collapsing Soviet system attracted massive audiences wishing to learn more about the hitherto taboo topics of frigidity, impotence, homosexuality, orgasm and other sexual questions.

The Soviet ideologues themselves admitted that marriage became a means for securing registration in a desirable city, and after completing university or specialized vocational studies, marriage was a way to get a good job together with one's beloved. Marriage and family status was also one of the conditions for improved material conditions for Soviet citizens, beginning with everyday household goods and ending with housing and a car. Starting in the late 1970s, in Lithuania as in other Soviet republics, 'character irreconcilability' and 'lack of spiritual connection' became the most common reasons for divorce. At the same time, the work collective had great power and was responsible for solving problems within the marriage, and in case of divorce, even for dividing up of the couple's property.

The court system in post-war Lithuania was reorganized according to the Soviet model and divorce cases were heard twice by two different courts: the People's Court and the Supreme Court. The People's Courts did not handle divorce cases on their merits. The goal of the People's Courts was to try to reconcile the two parties and to determine whether a life together henceforth was possible. The Supreme Court heard divorce cases as the court of first instance and as the court of cassation. The two-instance divorce proceedings system was abolished in Lithuania on 10 December 1965 when the Presidium of the USSR Supreme Soviet announced court system reforms. Under their new jurisdiction, the People's Courts were authorized to continue performing their mediation function attempting to reconcile the partners. However, in the event that they were not successful, the court would consider cases on their merits.

The occupation and crimes committed by the Soviet regime affected interpersonal relations. Until Stalin's death in March of 1953, a number of disappeared divorce petitioners and respondents never returned to the courtroom. They were exiled, imprisoned, persecuted and killed. Marriages were not always able to withstand the regime, violence and chaos of the post-war era. Having one's spouse exiled or imprisoned often became an unbearable burden and grounds for divorce. Repression, constant material shortages and everyday fears inevitably inflamed aggression, alcoholism and violence in the family. It was no accident that from the end of the war until the early 1960s, the most common grounds for divorce were violence, alcoholism and marital infidelity. In the late 1970s, alcohol abuse became the second most common reason for divorce among the families of professionals; the first was 'character incompatibility'.

Divorce rates in the three Baltic Soviet republics surpassed those of the rest of the USSR. In 1950, of 100 registered marriages in Lithuania, there were 2.7 divorces; in 1960, the rate increased to 8.4 divorces, and in 1970, there were 23.1 divorces. In 1979, the number increased to 33.9 divorces per 100 marriages. In 1976 in Latvia, of 100 marriages, 52 ended in divorce, 1.4 times more the Soviet average.

Eventually, few in Soviet Lithuania believed in happy marriages. In 1984–5, barely half of marrying couples evaluated their family and marriage prospects optimistically, and on their wedding day only 49 per cent of brides and 60 per cent of grooms still believed that their marriage would be happy and that it would bring them personal satisfaction. Married life and family began to be conceived of as hard work full of conflicts that would have to be suffered and resolved. This conception of marriage and family remained until the end of the 1990s. The number of unhappy marriages increased throughout the USSR. In 1980, sexologist Michail Stern, generalizing the subject of his study, published results which revealed 74 per cent of couples were living in constant conflict.

Regardless that officially Soviet demographic policies aimed to increase birth rates, domestic reality had solidified the small-family model. The ideal family with one or two children certainly corresponded to the demographic situation in Lithuania: in 1971, 34.4 per cent of professional families and 26.2 per cent of workers' families were raising two children. In 1979, in Lithuania, families corresponding to the socially accepted, normative family size made up the majority: 42.8 per cent of families were raising one child and 37.3 per cent of all families had two children. In 1989, the number of small families increased even more: families with only one child made up 50.4 per cent and those with two children made up 39.7 per cent of all families.

On 1 April 1956, pregnancy and birth leave were extended to 112 calendar days: all women (except for *kolkhoz* workers) were provided with eight weeks of fully paid maternity leave before the birth and an equal number of weeks afterwards. This legal provision was changed only in 1981 when partially paid family leave was granted until the child turned 1. In 1987, for the first time, a resolution was adopted which provided improved flexibility for mothers in the workplace: mothers of children under the age of 8 could take advantage of the opportunity to work part time. On 22 March 1989 maternity leave was once again extended until the child turned 1.5 years, allowing unpaid leave until age 3 with guaranteed job status.

Despite the Soviet government's promise to fully develop a *network* of *preschool institutions* it came true only in the last decade of the regime. In the 1950s, 80 per cent of working age women in the USSR held state-paid jobs, but only 13 per cent of children under the age of 6 were enrolled in preschool facilities. The number of preschools did increase in 1965, but still only 22.5 per cent of city dwellers and 12 per cent of residents of rural districts were able to enrol their preschool-aged children in day schools or seasonal preschool institutions. Some data from the 1980s suggest that approximately 70 per cent of children under 7 were enrolled in preschool facilities in the USSR. Although statistics on the availability of preschool institutions in the USSR in the mid-1980s may vary, families that placed themselves on waiting lists for creche-kindergartens before their child was born could expect to get a spot for their child in preschool facilities. However, financial benefits paid by the state were insufficient, and mothers could only make use of the maternity leave granted by the 1981 and 1989 resolutions, which provided partially paid or unpaid childcare if they could demonstrate that they had supplementary financial funds.

Women who did shift work found it difficult to find time to spend with their children. In 1970, the magazine *Tarybinė moteris* surveyed readers on how they reconciled the responsibilities of work and home. The 1,291 Lithuanian women who responded wrote that the third shift, that is unpaid work at home, was the most exhausting because it drained them of all their energy. Children, whose mothers worked irregular hours and didn't have close friends or family to help out, inevitably spent some of their time alone, without adult supervision. These kids were easily identifiable on the streets or in the courtyards of every Soviet republic by the latchkey that hung around their necks. Without other alternatives, parents used the tried and tested traditional method, namely, assigning childcare to their elder sons and daughters. In such cases, older children became responsible for their younger siblings' care and safety. Some young mothers would choose their mothers' help, but that often meant leaving their husbands and going to another city or to the countryside. This practice of raising children became particularly popular in Lithuania in the 1980s when maternity leave was considerably longer and young families did not have their own space for raising children under the age of 3. Mothers raising disabled children had no choice but to stay home. Mothers of children with psychological disabilities in particular could not work because, until late 1960s, the state did not provide any special assistance to disabled children or financial assistance to their parents.

Although in almost every interview conducted in Lithuania (1989–2005), women stressed that family and children were their most important concern and life goal, only a very few of those women were not working in an official job and devoting all their time to their families. Mothers who cared for their own children at home but wanted to earn a state salary could expect only the most basic physical and unqualified work, regardless of their education. Interviews with the women of Lithuania testify to the fact that women often worked for their children and family under very unfavourable conditions. In the 1990s, after Lithuania regained independence, hundreds of thousands of young women of Lithuania left their paid jobs or simply did not look for a job outside the home, opting instead for the role of homemaker and mum.

Lack of the living space was another issue that faced Soviet families. After the war, every half-meter of living space was important as families of three or more were being accommodated in spaces as tiny as 7–12 square meters. As centralized plans for the distribution of living space were being enacted in post-war Lithuania, the Soviet government made sure that no single person would be allotted any more space than the norms allowed. Prisoners returning from the GULAG camps and places of exile were unable to reclaim their property or they would find their family homes had been destroyed by strangers and even neighbours. Regardless of the mass construction of residential properties, for most people in Lithuania, an apartment of their own was a dream that remained difficult to realize. In 1970, approximately 70 per cent of newly-weds began their new lives living in the parental home of one of the spouses.

After experiencing material hardships in the post-war era, the Lithuanian population had actively and enthusiastically embraced the cultivated and aesthetic lifestyle being propagated by Khrushchevian ideology. But without any realistic means for providing materially for their families according to publicly advertised Western standards, most Lithuanian citizens were forced to use informal initiatives like the *blat* or lodging complaints and making requests. By lodging complaints, average Soviet citizens were not seeking to inform on anyone or to get them punished;; rather they hoped to solve the problems of everyday life and alleviate the deprivations of their family's material conditions. Informal economic initiatives were tolerated in Soviet everyday life. The *blat* and complaint writing were understood as unavoidable Soviet practices as well as a form of resistance against the system and a way of influencing the bureaucracy.

However, the writing of complaints solely for consumerist goals formed the egotistical aspects of Soviet Lithuanian society. After they had mastered Soviet demagoguery and figured out its meaning in everyday life as well as understood the utility of the patron-client relationship, the writers of complaints took on the role of abused victims within the patron-petitioner environment they created. Ordinary women without useful social connections, well-paying jobs or husbands holding important positions in society inevitably made up the greater part of this practice. Writing complaints with pragmatic and exceptionally consumerist aims fostered egotistic individualism in Soviet Lithuania. Having perfectly mastered principles of Soviet demagogy and being fully aware of its importance in everyday life, knowing the advantages given by equilibristic patron-client relationships, authors of complaints identified themselves with constantly suffering victims, thus creating a milieu of professional petitioners.

Notes

Introduction

1 *Lietuva 1940–1990 m.* (Lithuania, 1940–1990) (Vilnius: Lietuvos gyventojų genocido ir rezistencijos tyrimų centras, 2005), 288–9.
2 Donald Filtzer, *Soviet Workers and De-Stalinization* (Cambridge, UK: Cambridge University Press, 1992), 7. Melanie Ilič, 'Women in the Khrushchev Era: An Overview', in *Women in the Khrushchev Era*, ed. Melanie Ilič, Susan E. Reid and Lynne Attwood (London: Palgrave Macmillan, 2004), 44.
3 Sveikatos apsaugos ministro pavaduotojo Lazutkos raštas M. Kaunaitei (Deputy Health Minister Lazutka's Note to M. Kaunaitė), 12 May 1951, LCSA, F. 1771, Ap. 103, B. 4, L. 6. Tauragės rajono Darbo Tarp Moterų Skyriaus ataskaita už 1953 m. (Tauragė District Work Among Women Division Report on the Year 1953), LCSA, F. 1771, Ap. 145, B. 7, L. 5.
4 'Ar tai tikroji, tvirta draugystė?' (Is This a True, Solid Friendship?), *Komjaunimo tiesa*, 7 April 1957.
5 *Blat* is a Russian word (Russian: блат) used to define a form of corruption which was the system of informal agreements, exchanges of services, connections, Communist Party contacts or black market deals to achieve results or get ahead.
6 Marija Drėmaitė, 'Apdovanotieji: masinė gyvenamoji architektūra ir sovietiniai architektūriniai apdovanojimai' (Award Winners: Mass Produced Architecture and Soviet Architectural Prizes), in *Masinės statybos gyvenamųjų rajonų architektūra Lietuvoje*, ed. I. Nekrošius, V. Petrušonis and E. Riaubienė (Vilnius: VGTU leidykla Technika, 2017), 45–65, 50.
7 I. Nekrošius, V. Petrušonis and E. Riaubienė, eds. *Masinės statybos gyvenamųjų rajonų architektūra Lietuvoje* (The Architecture of Mass-produced Residential Districts in Lithuania) (Vilnius: VGTU leidykla Technika, 2017), 10.
8 Susan E. Reid, 'Everyday Aesthetics in the Khrushchev-Era Standard Apartment', in *Everyday Life in Russia: Past and Present*, ed. Choi Chatterjee, David L. Ransel, Mary Cavender and Karen Petrone (Bloomington: Indiana University Press, 2015), 204. Deborah A. Field, 'Everyday Life and the Problem of Conceptualizing Public and Private during the Khrushchev Era', in ibid., 163–80.

9 Н. Н. Соловьев, *Брак и семья сегодня* (Marriage and Family Today) (Вильнюс: Минтис, 1977), 104.

1 Soviet family policy

1. 'Santuokos įstatymas' (Marriage Law), *Vyriausybės žinios* 725, 15 August 1945, Kaunas. Respublikos Prezidento kanceliarija (Chancellery of the Office of the President of the Republic), 266.
2. Donald Filtzer, 'Women Workers in the Khrushchev Era', in *Women in the Khrushchev Era*, ed. Melanie Ilič, Susan E. Reid and Lynne Attwood (New York: Palgrave Macmillan, 2004), 71.
3. Dalia Marcinkeviciene and Rima Praspaliauskiene, 'Prostitution in Post-war Lithuania', *Women's History Review* 12, no. 4 (2003), 651–60.
4. Ibid., 655.
5. The *Supreme Soviet* was the common name for the legislative bodies (parliaments) of the Soviet socialist republics (SSR) in the Union of Soviet Socialist, including Soviet Lithuania. After the first free elections were held in February 1990 in Lithuania the Act of the Re-establishment of the State of Lithuania was adopted and the former Supreme Soviet was renamed itself the *Supreme Council of the Republic of Lithuania*
6. Lietuvos TSR Aukščiausiosios Tarybos ir Vyriausybės žinios (News of the Lithuanian Socialist Republic Supreme Soviet) 30 June 1958, 173.
7. Lietuvos TSR Aukščiausiosios Tarybos ir Vyriausybės žinios, 28 June 1966, 91.
8. Donald Filtzer, *The Khrushchev Era: De-Stalinisation and the Limits of Freedom of Reform in the USSR, 1953–1964* (London: Macmillan, 1993), 9.
9. Rokiškio apskrities Moterų skyriaus vedėjos Paradauskienės ataskaita už 1945 m. lapkričio–gruodžio mėn (Rokiškis County Women's Department Director Paradauskienė's Report on November–December 1945), LCSA, F. 1771, Ap. 8, B. 335.
10. Šakių apskrities liaudies švietimo skyriaus darbuotojo Antano Pakarklio laiškas M. Kaunaitei (Letter of Šakiai County People's Department of Education Employee Antanas Pakarklis to M. Kaunaitė) LCSA, F. 1771, Ap. 39, B. 500.
11. LCP CK instruktorės Povilaitytės raštas A. Sniečkui (Letter from LCP CC Instructor Povilaitytė to A. Sniečkus), 14 November 1948, LCSA, F. 1771, Ap. 39, B. 500.
12. Kauno apskrities Darbui tarp moterų skyriaus ataskaita už 1947 m. gruodžio mėn (The Report of LSSR Work Among Women Division, the Alytus county, 1947, LCSA, F. 1771, Ap. 82, B. 7, L. 8.
13. Pažyma apie darbą tarp moterų LTSR (Note on LSSR Work Among Women), 1950, LCSA, F. 1771, Ap. 82, B. 1, L. 10–11.

14 M. Kaunaitės ataskaita už 1948 m. (M. Kaunaitė's Report on 1948), LCSA, F. 1771, Ap. 39, B. 499.
15 Pažyma apie darbą tarp moterų LTSR (Note on LSSR Work Among Women), 1950, LCSA, F. 1771, Ap. 82, B. 1, L. 13.
16 Alytaus apskrities Darbo tarp moterų skyriaus žinios (Alytus County Work Among Women Division News), 1948, LCSA, F. 1771, Ap. 11, B. 493.
17 Nakaitės raštas M. Kaunaitei (Note from Nakaitė to M. Kaunaitė), LCSA, F. 1771, Ap. 39, B. 500. 1948 m. Panašus skundas dėl darbo (Similar Complaint about Work), see F. 1771, Ap. 8, B. 335. Biržų apskrities Darbo tarp moterų skyriaus vedėjos raštas (Note by the Biržai County Department of Work Among Women), 1945.
18 LCSA, F. 1771, Ap. 8, B. 335. Rokiškio apskrities Darbo tarp moterų skyriaus vedėjos Paradauskienės ataskaita M. Kaunaitei už 1945 m. spalio mėn (Report on October 1945 to M. Kaunaitė from Rokiškis County Work Among Women Department Director Paradauskienė), LCSA, F. 1771, Ap. 9, B. 455. Panevėžio apskrities Darbo tarp moterų skyriaus ataskaita už 1946 m. vasario mėn (Panevėžys County Work Among Women Report on February 1946), LCSA, F. 1771, Ap. 11, B. 495. už 1947 m. For more on meetings at the factories, see F. 1771, Ap. 8, B. 334.
19 M. Kaunaitės ataskaita apie Šakių apskrities Darbo tarp moterų skyrių (Report by M. Kaunaitė on the Šakiai County Department of Work Among Women), 9 February 1948, LCSA, F. 1771, Ap. 39, B. 500.
20 Biržų apskrities Darbo tarp moterų skyriaus ataskaita (Report from the Biržai County Department of Work Among Women), 31 December 1945, LCSA, F. 1771, Ap. 8, B. 334. Alytaus apskrities Darbo tarp moterų skyriaus ataskaita už 1948 m. gegužės–birželio mėn (Report from the Alytus County Department of Work Among Women for May–June 1948) LCSA, F. 1771, Ap. 11, B. 493. Biržų apskrities Darbo tarp moterų skyriaus ataskaita (Report from the Biržai County Department of Work Among Women), 1 June 1946, LCSA, F. 1771, Ap. 9, B. 454.
21 Pažymoje apie darbą tarp moterų LTSR, 1950 m. teigiama, kad Moterų tarybos Lietuvoje pradėtos kurti 1948 m. (This 1950 report on the LSSR Work Among Women claims that Women's Councils began to be established in Lithuania in 1948), LCSA, F. 1771, Ap. 82, B. 1, L. 13.
22 Vilniaus srities Darbo tarp moterų skyriaus ataskaita už 1950 m (Vilnius District Work Among Women Division Report for the Year 1950), LCSA, F. 1771, Ap. 103, B. 2.
23 Pažyma apie darbą tarp moterų LTSR, 1950 m. (1950 Report on Work Among Women in the LSSR), LCSA, F. 1771, Ap. 82, B. 1, L. 13.
24 Biržų apskrities Darbo tarp moterų skyriaus ataskaita už 1946 m. rugsėjo-lapkričio mėn (Report on September–November 1946 by the Biržai County Department of Work Among Women), LCSA, F. 1775, Ap. 9, B. 454.

25 Marijampolės apskrities Darbo tarp moterų skyriaus ataskaita už 1948 m. gegužės-birželio mėn (Report on May–June 1948 by the Marijampolė County Department of Work Among Women), LCSA, F. 1771, Ap. 11, B. 495.
26 Apie darbą tarp moterų Šiaulių rajone, 1953 m. (On Work Among Women in the Šiauliai district, 1953), LCSA, F. 1771, Ap. 145, B. 1, L. 10.
27 For more on forms of Work Among Women Division activities, see LCSA, F. 1771, Ap. 9, B. 453; Ap. 9, B. 454; Ap. 39, B. 16; Ap. 11, B. 501; Ap. 8, B. 335; Ap. 9, B. 455; Ap. 8, B. 335; Ap. 11, B. 493; Ap. 11, B. 495.
28 LCSA, F. 1771, Ap. 9, B. 455, L. 26.
29 LCSA, F. 1771, Ap. 9, B. 453, L. 22.
30 LCSA, F. 1771, Ap. 9, B. 455, L. 145.
31 The MGB was the repressive structure which dealt with internal and external security issues: secret police duties, foreign and domestic intelligence, and counterintelligence, among others.
32 Alytaus apskrities Darbo tarp moterų skyriaus ataskaita už 1948 m. Kovo ir balandžio mėn (Report on March–April 1948, Alytus County Department of Work Among Women), LCSA, F. 1771, Ap. 11, B. 493, L. 5.
33 Tarnybinis raštas Anykščių LCP(b) CK I sekretoriui (Official letter to the First Secretary of the Anykščiai LCP(b) CC), LCSA, F. 1771, Ap. 11, B. 493, L. 42.
34 Alytaus apskrities Darbo tarp moterų skyriaus ataskaita už 1948 m. Rugsėjo ir spalio mėn (Report on September–October 1948, Alytus County Department of Work Among Women), LCSA, F. 1771, Ap. 11, B. 493, L. 26.
35 T. A. Ždanko, ed., *Semejnyj byt narodov CCCR* (Family Life of the People of the USSR) (Moscow: Nauka, 1990), 161.
36 Sveikatos apsaugos ministro pavaduotojo Lazutkos raštas M. Kaunaitei (Letter to M. Kaunaitė from Deputy Minister of Health Lazutka), 12 May 1951, LCSA, F. 1771, Ap. 103, B. 4, L. 6. Tauragės rajono Darbo tarp moterų skyriaus ataskaita už 1953 m. (Tauragė District Department of Work Among Women report on 1953), 1771, Ap. 145, B. 7, L. 5.
37 Yulia Gradskova and Ildikó Asztalos Morell, eds, *Gendering Post-socialism: Old Legacies and New Hierarchies* (London: Routledge, 2018), 3–4. See also Sarah Ashwin, 'Introduction', in *Gender, State and Society in Soviet and Post-Soviet Russia* ed. Sarah Ashwin (London: Routledge, 2000), 17.
38 *Lietuva 1940–1990 m.* (Lithuania, 1940–1990) (Vilnius: Lietuvos gyventojų ir rezistencijos tyrimų centras, 2005), 450.
39 B. Petravys, 'Remiamos daugiavaikės ir vienišos motinos' (Mothers of Large Families and Single Mothers Are Receiving Support), *Tarybų Lietuva*, 14 June 1945.
40 Ibid., 8–10.
41 TSRS Aukščiausiosios Tarybos Prezidiumo nutarimas dėl priemonių savalaikiam daugiavaikių motinų apdovanojimui bei ordinų ir medalių įteikimui užtikrinti

(Resolution of the Presidium of the USSR Supreme Soviet on Measures for Ensuring the Timely Honouring and Presenting of Orders and Medals to Mothers of Large Families). *LTSR Aukščiausiosios Tarybos ir Vyriausybės žinios*, no. 5 (185), 15 April 1954, 4–5.

42 Alina Zvinklienė, 'The State of Family Studies in Lithuania', *Marriage and Family Review* 22, no. 3 (n.d.), 203–2, 226.

43 G. Ickovičiūtė, 'Motinos ir vaiko sveikatos sargyboje' (Looking Out for the Health of Mothers and Children), *Tiesa*, 7 December 1946.

44 L.Veržbavičius, 'Motinystės ir vaikystės globa Tarybų Lietuvoje' (Caring for Mothers and Children in Soviet Lithuania), *Tiesa*, 8 July 1945.

45 I. Kielienė, 'Priešmokyklinis auklėjimas Lietuvoje' (Preschool Education in Lithuania), *Tarybinė mokykla* 9 (1947), 34.

46 M. Kaniauskas, 'Ką davė Tarybų valdžia moterims?' (What Did the Soviet Government Provide for Women?), *Tiesa*, 20 January 1946.

47 Lietuvos Tarybų Socialistinės Respublikos Aukščiausiosios Tarybos Prezidiumo įsakas *Dėl Vyriausiosios Karių Šeimų Valstybinio Aprūpinimo ir Buities Sutvarkymo Valdybos prie Lietuvos TSR Liaudies Komisarų Tarybos ir Karių Valstybinio Aprūpinimo ir Buities Sutvarkymo skyrių prie miestų, miestų rajonų ir apskričių vykdomųjų komitetų sudarymo* (Order of the Presidium of the Supreme Soviet of the Soviet Socialist Republic of Lithuania on the Establishment of a Board Providing State Provisions for the Well-being of Soldiers' Families Under the Council of People's Commissars of the LSSR and the Department for Providing State Provisions for the Well-being of Soldiers' Families at the City, City District and County Levels), *LTSR Aukščiausiosis Tarybos ir Vyriausybės žinios* 1, no. 10, 28 October 1944, 14–15.

48 Lietuvos Tarybų Socialistinės Respublikos Aukščiausiosios Tarybos Prezidiumo nutarimas *Dėl papildomos socialinės pagalbos kare žuvusių karių šeimoms* (Resolution of the Presidium of the Supreme Soviet of the Soviet Socialist Republic of Lithuani On Supplemental Social Benefits for Families of Soldiers Who Perished at War), *LTSR Aukščiausiosios Tarybos ir Vyriausybės žinios* 3, no. 152, 12 March 1952, 1–3.

49 Lietuvos Tarybų Socialistinės Respublikos Ministrų Tarybos nutarimas *Dėl tolesnio žuvusių kare šeimų buities sąlygų gerinimo* (Resolution of the LSSR Council of Ministers on Further Improvements to the Well-being of Families of Soldiers), *LTSR Aukščiausiosios Tarybos ir Vyriausybės žinios*, 30 June 1970.

50 Lietuvos Tarybų Socialistinė Respublikos Aukščiausiosios Tarybos Prezidiumo nutarimas *Dėl Lietuvos TSR vietinių Darbo žmonių deputatų tarybų nuolatinių komisijų nuostatų* patvirtinimo (Resolution of the Presidium of the Supreme Soviet on the Regulations Issued by the Standing Commissions of the Deputies of the

Local Councils of Working People of the LSSR), *LTSR Aukščiausiosios Tarybos ir Vyriausybės žinios* 8–9, nos 134–5, 20 July 1951, 3, 7.

51 Lietuvos Tarybų Socialistinės Respublikos Aukščiausiosios Tarybos nutarimas *Dėl mokinių, gyvenančių kaimo vietovėse nemokamo vežiojimo* (Resolution of the Supreme Soviet of the LSSR on Free Travel for Pupils Living in Rural Areas), *LTSR Aukščiausiosios Tarybos ir Vyriausybės žinios*, 30 September 1965, 610.

52 Lietuvos Tarybų Socialistinės Respublikos Ministrų Tarybos nutarimas *Dėl kaime gyvenančių mokinių pavežėjimo* (Resolution adopted by the Lithuanian Council of Ministers on Transport of Pupils Living in Rural Areas), *LTSR Aukščiausiosios Tarybos ir Vyriausybės žinios*, 31 January 1966, 43–5.

53 Lietuvos Tarybų Socialistinės Respublikos Ministrų Tarybos nutarimas *Dėl priemonių pramonei vaikams skirtų maisto produktų gamybai toliau didinti ir vaikų maitinimui organizuoti* (Resolution of the Lithuanian Council of Ministers on Measures for Industry to Further Increase Food Production for Children and to Administer Programme for Feeding Children), *LTSR Aukščiausiosios Tarybos ir Vyriausybės žinios*, 20 December 1965, 709.

54 Lietuvos TSR Ministrų Tarybos nutarimas *Dėl mėnesinių pašalpų invalidams nuo vaikystės* (Resolution of the LSSR Council of Ministers on Monthly Benefits for Those Handicapped since Childhood), *LTSR Aukščiausiosios Tarybos ir Vyriausybės žinios*, 20 December 1967, 568–9.

55 V. Daunoravičius, 'Pašalpos vaikystės invalidams' (Assistance for the Handicapped since Childhood), *Mūsų žodis* 2 (1968), 23.

56 Lietuvos Tarybų Socialistinės Respublikos Ministrų Tarybos nutarimas *Dėl profesinių technikos ir specialiųjų vidurinių mokyklų moksleivių našlaičių ir netekusių tėvų globos aprūpinimo* (Resolution of the LSSR Council of Ministers on Providing for Students Attending Vocational, Technical and Specialized Secondary Schools Who Are Orphans or Who Have Lost Their Parental Guardians), *LTSR Aukščiausiosios Tarybos ir Vyriausybės žinios*, 30 March 1970, 66–7.

57 Lietuvos Tarybų Socialistinės Respublikos Ministrų Tarybos nutarimas *Dėl pašalpų mokėjimo maitintojo netekusiems vidurinių bendrojo lavinimo mokyklų XI klasių moksleiviams* (Resolution of the LSSR Council of Ministers on the Payment of Assistance to Students of General Secondary Schools, Grades One Through Eleven Who Have Lost Their Breadwinner), *LTSR Aukščiausiosios Tarybos ir Vyriausybės žinios*, 21 September 1970, 215.

58 Lietuvos Tarybų Socialistinės Respublikos Ministrų Tarybos potvarkis *Dėl tėvų atleidimo nuo mokesčio už vaiko išlaikymą, kai jis nelanko vaikų įstaigos eilinių tėvo atostogų metu* (Resolution of the Council of Ministers of the LSSR on Exemptions from Child Support for Fathers While Their Child Is Not Attending Childcare Institutions during Paternity Leave), *LTSR Aukščiausiosios Tarybos ir Vyriausybės žinios*, 10 June 1970, 112–13.

59 Lietuvos Tarybų Socialistinės Respublikos Ministrų Tarybos potvarkis *Dėl mokesčio ėmimo už auklėtinių išlaikymą mokyklose internatuose sutvarkymo* (Resolution of the Council of Ministers of the LSSR on the Issuing of Fees for Room and Board of Pupils Attending Boarding Schools for the Needy), *LTSR Aukščiausiosios Tarybos ir Vyriausybės žinios*, 30 October 1973, 279–80.

60 I. Katkova, 'Maternal Care of Infants', in *Women, Work and Family in the Soviet Union*, ed. Gail W. Lapidus (New York: Routledge, 1982), 237.

61 LTSR CK ir LTSR Ministrų Tarybos ir Lietuvos respublikinės profesinių sąjungų tarybos nutarimas *Dėl priemonių vaikų ir paauglių vasaros poilsio organizavimui toliau gerinti* (Resolution of the Central Committee of the LSSR, Council of Ministers of the LSSR and the LSSR Council of Trade Unions on Measures for Further Improving the Management of Summer Recreation for Children and Adolescents), *LTSR Aukščiausiosios Tarybos ir Vyriausybės žinios*, 20 April 1973, 99–100.

62 Aušra Steckienė, 'Šeimos politikos pokyčiai Lietuvoje pereinant iš socializmo į kapitalizmą' (Changes in Family Policy in Lithuania's Transition from Socialism to Capitalism) (Master's Thesis, Vilnius University, 2008), 42.

63 Ibid., 35.

64 Agenda for OSBMLFSM branch staff seminar in Vilnius, 21–25 May 1944, Lithuanian Central State Archive (LCSA), F. R.-164, Ap. 14, B. 1, L. 4.

65 'Apie valstybines pašalpas daugiavaikėms ir vienišoms motinoms' (On State Assistance for Mothers of Large Families and Single Mothers), *Tiesa*, 16 November 1944.

66 Petras Kalnius, 'Miesto šeimos etnodemografiniai bruožai ir vidaus organizacija XIX-XX a.' (Ethnodemographic Characteristics and Internal Organization of Urban Families in the nineteenth-twentieth centuries), in *Lietuvių šeima ir papročiai* (The Lithuanian Family and Its Traditions), ed. Angelė Vyšniauskaitė, Petras Kalnius and Rasa Paukštytė (Vilnius: Mintis, 1995), 182–8.

67 S. Zakharov, 'Russian Federation: From the First to Second Demographic Transition', *Demographic Research* 19, no. 24 (2008), 955. В. Станкунене, 'Vosproizvodstvo naselenija Litvy', in *Demografičeskoe razvitie Litvy: retrospektiva, sovremenye problemy, sravnitelnyj analiz*, ed. V. Kanopiene, A. Sipaviciene, V. Stankuniene and V. Januškevčius (Vilnius: Institut Ekononmiki Akademii Nauk Litovskoj SSR, 1989), 31.

68 Petras Kalnius, 'Miesto šeimos etnodemografiniai bruožai ir vidaus organizacija XIX-XX a.' (Ethnodemographic Characteristics and Internal Organization of Urban Families in the nineteenth-twentieth centuries), in *Lietuvių šeima ir papročiai* (The Lithuanian Family and Its Traditions), ed. Angelė Vyšniauskaitė, Petras Kalnius and Rasa Paukštytė (Vilnius: Mintis, 1995), 161–3.

69 Arvydas Anušauskas, ed, *Lietuva 1940–1990* (Vilnius: n.p., 2005), 395.

70 Ibid., 394.
71 Deputy LSSR Finance Commissariat J. Genys, note of 6 October 1945, LCSA, F. R.-164, Ap. 14, B. 1, L. 17.
72 Agenda of the metropolitan Vilnius branch of the OSBMLFSM, 1945, LCSA, F. R.-164, Ap. 14, B. 4, L. 6.
73 Šiauliai branch of the OSBMLFSM plan for disseminating information about the law, 1946, LCSA, F. R.-164, Ap. 14, B. 4, L. 14.
74 Prienai county finance and OSBMLFSM branches, fourth quarter work plan, 1947, LCSA, F. R.-164, Ap. 14, B. 7, L. 229.
75 LSSR Finance Minister's order to the OSBMLFSM branches, 14 November 1946, LCSA, F. R.-164, Ap. 14, B. 3, L. 66.
76 Agenda for 25–30 October 1945 seminar for the OSBMLFSM branches, LCSA, F. R.-164, Ap. 14, B. 1, L. 22. Agenda for 25–30 March OSBMLFSM branch seminar, LCSA, F. R.-164, Ap. 14, B. 3, L. 18.
77 Protocol materials for 7–10 July 1947 seminar for the OSBMLFSM branches, LCSA, F. R.-164, Ap. 14, B. 6, L. 49.
78 As the Commissar changed to ministry, Genys's designation changed accordingly.
79 Deputy LSSR Finance Minister J. Genys's note to J. Paleckis, 20 September 1946, LCSA, F. R.-164, Ap. 14, B. 5, L. 10.
80 Vilkaviškis branch of the OSBMLFSM, 5 October 1946 work plan, LCSA, F. R.-164, Ap. 14, B. 4, L. 2.
81 OSBMLFSM board, fourth quarter work plan, 1946, Šakiai county, LCSA, F. R.-164, Ap. 14, B. 4, L. 8.
82 OSBMLFSM board, third quarter work plan, 1947, LCSA, F. R.-164, Ap. 14, B. 7, L. 98.
83 USSR Finance Ministry commentary on the OSBMLFSM board's 1946 third quarter work plan, LCSA, F. R.-164, Ap. 14, B. 7, L. 42.
84 OSBMLFSM Board Director M. Kymantaitė's report on the 1946 fourth quarter work plan, LCSA, F. R.-164, Ap. 14, B. 7, L. 33.
85 Jurbarkas branch of the OSBMLFSM, third quarter work plan, 1948, and Pagėgiai county 1948 fourth quarter work plan, LCSA, F. R.-164, Ap. 14, B. 9, L. 56, 133.
86 'Progress on Rewarding Mothers of Large Families', LSSR Supreme Soviet resolution, 10 April 1947, LCSA, F. R.-164, Ap. 14, B. 6, L. 36–7.
87 Kėdainiai county VK finance department director's note to the OSBMLFSM Board, 31 December 1945, LCSA, F. R.-164, Ap. 14, B. 2, L. 6.
88 LSSR People's Commissariat for Finance decree, 20 December 1945, LCSA, F. R.-164, Ap. 14, B. 2, L. 1.
89 OSBMLFSM board's note, 1946, LCSA, F. R.-164, Ap. 14, B. 2, L. 13.
90 LSSR Deputy Fianance Minister V. Kuznecovas's note, 6 October 1950, LCSA, F. R.-164, Ap. 14, B. 16, L. 32.

91 Regarding the Tauragė, Švenčionys, Utena, Prienai, Varėna, Kaišiadorys, Trakai and Alytus county branches of the OSBMLFSM and the Tauragė, Švenčionys, Utena and Lazdijai Savings Banks audit, 30 December 1946, LCSA, F. R.-164, Ap. 14, B. 3, L. 71. Regarding the audits conducted in the Biržai, Marijampolė and Vilkaviškis OSBMLFSM branches. Deputy LSSR Finance Minister J. Genys's note of 30 May 1946, LCSA, F. R.-64, Ap. 14, B. 3, L. 38.
92 Deputy LSSR Finance Minister J. Genys's note of 30 May 1946, LCSA, F. R.-64, Ap. 14, B. 3, L. 38, 71–2.
93 Ibid.
94 Note written by OSBMLFSM board director M. Kymantaitė and the LSSR People's Commissariat for Finance A. Drobnys to the LCP(b) CC, 6 July 1946, LCSA, F. R.-164, Ap. 14, B. 5, L. 5.
95 Kaunas county branch of the OSBMLFSM, audit data, 29 January 1949, LCSA, F. R.-164, Ap. 14, B. 12, L. 3.
96 Alytus county branch of the OSBMLFSM, audit data, 20 October 1949, LCSA, F. R.-164, Ap. 14, B. 12, L. 43.
97 Pagėgiai county branch of the OSBMLFSM, audit data, 20 February 1948.
98 LSSR Finance Minister's order regarding work at the Lazdijai branch of the OSBMLFSM, 28 June 1950, LCSA, F. R.-164, Ap. 14, B. 15, L. 38.
99 LSSR Interim Finance Minister A. Sinaiskis's order regarding work at the Šilutė county branch, 24 October 1947, L. 92–3. A. Drobnys's order regarding work at the Šilutė county branch, L. 103. Director of the LSSR Council of Ministers M. Gedvilas's resolution regarding work at the Šilutė county branch, 31 December 1947, LCSA, F. R.-164, Ap. 14, B. 6, L. 112.
100 Mažeikiai county branch of the OSBMLFSM, audit data, 20 May 1950, LCSA, F. R.-164, Ap. 14, B. 16, L. 77.
101 Pagėgiai county branch of the OSBMLFSM, audit data, 20 February 1948, LCSA, F. R.-164, Ap. 14, B. 11, L. 8. Report from the Joniškis county OSBMLFSM branch, 24 May 1950, LCSA, F. R.-164, Ap. 14, B. 16, L. 47.
102 Report on the third quarter of 1946 by the director of benefits of the Kaišiadoriai county executive committee branch, finance department, LCSA, F. R.-164, Ap. 14, B. 7, L. 84.
103 Kėdainiai county branch of the OSBMLFSM, audit results, 23 February 1948, LCSA, F. R.-164, Ap. 14, B. 11, L. 11. Tauragė county state savings bank audit results, 20 February 1948, LCSA, F. R.-164, Ap. 14, B. 11, L. 6. Order of the LSSR Finance Ministry regarding the work of the Joniškis district OSBMLFSM branch, 21 November 1950, LCSA, F. R.-164, Ap. 14, B. 15, L. 66. Regarding the work of the Šiauliai region OSBMLFSM branch, 11 October 1951, LCSA, F. R.-164, Ap. 14, B. 20, L. 59–60.

104 Pasvalys OSBMLFSM branch audit results, 3 June 1949, LCSA, F. R.-164, Ap. 14, B. 12, L. 24.
105 USSR Finance Ministry resolution regarding the work of the OSBMLFSM board, 1950 (more precise date unavailable), LCSA, F. R.-164, Ap. 14, B. 15, L. 16–23.
106 Biržai county OSBMLFSM branch director's memo to the board, 3 June 1950, LCSA, F. R.-164, Ap. 14, B. 16, L. 42.
107 Lazdijai county OSBMLFSM branch director's memo to the board, 12 April 1950, LCSA, F. R.-164, Ap. 14, B. 14.
108 Memo to the OSBMLFSM board from the Panevėžys county executive committee finance department director, 1945, LCSA, F. R.-164, Ap. 14, B. 2, L. 19.
109 Memo written by the director of benefits of the city of Panevėžys finance department, 1945, LCSA, F. R.-164, Ap. 14, B. 2, L. 18.
110 Memo written by the Kaunas county OSBMLFSM branch director, 1946, LCSA, F. R.-164, Ap. 14, B. 2, L. 4.
111 Note, Biržai county finance department, 22 December 1945, LCSA, F. R.-164, Ap. 14, B. 2, L. 2.
112 M. Kymantaitė memo to the Pagėgiai branch of the OSBMLFSM, July 1946, LCSA, F. R.-164, Ap. 14, B. 4, L. 15.
113 LSSR People's Commissar Commission's decree project on the work of the OSBMLFSM boad, 13 April 1945, LCSA, F. R.-164, Ap. 14, B. 1, L. 5–6.
114 Dėl Ukmergės apskrities OSBMLFSM skyriaus patikrinimo (On the Audit of the Ukmergė District OSBMLFSM Division), LSSR Deputy Finance Minister Genys's note, 14 November 1946, LCSA, F. R.-164, Ap. 14, B. 3, L. 66–7.
115 Deputy LSSR Finance Minister Genys's note regarding the work of the Kėdainiai county branch of the OSBMLFSM, 10 April 1946, LCSA, F. R.-164, Ap. 14, B. 6, L. 22.
116 LSSR Finance Minister A. Drobnys's order regarding the work of the OSBMLFSM board, 7 September 1947, LCSA, F. R.-164, Ap. 14, B. 6, L. 75.
117 Order of the USSR Finance Ministry, 10 May 1950, LCSA, F. R.-164, Ap. 14, B. 15, L. 26–7.
118 LSSR Finance Minister A. Drobnys's note regarding the work of the OSBMLFSM board, 27 December 1951, LCSA, F. R.-164, Ap. 14, B. 20, L. 20
119 Šiauliai county executive commitee finance department director's note regarding the work of the OSBMLFSM branch, 26 January 1952, LCSA, F. R.-164, Ap. 14, B. 20, L. 15, 2. Order of USSR Finance Minister A. Zverev No. 84, 18 January 1951, LCSA, F. R.-164, Ap. 14, B. 20, L. 121. Note written by the director of the Kaunas county executive committee finance department regarding the work of the OSBMLFSM branch, 18 February 1952, LCSA, F. R.-164, Ap. 14, B. 20, L. 5.
120 From the OSBMLFSM board of the Trakai county branch, 14 October 1949, LCSA, F. R.-164, Ap. 14, B. 14, L. 21. LSSR Finance Ministry audit of the Joniškis district

OSBMLFSM branch, 21 November 1950, LCSA, F. R.-164, Ap. 14, B. 15, L. 67. Šiauliai region executive committee finance department director's note, 6 March 1952, LCSA, F. R.-164, Ap. 14, B. 20, L. 14.
121 Susan E. Reid, 'Women in the Home', in *Women in the Khrushchev Era*, ed. Melanie Ilič, Susan E. Reid and Lynne Attwood (New York: Palgrave Macmillan, 2004), 154.

2 Marriage and divorce

1 Dalia Leinarte, *The Lithuanian Family in Its European Context, 1800–1914: Marriage, Divorce and Flexible Communities* (London: Palgrave Macmillan, 2017), 47.
2 *1940 m. Santuokos įstatymas* (1940 Marriage Law), *Vyriausybės žinios*, 15 August 1940, 619.
3 Ibid., 623.
4 Ibid.
5 Ibid., 619.
6 Ibid., 620.
7 Ibid., 620, 626.
8 Dalia Leinarte, *Adopting and Remembering Soviet Reality: Life Stories of Lithuanian Women, 1945–1970* (Amsterdam: Rodopi, 2010), 116.
9 The law was not in effect during Nazi occupation, 1941–4.
10 LTSR Aukščiausiosios Tarybos įsakas *Dėl veikiančių Lietuvos TSR teritorijoje Santuokos, šeimos ir globos įstatymų kodekso ir Civilinio procesinio kodekso pakeitimų* (The LSSR Supreme Soviet decree on Marriage, Family and Guardianship Code of Law and Civilian in Effect in the Territory of the LSSR and Amendments to the Code of Civil Procedure), *LTSR Aukščiausiosios Tarybos ir Vyriausybės žinios* 17, 5 August 1946, 1–4.
11 *LTSR Aukščiausiosios Tarybos ir Vyriausybės žinios* 12–13, 30 June 1947, 23.
12 'Įsakymas Dėl Lietuvos TSR teritorijoje veikiančio Santuokos, šeimos ir globos įstatymų kodekso pakeitimų' (Law: On the Changes to the Marriage, Family and Guardianship Laws in Effect in the Territory of the LSSR), *LTSR Aukščiausiosios Tarybos ir Vyriausybės žinios*, 12 February 1954, 2.
13 Pranas Dičius, *Santuoka ir šeima Tarybų Lietuvoje* (Marriage and Family in Soviet Lithuania) (Vilnius: Minties Leidykla, 1974), 17.
14 'Dėl *Lietuvos TSR santuokos ir šeimos kodekso* įsigaliojimo tvarkos' (On the Procedure for Implementing the Marriage and Family Code of the LSSR), *LTSR Aukščiausiosios Tarybos ir Vyriausybės žinios*, 10 December 1969, 604.
15 *1957 m. Liepos 17 d. Instrukcijos dėl civilinės metrikacijos tvarkos LTSR* (17 July 1957 Instructions on Civilian Metrics Procedures in the LSSR), *Lietuvos*

Tarybų Socialistinės Respublikos Aukščiausiosios Tarybos ir Vyriausybės žinios, 30 August 1958.

16 *1958 m. August 20 d. Instrukcijos dėl civilinės metrikacijos tvarkos LTSR* (20 August 1958 Instructions on Civil Metrics Procedures in the LSSR), *LTSR Aukščiausiosios Tarybos ir Vyriausybės žinios*, 31 May 1960, 311.

17 *1958 m. August 20 d. Instrukcijos dėl civilinės metrikacijos tvarkos LTSR*, 1 ir 4 punktų pakeitimo (Changes to Points 1–4 of on Civil Metrics Instructions in the LSSR), *LTSR Aukščiausiosios Tarybos ir Vyriausybės žinios*, 20 August 1963, 189.

18 '*1970 m. Sausio 4 d. LTSR Ministrų Tarybos nutarimas Dėl civilinės metrikacijos instrukcijos patvirtinimo* (Resolution of the Council of Ministers of the LSSR on the Approval of the Instructions on Civilian Metrics), *LTSR Aukščiausiosios Tarybos ir Vyriausybės žinios*, 20 February 1970, 79–110.

19 Dalia Leinarte, *Adopting and Remembering Soviet Reality: Stories of Lithuanian Women, 1945–1970* (Amsterdam: Rodopi, 2010), 79.

20 A. Grigonis, 'Jaunos šeimos istorija' (The Story of a Young Family), *Komjaunimo tiesa*, 25 August 1946.

21 N. Solovjovas, 'Apie šeimos laimę' (On Happiness in Marriage), 6. 'Religija nepadeda' (Religion Does Not Help), *Komjaunimo tiesa*, 24 May 1957.

22 Ibid.

23 D. Šniukas, 'Sutuoktuvių liudijimas Nr.1' (Witness to a Marriage No. 1), *Tiesa*, 24 July 1964.

24 P. Leonas, 'Mano pergyvenimai ir atsiminimai' (My Experiences and Memories), D. 1, 1934 m., Manuscript Department of the Wroblewski Library of the Lithuanian Academy of Sciences (hereafter MARS), F. 117–1074, L. 4–5.

25 J. Šliūpas, 'Autobiografija' (Autobiography), Rare Books and Manuscripts Unit of the National Library of Lithuania (hereafter NBRS), F. 1–17, L.13.

26 Divorce case, 1959, LCSA, F. R.-808, Ap. 2, B. 723, L. 14.

27 Divorce case of Povilas and Elena M., 1947–8, LCSA, F. R.-808, Ap. 2, B. 27, L. 22.

28 Divorce case, 1957, LCSA, F. R.-808, Ap. 2, B. 503, L. 31.

29 Divorce case of Vladas K. and Otilija K., 1940, LCSA, F. R.-808, Ap. 2, B. 5, L. 1.

30 'Kuris teisus? Skaitytojos laiškas' (Which of Us Is Right? Letter to the Editor), *Tarybinė moteris* 4 (1958), 17.

31 Divorce case, 1956, LCSA, F. R.-808, Ap. 2, B. 379, L. 159.

32 Н. Н. Соловьев, *Брак и семья сегодня* (Marriage and Family Today) (Вильнюс: Минтис, 1977), 7, 19.

33 *Pagrindiniai 1989 metų gyventojų surašymo duomenys* (Essential Data from the 1989 Census) (Vilnius: Lietuvos valstybinis statistikos komitetas, 1990), 53.

34 T. A. Ždanko, ed., *Semejnyj byt narodov CCCR* (Moskva: Nauka, 1990), 163.

35 V. Čekalinas, *Meilė ir šeima* (Love and Family) (Vilnius: Mintis, 1968), 122.

36 'Koks turi būti šeimos gyvenimas – uždaras ar atdaras?' (Should Family Life Be Open or Closed?), *Tarybinė moteris* 6, no. 2 (1970).
37 Alekseičikas, 'Ant ko laikosi šeima?' (What Is the Foundation of a Family?), *Tarybinė šeima* 8 (1970), 14.
38 Dalia Leinarte, *Adopting and Remembering Soviet Reality: Life Stories of Lithuanian Women, 1945–1970* (Amsterdam: Rodopi, 2010), 147.
39 A. Kaluzevičius, 'Apie santuoką' (On Marriage), *Tarybinė moteris* 10 (1958), 17.
40 A. Šalčiūtė, 'Noriu vesti' (I Want to Marry), *Jaunimo gretos* 5 (1964), 27–8.
41 T. A. Ždanko, ed., *Semejnyj byt narodov CCCR* (Moskva: Nauka, 1990), 166.
42 Pranas Dičius. *Santuoka ir Šeima Tarybų Lietuvoje* (Marriage and Family in Soviet Lithuania) (Vilnius: Minties Leidykla, 1974), 38. V. Gaidys, *Visuomenės pagalba šeimai. Praktika ir problemos* (Social Assistance to Families: Practice and Problems) (Vilnius: Lietuvos TSR Žinijos draugija, 1984), 11.
43 Н. Н. Соловьев, Брак и семья сегодня (Marriage and Family Today) (Вильнюс: Минтис, 1977), 104.
44 N. Sidorkaitė, 'Motina ir sūnus' (Mother and Son), *Tarybinė moteris* 6 (1954), 4.
45 Gyvenamojo ploto atidalijimo byla (Case on dividing up living space), 1979–80, LCSA, F. R.-808, Ap. 2, B. 1611, L. 95.
46 T. A. Ždanko, ed., *Semejnyj byt narodov CCCR* (Moskva: Nauka, 1990), 186.
47 Irving Singer, *The Nature of Love, Vol. 2: Courtly and Romantic* (Chicago: University of Chicago Press, 1984), 292–5.
48 Ibid., 361.
49 Denis de Rougemont, *Love in the Western World* (New York: Fawcett, 1956), 53.
50 William Jankowiak, ed., *Romantic Passion. A Universal Experience?* (New York: Columbia University Press, 1995), 4.
51 Denis de Rougemont, *Love in the Western World* (New York: Fawcett, 1956), 53.
52 In contrast, in the West since the beginning of the twentieth century as middle-class values became increasingly prevalent, societies tried to find cultural 'brakes' to put on sexual love. In this case, Denis de Rougemont discusses the primitivization and banalization of passion in Western mass culture. According to him, literature, film and theatre sought to reconcile and offer to Western consumers two irreconcilable things: passionate love and the happy ending. On tamed and domesticated passion as a refusal to suffer in American culture, see Eva Illouz's fine analysis: Eva Illouz, *Consuming the Romantic Utopia: Love and the Cultural Contradictions of Capitalism* (Berkeley: University of California Press, 1997).
53 Wendy Z. Goldman, *Women, the State and Revolution, Soviet Family Policy and Social Life: 1917–1936* (Cambridge, UK: Cambridge University Press, 1993), 34.
54 Elizabeth A. Wood, *The Baba and the Comrade* (Bloomington: Indiana University Press, 1997), 3.
55 Ibid., 107–8.

56 Barbara Alpern Engel and Anastasia Posadskya-Vanderbeck, eds, *A Revolution of Their Own: Voices of Women in Soviet History* (Boulder, CO: Westview Press, 1998).
57 Ibid., 169.
58 Ibid., 145.
59 Vladimir Shlapentokh, *Love, Marriage, and Friendship in the Soviet Union: Ideals and Practices* (New York: Praeger, 1984), 22.
60 Elizabeth A. Wood, *The Baba and the Comrade* (Bloomington: Indiana University Press, 1997), 3. Ibid., 106–8. Eric Naiman, *Sex in Public: The Incarnation of Early Soviet Ideology* (Princeton, NJ: Princeton University Press, 1997), 137.
61 Eric Naiman, *Sex in Public: The Incarnation of Early Soviet Ideology* (Princeton, NJ: Princeton University Press, 1997), 137.
62 Rosalind Marsh, 'Women Writers of the 1930s: Conformity or Subversion?', in *Women in the Stalin Era*, ed. Melanie Ilič (New York: Palgrave Macmillan, 2001), 184.
63 A. Maslauskaitė, *Meilė ir santuoka pokyčių Lietuvoje* (Vilnius: Mokslo Aidai, 2004), 58–61.
64 M. Mašiotienės laiškas M. Mašiotaitei (Letter of M. Mašiotienė to M. Mašiotaitė), 1924, NBRS, F. 14–578, L. 15.
65 M. Urbšienės laiškai J. Urbšiui į Berlyną (M. Urbšienė's letters to J. Urbšys in Berlin), 1926, NBRS, F. 14–449.
66 Vlado Šimaičio laiškai Aldonai Dirmantaitei (Letters of Vladas Šimaitis to Aldona Dirmantaitė), 1935, NBRS, F. 62–188, L. 14.
67 Vlado Šimaičio laiškai Aldonai Dirmantaitei (Letters of Vladas Šimaitis to Aldona Dirmantaitė), 1934, NBRS, F. 62–188, L. 9.
68 Vlado Šimaičio laiškai Aldonai Dirmantaitei (Letters of Vladas Šimaitis to Aldona Dirmantaitė), 1934, NBRS, F. 62–188.
69 J. Puzino laiškas žmonai Konstancijai iš Heidelbergo (J. Puzinas's letter to his wife Konstancija from Heidelberg), 27 May 1930, NBRS, F. 52–96.
70 J. Puzino laiškas žmonai Konstancijai iš Heidelbergo (J. Puzinas's letter to his wife Konstancija from Heidelberg), 15 December 1932, NBRS, F. 52–96.
71 Marijos Bilevičiūtės-Vasiliauskienės dienoraštis (Diary of Marija Bilevičiūtė-Vasiliauskienė), 1922–1925, MARS, F. 205, Part I, p. 52..
72 A. Griginis, 'Jaunos šeimos istorija' (The Story of a Young Family), *Komjaunimo tiesa*, 25 August 1946.
73 Ibid.
74 I. Mikšytė, 'Dar kartą apie meilę', *Jaunimo gretos* 7 (1954), 13.
75 E. Levanienė, 'Berniukų ir mergaičių draugystė' (Friendship between Boys and Girls), *Tarybinė moteris* 11 (1954), 18.
76 Interview by author with Bronė Sopienė, Vilnius, 2004.

77 E. Levanienė, 'Berniukų ir mergaičių draugystė' (Friendship between Boys and Girls), *Tarybinė moteris* 11 (1954), 18.
78 Interview by author with Natalija J., Vilnius, 2001.
79 Kristin Roth-Ey, ' "Loose Girls" on the Lose?: Sex, Propaganda and the 1957 Youth Festival', in *Women in the Khrushchev Era*, ed. Melanie Illič, Susan E. Reid and Lynne Attwood (New York: Palgrave Macmillan, 2004), 88.
80 Josephine Woll, *Real Images. Soviet Cinema and the Thaw* (London: I. B. Tauris, 2000), 187.
81 Vladimir Shlapentokh, *Love, Marriage, and Friendship in the Soviet Union: Ideals and Practices* (New York: Praeger, 1984), 50, 55.
82 Ibid., 53.
83 K. Daukšas, 'Apie šeimos patvarumą' (On the Family's Stability), *Tarybinė moteris* 10 (1959), 12.
84 S. Pakalnis, *Jaunimo gretos* 11 (1955), 23, emphasis in original.
85 M. Garmuvienė 'Gerbiamoji redakcija!' (Dear Editors!), *Tarybinė moteris* 2 (1958), 13.
86 E. Matuzevičius, 'Meilę reikia branginti ir saugoti!' (Love Must Be Cherished and Protected!), *Jaunimo gretos* 7 (1955), 19.
87 V. Petkevičius, 'Jūsų žodis, Viktorai!' (Your Message to Victoria), *Jaunimo gretos* 1 (1966).
88 Č. Grizickas, 'Jaunystės problemos' (Problems of Youth), *Mokslas ir gyvenimas* 10 (1966), 33.
89 A. Baltrūnienė, 'Ne, nefantazija' (No, It's not a Fantasy), *Jaunimo gretos* 8 (1963), 16.
90 K. Klimavičius, 'Meilė puošia žmogų' (Love Makes Us Beautiful), *Komjaunimo tiesa*, 25 March 1955.
91 N. Solovjovas, 'Meilė – tai jausmas, širdis ir protas' (Love Is a Feeling, Heart and Mind), *Komjaunimo tiesa*, 7 May 1957.
92 Kristin Roth-Ey, ' "Loose Girls" on the Lose?: Sex, Propaganda and the 1957 Youth Festival', in *Women in the Khrushchev Era*, ed. Melanie Illič, Susan E. Reid and Lynne Attwood (New York: Palgrave Macmillan, 2004), 81.
93 A. Levšinas, 'Apie šeimos laimę' (On Happiness in Marriage), *Komjaunimo tiesa*, 22 September 1956.
94 K. Daukšas, 'Dar apie šeimos patvarumą' (More on Marriage Stability), *Tiesa*, 15 July 1959. J. Baltušis, 'Baimės akys didelės' (Fear Has Big Eyes), *Tiesa*, 15 July 1959.
95 N. Putinaitė, *Nenutrūkusi styga: Prisitaikymas ir pasipriešinimas sovietų Lietuvoje* (Vilnius: Aidai, 2007).
96 J. Valiulytė, 'Ir meilės reikia mokytis' (Even Love Must Be Learnt), *Tarybinė moteris* 1 (1960), 9.
97 K. Daukšas, 'Apie šeimos patvarumą', *Tarybinė moteris* 10 (1959), 12.

98 Н. Н. Соловьев, Брак и семья сегодня (Marriage and Family Today) (Вильнюс: Минтис, 1977), 144. N. Solovjovas, *Meilė, santuoka ir šeima* (Vilnius: Valstybinė politinės ir mokslinės literatūros leidykla, 1958), 22.
99 Divorce case, 1955, LCSA, F. R.-808, Ap. 2, B. 293, L. 22.
100 'Kilnūs ir taurūs tarybinio žmogaus jausmai' (Noble and Innocent Feelings of the Soviet Person), *Tiesa*, 10 January 1960.
101 Ibid.
102 O. Poškienė, 'Tu ir santuoka' (Marriage and You), *Tarybinė moteris* 6 (1969), 10.
103 T. Stungurys, 'Vedybos – rimtas žingsnis' (Marriage Is a Serious Step), *Tarybinė moteris* 12 (1959), 12–13.
104 E. Levanienė, 'Berniukų ir mergaičių draugystė' (Friendship between Boys and Girls), *Tarybinė moteris* 11 (1954), 18.
105 G. Sabaliauskiatė, 'Tave aplankė meilė' (Love Visited You), *Švyturys* 14 (1964), 21.
106 M. Sluckis, 'Tegyvuoja gilus jausmas ir skaisti svajonė' (May Deep Feelings and Innocent Dreams Flourish), *Tiesa*, 13 December 1959.
107 Vladimir Shlapentokh, *Love, Marriage, and Friendship in the Soviet Union: Ideals and Practices* (New York: Praeger, 1984), 62. A. Mockus, 'Viskas apie meilę' (Everything on Love), *Jaunimo gretos* 12 (1965), 30.
108 Vladimir Shlapentokh, *Love, Marriage, and Friendship in the Soviet Union: Ideals and Practices* (New York: Praeger, 1984), 45.
109 Interview by author with Juzefa Aišmantienė, Vilnius, 2002.
110 Interview by author with Marytė Karpavičiūtė-Sadūnaitė, Vilnius, 2005.
111 M. Sluckis, 'Meilės ir fiziologiniai instinktai?' (Instincts of Love and Physiology), *Tiesa*, 18 October 1959. I. Sodaitytė, 'Nepinkime meilei vainikų' (Let's Not Make Wreaths for Love), *Tiesa*, 29 November 1959. 'Kilnūs ir taurūs tarybinio žmogaus jausmai', *Tiesa*, 10 January 1960. Josephine Woll, *Real Images: Soviet Cinema and the Thaw* (London: I. B. Tauris, 2000), 32.
112 Interview by author with Aldona Kvedarienė, 2002.
113 Melanie Ilič, Susan E. Reid and Lynne Attwood, eds. *Women in the Khrushchev Era* (New York: Palgrave Macmillan, 2004), 12.
114 J. Riurikovas, 'Mįslingiausias jausmas' (The Most Mysterious Emotion), *Jaunimo gretos* 1 (1969), 25, 30–1.
115 I. Butautienė, 'Dar apie šeimos židinį' (More on the Family Hearth), *Tarybinė moteris* 7 (1959), 13.
116 M. Stern and A. Stern, *Sex in the USSR* (New York: Times Books, 1980), 97, 100.
117 V. Gaidys, *Visuomenės pagalba šeimai: Praktika ir problemos* (Public Assistance to Families: Applications and Problems) (Vilnius: Lietuvos TSR Žinijos draugija, 1984), 6, 14.
118 Kastytis Vijūnas, 'Nakties laiškai' (Letters at Night), *Tarybinė moteris* 8 (1985), 21.

119 Vladimir Shlapentokh, *Love, Marriage, and Friendship in the Soviet Union: Ideals and Practices* (New York: Praeger, 1984), 55.
120 Alina Zvinklienė, 'The State of Family Studies in Lithuania', *Marriage and Family Review* 22, no. 3 (1996), 223.
121 Deborah A. Field, 'Everyday Life and the Problem of Conceptualizing Public and Private during the Khrushchev Era', in *Everyday Life in Russia: Past and Present*, ed. Chatterjee, Choi, David L. Ransel, Mary Cavender and Karen Petrone (Bloomington: Indiana University Press, 2015), 106. Sue Bridger, 'Young Women and Presetroika', in *Women and Society in Russia and the Soviet Union*, ed. Linda Edmondson (Cambridge: Cambridge University Press, 1990), 179.
122 A. Grigonis, 'Jaunos šeimos istorija' (The Story of a Young Family), *Komjaunimo tiesa*, 25 September 1946.
123 Ibid.
124 *Tarybinė moteris* 12 (1960), 10.
125 Н. Н. Соловьев, Брак и семья сегодня (Marriage and Family Today) (Вильнюс: Минтис, 1977), 102.
126 Ibid., 154, 160.
127 A. Žvinklienė and R. Savulionienė, 'Kodėl kuriamos šeimos' (Why We Form Families), in *Žvilgnsis į šeimą* (A Look at Families) (Vilnius: Lietuvos mokslų akademija, 1990), 25.
128 T. A. Ždanko, ed., *Semejnyj byt narodov CCCR* (Moskva: Nauka, 1990), 10.
129 Н. Н. Соловьев, Брак и семья сегодня (Marriage and Family Today) (Вильнюс: Минтис, 1977), 107. Angelė Vyšniauskaitė, Petras Kalnius and Rasa Paukštytė-Šaknienė, eds, *Lietuvių šeima ir papročiai* (The Lithuanian Family and Its Traditions) (Vilnius: Mintis, 2008), 23. A. Žvinklienė, R. Savulionienė, 'Kodėl kuriamos šeimos' (Why We Form Families), in *Žvilgsnis į šeimą* (A Look at Families) (Vilnius: Lietuvos mokslų akademija, 1990), 226.
130 'Koks turi būti tavo vyras' (What Kind of Husband Should You Choose?), *Tarybinė moteris* 12 (1956), 8.
131 R. Pauraitė, 'Būkite laimingi, Nijole ir Alfredai!' (Best Wishes, Nijolė and Alfredas!), *Komjaunimo tiesa*, 18 August 1964.
132 N. Indrašius, 'Už ko tekėti?' (Who Should I Marry?), *Švyturys* 8 (1966), 18–19.
133 Ibid.
134 'Kelias į šeimą' (Journey to Having a Family), *Jaunimo gretos* 5 (1967), 28–9.
135 A. Kancleris, 'Optimali žmona' (The Perfect Wife), *Jaunimo gretos* 2 (1970), 30–1. V. Pekelis, 'Meilės patarėjas' (The Love Adviser), *Mokslas ir technika* 1 (1970), 34–5.
136 Skyrybų ir alimentų išieškojimo byla (Case Seeking Divorce and Alimony), 1972, LCSA, F. R.-808, Ap. 2, L. 5, 32.

137 A. G. Kharchev and M. S. Matskovskii, 'Changing Family Roles and Marital Instability', in *Women, Work and Family in the Soviet Union*, ed. Gail W. Lapidus (New York: Routledge, 1982), 197.
138 Francine du Plessix Gray, *Soviet Women Walking the Tightrope* (New York: Doubleday, 1989), 54.
139 Peter H. Juviler, 'Cell Mutation in the Soviet Union: The Family', Final Report to National Council for Soviet and East European Research (New York: Columbia University Press, 1987), 11.
140 A. Žvinklienė, R. Savulionienė, 'Kodėl kuriamos šeimos' (Why We Form Families), in *Žvilgsnis į šeimą* (A Look at Families) (Vilnius: Lietuvos mokslų akademija, 1990), 22.
141 Ibid., 26.
142 A. Alekseičikas, 'Optimistinis žvilgsnis į šeimą' (An Optimistic Look at the Family), No. 11 (1981), 14.
143 M. Stern and A. Stern, *Sex in the USSR* (New York: Times Books, 1980), 104. Н. Н. Соловьев, Брак и семья сегодня (Marriage and Family Today) (Вильнюс: Минтис, 1977), 57–8.
144 *Законы о разводе православного и неправославного исповедания* (Moscow, 1909), 258.
145 V. Andriulis, 'Santuokos nutraukimas ir jos pripažinimas negaliojančia senojoje Lietuvos teisėje' (The Annulment of Marriage and the Recognition of Its Invalidity in Early Lithuanian Law), *Socialistinė teisė* 1 (1975), 57.
146 *Vyriausybės žinios*, 15 August 1940, 621.
147 Pranas Dičius, *Santuoka ir šeima Tarybų Lietuvoje* (Marriage and Family in Soviet Lithuania) (Vilnius: Minties leidykla, 1974), 17.
148 Divorce case of V. M. and O. V., LCSA, F. R.-808, Ap. 2, B. 5, L. 1.
149 Divorce case of Vladisalva A. and Vladas A., 1945, LCSA, F. R.-808, Ap. 2, B. 3, L. 19.
150 Divorce case, 1956, LCSA. F. R.-808, Ap. 2, B. 382, L. 17.
151 Divorce case of Genovefa K. and Aleksas K., 1965, LCSA, F. R.-808, Ap. 2, B. 1354, L. 11.
152 Dovilė Sagatienė, 'Sovietinių teismų atkūrimas ir raida Lietuvoje 1944–1956 metais' (The Founding of the Soviet Courts and Their Development in Lithuania 1944–56), *Socialinių Mokslų Studijos* 5, no. 1 (2013), 195.
153 Case regarding return of child's custody to the mother, 1962–63, LCSA F. R.-808, Ap. 2, B. 1038.
154 Lietuvos Tarybų Socialistinė Respublikos Aukščiausiosios tarybos įsakas dėl veikiančių Lietuvos TSR teritorijoje *Santuokos, šeimos ir globos įstatymų kodekso* ir *Civilinio proceso kodekso* pakeitimų (Order of the Supreme Soviet of the LSSR on Amendments to the Code of Marriage, Family and Custody Laws and the Code

of Civil Procedure Operating in the Territory of the LSSR), *LTSR Aukščiausiosios Tarybos ir Vyriausybės žinio*, 5.
155 Olga Khazova, 'Marriage and Divorce Law in Russia and the Baltic States: Overview of Recent Changes', in *And They Lived Happily Ever After: Norms and Everyday Practices of Family and Parenthood in Russia and Eastern Europe*, ed. Helene Carlback, Youlia Gradskova and Zhanna Kravchenko (Budapest: CEU Press, 2012).
156 Divorce case of Vladas K. and Otilija K., 1944, LCSA, F. R.-808, Ap. 2, B. 5, L. 39.
157 Dovilė Sagatienė, 'Sovietinių teismų atkūrimas ir raida Lietuvoje 1944–1956 metais' (Re-establishing the Soviet Courts and Their Development in Lithuania), *Socialinių Mokslų Studijos* 5, no. I (2013), 199, 207.
158 Divorce case of Kazimiera G. and Steponas G., LCSA, F. R.-808, Ap. 2, B. 499, L. 2. 1956-7
159 Dovilė Sagatienė, 'Sovietinių teismų atkūrimas ir raida Lietuvoje 1944–1956 metais' (The Founding of the Soviet Courts and Their Development in Lithuania 1944–56), *Socialinių Mokslų Studijos* 5, no. 1 (2013), 197, 207.
160 Divorce case, LCSA, F. R.-808, Ap. 2, B. 55, L. 20. 1946.
161 Divorce case, 1955-6, LCSA, F. R.-808, Ap. 2, B. 382, L. 48, 49.
162 'Dėl TSRS Aukščiausiosios Tarybos Prezidiumo 1965 m. gruodžio 10 d. Įsako "Dėl Tam Tikro Ištuokos Bylų Teisminio Nagrinėjimo Tvarkos Pakeitimo"' (On the Presidium of the Supreme Soviet of the USSR on the Orders of 10 December 1965 'On a Certain Change in Procedure for Legal Proceedings in Divorce Cases'), *LTSR Aukščiausiosios Tarybos ir Vyriausybės žinios*, 30 November 1966, 459, 461.
163 "Dėl *Lietuvos TSR Santuokos ir Šeimos Kodekso* Įsigaliojimo Tvarkos' (On the Procedure for Implementing the Marriage and Family Code of the LSSR), *LTSR Aukščiausiosios Tarybos ir Vyriausybės žinios*, 10 December 1969, 604.
164 "Dėl *Civilinės Metrikacijos Instrukcijos* Patvirtinimo' (On the Ratification of the Civil Registry Guidelines Law), *LTSR Aukščiausiosios Tarybos ir Vyriausybės žinios*, 20 February 1970, 79.
165 Dalia Leinarte, *The Lithuanian Family in its European Context, 1800–1914: Marriage, Divorce and Flexible Communities* (London: Palgrave Macmillan, 2017), 158.
166 Divorce case, LCSA, F. R.-808, Ap. 2, B. 106, L. 1.
167 LTSR Aukščiausiojo teismo civilinių bylų teisminės kolegijos I instancijos eigos knyga, 1947 m. (Book of Proceedings of the First Instance of the Judicial Chamber of Civil Cases of the LSSR Supreme Court, 1947), LCSA, F. R.-808, Ap. 2, B. 20.
168 LTSR Aukščiausiojo teismo civilinių bylų teisminės kolegijos I instancijos eigos knyga, 25 February 1948–6 January 1949 (Book of Proceedings of the First Instance of the Judicial Chamber of Civil Cases of the LSSR Supreme Court), LCSA, F. R.-808, Ap. 2, B. 49.

169 Data are from the LCSA, F. R.-808, Ap. 2, B. 456, 468, 483, 494, 504, 510, 515, 525, 534, 536, 543. LTSR Aukščiausiojo teismo civilinių bylų teisminės kolegijos I instancijos priimti sprendimai (First Instance Rulings on Civil Cases of the LSSR Supreme Court Judicial Chamber, 1957).

170 T. A. Ždanko, ed., *Semejnyj byt narodov CCCR* (Moskva: Nauka, 1990), 182.

171 В. А. Сысенко, *Устойчивость брака: проблемы, факторы, условия* (Москва: Финансы и статистика, 1981), 132.

172 V. Gaidys, 'Demografinės situacijos Lietuvoje bruožai' (Šeimos ir Santuokos Aspektai), *Žvilgsnis į šeimą* (Vilnius: Lietuvos mokslų akademija, 1990), 157.

173 Alina Žvinklienė, 'The State of Family Studies in Lithuania', *Marriage and Family Review* 22, no. 3, 222.

174 A. G. Kharchev and M. S. Matskovskii, 'Changing Family Roles and Marital Instability', in *Women, Work and Family in the Soviet Union*, ed. Gail W. Lapidus (New York: Routledge, 1982), 193. Pranas Dičius, *Santuoka ir Šeima Tarybų Lietuvoje* (Marriage and Family in Soviet Lithuania) (Vilnius: Minties leidykla, 1974), 183.

175 Н. Н. Соловьев, *Брак и семья сегодня* (Marriage and Family Today) (Вильнюс: Минтис, 1977), 115.

176 Peter H. Juviler, 'Cell Mutation in Soviet Society: The Family', Final Report to the National Council for Soviet and East European Research (New York: Columbia University Press, 1987), 49.

177 Divorce case of Vladas and Otilija K., 1945, LCSA, F. R.-808, Ap. 2, B. 5, L. 109.

178 Divorce case of M. V. and O. V., 1946, LCSA, F. R.-808, Ap. 2, B. 2, L. 43.

179 Divorce case, 1953, LCSA, F. R.-808, Ap. 2, B. 148, L. 154 and Divorce case, 1948, LCSA, F. R.-808, Ap. 2, B. 2, L. 153.

180 Divorce case, 1963–5, LCSA, F. R.-808, Ap. 2, B. 1321, L. 29.

181 Divorce case. LCSA, F. R.-808, Ap. 2, B. 2, p. 3.

182 Decree Regarding the Marriage, Family and Guardianship Code and Amendments to the Code of Civil Procedure in Effect on the Territory of the LSSR, *Lietuvos TSR Aukščiausiosios Tarybos Žinios*, 5 August 1946, 2.

183 Divorce case, 1961–2, LCSA, F. R.-808, Ap. 2. B. 942, L. 1.

184 Divorce case, 1954–5, LCSA, F. R.-808, Ap. 2, B. 264, L. 2.

185 Divorce case, 1960, LCSA, F. R.-808, Ap. 2, B. 795, L. 30.

186 Divorce case of Jonas and Elena K., 1957–8, LCSA, F. R.-808, Ap. 2, B. 591, L. 3.

187 Polygamy case, 1956–7, LCSA, F. R.-808, Ap. 2, B. 497, L. 14.

188 Marriage determined to be invalid, 1957–8, LCSA, F. R.-808, Ap. 2, B. 591, L. 58.

189 Divorce case, 1953, LCSA, F. R.-808, Ap. 2, B. 141, L. 57.

190 Divorce case of V. K. and O. K., 1944, LCSA, F. R.-808, Ap. 2, B. 5, L. 26.

191 Divorce case, LCSA, F. R.-808, Ap. 2, B. 379, L. 148.

192 Divorce case, LCSA, F. R.-808, Ap. 2, B. 179, L. 45.

193 Divorce case of P. and E. P., 1961, LCSA, F. R.-808, Ap. 2, B. 891, L. 4
194 Divorce case, 1954, LCSA, F. R.-808, Ap. 2, B. 179, L. 47.
195 Divorce case, 1961, LCSA, F. R.-808, Ap. 2, B. 891, L. 9.
196 Divorce case, 1964–5, LCSA, F. R.-808, Ap. 2, B. 1212, L. 40.
197 Dalia Leinarte, *Adopting and Remembering Soviet Reality: Life Stories of Lithuanian Women, 1945–1970* (Amsterdam: Rodopi, 2010), 77.
198 Divorce case of Antosė O., 1950, LCSA, F. R.-808, Ap. 2, B. 111, L. 30
199 Divorce case, 1957, LCSA, F. R.-808, Ap. 2, B. 490, L. 39.
200 Divorce case, 1964, LCSA, F. R.-808, Ap. 2, B. 1308.
201 Н. Н. Соловьев, *Брак и семья сегодня* (Marriage and Family Today) (Вильнюс: Минтис, 1977), 121.
202 Divorce case, 1963, LCSA, F. R.-808, Ap. 2, B. 1130, L. 2
203 Ibid.
204 'Dėl kovos su girtavimu sustiprinimu ir dėl prekybos stipriausiais svaiginamaisiais gėrimais sutvarkymo' (On the Intensified Battle with Drunkenness and the Regulation of Commerce of Strong, Intoxicating Alcoholic Beverages), *LTSR Aukščiausiosios Tarybos ir Vyriausybės žinios*, 1 February 1959, 40. 'Dėl kovos su girtavimu sustiprinimo' (On the Intensified Battle with Drunkenness), *LTSR Aukščiausiosios Tarybos ir Vyriausybės žinios*, 20 June 1961, 183. 'Dėl piktybinių girtuoklių (alkoholikų)' (On the Treatment of Alcoholics and Drug Addicts), *LTSR Aukščiausiosios Tarybos ir Vyriausybės žinios*, 31 August 1966, 445. "Dėl priemonių kovai su girtavimu ir alkoholizmu sustiprinti' (On the Improved Methods in the Battle with Drunkenness and Alcoholism), *LTSR Aukščiausiosios Tarybos ir Vyriausybės žinios*, 10 July 1972, 141.
205 Divorce case of Elena and Nikodemas M., 1956, LCSA, F. R.-808, Ap. 2, B. 361, L. 17, 37.
206 V. Gaidys, *Visuomenės pagalba šeimai. Praktika ir problemos* (Vilnius: Lietuvos TSR Žinijos draugija, 1984), 5.
207 Сысенко Виктор, *Супружеские конфликты* (Москва: Финансы и статистика, 1983), 62.
208 Divorce case, 1955, LCSA, F. R.-808, Ap. 2, B.356, L. 1. Divorce case, 1956–7, LCSA, F. R.-808, Ap. 2, B. 498, L. 2. Divorce case of Mečislovas V. and Ona V., 1944, LCSA, F. R.-808, Ap. 2, B. 5, L. 19.
209 Divorce case, 1953, LCSA, F. R.-808, Ap. 2, B. 141, L. 21. Divorce case, 1950, LCSA, F. R.-808, Ap. 2, B. 114, L. 2.
210 Divorce case of Algirdas P. and Juzė P., 1953, LCSA, F. R.-808, Ap. 2, B. 139, L. 27.
211 'Dėl kovos su venerinėmis ligomis stiprinimo' (On the Intensifying the Battle against Venereal Diseases), *LTSR Aukščiausiosios Tarybos ir Vyriausybės žinios*, 9 February 1967, 71.
212 Divorce case, 1955, LCSA, F. R.-808, Ap. 2, B. 267, L. 13.

213 Divorce case, 1958, LCSA, F. R.-808, Ap. 2, B. 649, L. 14.
214 Divorce case of Motiejus Š. And Ona-Elžbieta Š.'s, 1945, LCSA, F. R.-808, Ap. 2, B. 7, L. 1.
215 Divorce case of Z. Š. and K. Š., 1944, LCSA, F. R.-808, Ap. 2, B. 1, L. 1.
216 Divorce case, 1961–2, LCSA, F. R.-808, Ap. 2, B. 942, L. 26.
217 Divorce case of Bronė K. and Balys K., 1947, LCSA, F. R.-808, Ap. 2, B. 26, L. 1.
218 Divorce case, 1949, LCSA, F. R.-808, Ap. 2, B. 106, L. 2.
219 Divorce case, 1964–5, LCSA, F. R.-808, Ap. 2, B. 1224, L. 38.
220 Divorce case of Stanislava P., LCSA, F. R.-808, Ap. 2, B. 1186, L. 42., 1964.
221 Divorce case, 1954 LCSA, F. R.-808, Ap. 2, B. 174, L. 63. Divorce case of Mykolas R. and Elena R., 1964, LCSA, F. R.-808, Ap. 2, B. 1273 L. 1.
222 Divorce case of Asta G. -K., 1963, LCSA, F. R.-808, Ap. 2, B. 1064, L. 1.
223 Case regarding division of living space, 1979–80, LCSA, F. R.-808, Ap. 2, B. 1611, L. 3, 255.
224 Dalia Leinarte, *The Lithuanian Family in Its European Context, 1800–1914: Marriage, Divorce and Flexible Communities* (London: Palgrave Macmillan, 2017), 41–4.
225 Paternity test case, 1973–4, LCSA, F. R.-808, Ap. 2, B. 1491, L. 1.
226 Paternity case, 1975–6, LCSA, F. R.-808, Ap. 2, B. 1520, L. 132.
227 Paternity case, 1978–80, LCSA, F. R.-808, Ap. 2, B. 1598, L. 91, 208.
228 Paternity and alimony case, 1976–7, LCSA, F. R.-808, Ap. 2, B. 1551, L. 2.
229 Paternity and alimony case, 1973–4, LCSA, F. R.-808, Ap. 2, B. 1481, L. 43.
230 Case regarding refusal of paternity, 1975–6, LCSA, F. R.-808, Ap. 2, B. 1520, L. 2, 124.
231 Alina Zvinklienė, 'The State of Family Studies in Lithuania', *Marriage and Family Review* 22, no. 3, 223.
232 Paternity case, 1974–3, LCSA, F. R.-808, Ap. 2, B. 1486, L. 144.
233 Paternity case, 1971–2, LCSA, F. R.-808, Ap. 2, B. 1442, L. 205.
234 Paternity case, 1952, LCSA, F. R.-808, Ap. 2, B. 462, L. 13.
235 Case regarding the removal of paternity in the records, 1969–70, LCSA, F. R.-808, Ap. 2, B. 1413, L. 109.
236 Divorce case, 1964, LCSA, F. R.-808, Ap. 2, B. 1164, L. 36.
237 'Dėl Santuokos, šeimos ir globos įstatymo kodekso, galiojančio LTSR teritorijoje, pakeitimo' (On the Changes to the Marriage, Family and Guardianship Code in Effect in the Territory of the LSSR), *LTSR Aukščiausiosios Tarybos ir Vyriausybės žinios*, 31 October 1966, 428.
238 Withdrawal of alimony for ex-wife, 1956, LCSA, F. R.-808, Ap. 2, B. 431, L. 26, 66.
239 Alimony case, 1961–2, LCSA, F. R.-808, Ap. 2, B. 957, L. 40.
240 Divorce case of Adelė S. and Bronislovas S., 1948, LCSA, F. R.-808, Ap. 2, B. 40, L. 3.

241 Inheritance case, 1946, LCSA, F. R.-808, Ap. 2, B. 24, L. 31.
242 Inheritance case, 1951–5, LCSA, F. R.-808, Ap. 2, B. 295, L. 38.
243 Court of first instance decisions of civil cases, 1987, LCSA, F. R.-808, Ap. 2, B. 1729, L. 3.
244 Divorce and division of marital property case, 1981, LCSA, F. R.-808, Ap. 2, B. 1635, L. 235.
245 Divorce and return of custody case, 1958, LCSA, F. R.-808, Ap. 2, B. 608, L. 213.
246 On exchanging rooms, 1953, LCSA, F. R.-808, Ap. 2, B. 147, L. 58.
247 Division of property after divorce, 1981–2, LCSA, F. R.-808, Ap. 2, B. 1633, L. 23.
248 Divorce case, 1964, LCSA, F. R.-808, Ap. 2, B. 1247, L. 28.
249 Divorce and division of marital property case of Albertas B. and Vanda B, 1969, LCSA, F. R.-808, Ap. 2, B. 1405, L. 2.
250 Division of living space case, 1980–1, LCSA, F. R.-808, Ap. 2, B. 1618, L. 117.
251 Division of living space case, 1980–1, LCSA, F. R.-808, Ap. 2, B. 1618, L. 208.
252 Divorce case, 1961–2, LCSA, F. R.-808, Ap. 2, B. 937, L. 4.

3 Parents and their children

1 E. E. Novikova, V. S. Iazykova and Z. A. Iankova, 'Women's Work and the Family', in *Women, Work and Family in the Soviet Union*, ed. Gail W. Lapidus (New York: Routledge, 1982), 180.
2 Н. Н. Соловьев, *Брак и семья сегодня* (Marriage and Family Today) (Вильнюс: Минтис, 1977), 41.
3 Qtd in Aušra Steckienė, 'Šeimos politikos pokyčiai Lietuvoje pereinant iš socializmo į kapitalizmą' (Changes in Family Policy in Lithuania's Transition from Socialism to Capitalism) (Master's Thesis, Vilnius University, 2008), 21.
4 Alina Zvinklienė, 'The State of Family Studies in Lithuania', *Marriage and Family* 22 no. 3 (2010), 203–32, 223, 226.
5 Zillah Eisenstein, 'Eastern European Male Democracies', in *Gender Politics and Post-Communism: Reflections from Eastern Europe and the Former Soviet Union*, ed. Nanette Funk and Magda Mueller (New York: Routledge, 1993), 308. Sarah Ashwin, 'Gender, State and Society in Soviet and Post-Soviet Russia', in *Gender, State and Society in Soviet and Post-Soviet Russia*, ed. Sarah Ashwin (New York: Routledge, 2000), 10. Lynne Haney, *Inventing the Needy: Gender and the Politics of Welfare in Hungary* (Berkeley: University of California Press, 2002), 33.
6 K. Kovas 'Moterys įsitraukia į visuomeninį darbą' (Women Entering the Workplace), *Tarybų Lietuva*, 9 October 1945.
7 Lietuvos Tarybų Socialistinės Respublikos Ministrų Tarybos potvarkis *Dėl tėvų atleidimo nuo mokesčio už vaiko išlaikymą, kai jis nelanko vaikų įstaigų eilinių tėvo*

atostogų metu (Resolution of the Council of Ministers of the LSSR on Exemptions from Child Support for Fathers While Their Child Is Not Attending Childcare Institutions during Paternity Leave), *LTSR Aukščiausiosios Tarybos ir Vyriausybės žinios*, 10 June 1970, 112–13.

8. V. Gaidys, *Visuomenės pagalba šeimai: Praktika ir problemos* (Social Assistance to Families: Practice and Problems) (Vilnius: Lietuvos TSR Žinijos draugija, 1984), 3.

9. V. Aksomaitis, 'Kada Vilniuje bus įrengtas vaikų miestelis?' (When Will the Children's Village Open in Vilnius?), *Komjaunimo tiesa*, 5 August 1951.

10. L. Veržbavičius, 'Motinystės ir vaikystės globa Tarybų valstybėje' (Care for Mothers and Children in the Soviet State), *Tiesa*, 8 July 1945.

11. 'Tavo laisvalaikio valandos' (Your Leisure Time) (reprinted from the newspaper *Komsomolskaya pravda*) *Komjaunimo tiesa*, 5 August 1960.

12. 'Dėl priemonių mokykloms-internatams vystyti 1959–1965 metais' (On the Methods for Developing the Boarding Schools for the Needy from 1959 to 1965), *Tiesa*, 29 May 1959.

13. 'Dėl *respublikinių mokyklų-internatų*' (On the Republic's Boarding Schools for the Needy), LTSR Švietimo ministerijos įsakymas dėl metodinės komisijos sudarymo (LSSR Ministry of Education decree on Creating a Commission on Methods), 24 April 1978, 5.

14. *Mokymas ir auklėjimas internatinėse mokyklose* (Education and Upbringing in the Boarding Schools) (Kaunas: Šviesa, 1971), 68.

15. Lietuvos Tarybų Socialistinės Respublikos Ministrų Tarybos potvarkis *Dėl mokesčio ėmimo už auklėtinių išlaikymą mokyklose internatuose sutvarkymo* (Resolution of the Council of Ministers of the LSSR on the Issuing of Fees for Room and Board of Pupils Attending Boarding Schools for the Needy), *LTSR Aukščiausiosios Tarybos ir Vyriausybės žinios*, 30 October 1973, 279–80.

16. *Mokyklų-internatų vidaus tvarkos taisyklės auklėtiniams* (Boarding School Disciplinary Rules for Students) (Vilnius: RSFSR santuokos, šeimos ir globos kodeksas, Švietimo Misterija, 1962), 25, 22, 21, 20, 19.

17. *Jie-savo mokyklos-internato šeimininkai* (They Are the Directors of Their Own Boarding School) (Vilnius: Laikraščių ir Žurnalų Leidykla, 1966), 41.

18. *Apie auklėjimą mokyklose-internatuose ir vaikų namuose* (On Education at the Boarding Schools for the Needy and Orphanages) (Kaunas: Valstybinė Pedagoginė Literatūros Leidykla, 1960), 9, 14–15.

19. *Mokymas ir auklėjimas internatinėse mokyklose* (Education and Upbringing in the Boarding Schools) (Kaunas: Šviesa, 1971), 58.

20. *Jie-savo mokyklos-internato šeimininkai* (They Are the Directors of Their Own Boarding School) (Vilnius: Laikraščių ir Žurnalų Leidykla, 1966), 9.

21. Interview by author with Rūta Skatikaite, 2001, Vilnius University LSC Women's Memories Archive.

22 Dalia Leinarte, *Adopting and Remembering Soviet Reality: Life Stories of Lithuanian Women, 1945–1970* (Amsterdam: Rodopi, 2010), 177.
23 T. A. Ždanko, ed., *Semejnyj byt narodov CCCR* (Moskva: Nauka, 1990), 187.
24 M. Kaniauskas, 'Ką davė Tarybų valdžia moterims?' (What Did the Soviet Government Give Women?), *Tiesa*, 10 January 1946.
25 'Tavo laisvalaikio valandos' (Your Leisure Time) (reprinted from the newspaper *Komsomolskaja pravda*) *Komjaunimo tiesa*, 5 August 1960.
26 A.Ваržgalys and P. Mikuckas, 'Kad moteriai nereikėtų užsidaryti virtuvėje' (So Women Wouldn't Have to Hide in the Kitchen), *Tiesa*, 25 February 1960.
27 Ibid.
28 Barbar Alpern Engel, *Women in Russia: 1700–2000* (Cambridge, UK: Cambridge University Press, 2004), 237–8.
29 A. Petrauskas, 'Kolūkietės-motinos laukia sezoninių vaikų lopšelių' (Collective Farm Worker and Mother Awaits Seasonal Daycare for her Children), *Tiesa*, 23 June 1954.
30 T. A. Ždanko, ed., *Semejnyj byt narodov CCCR* (Moskva: Nauka, 1990), 187.
31 Resolution of the LSSR Council of Ministers, *Dėl Lietuvos TSR ministerijų ir žinybų vaikų darželių tipinių etatų patvirtinimo* (On the Management of LSSR Ministry and Company Kindergarten Staff), *LTSR Aukščiausiosios Tarybos ir Vyriausybės žinios*, 30 June 1958, 139.
32 Interview with Natalija J., 2001, Vilnius University LSC Women's Memories Archive.
33 T. A. Ždanko, ed., *Semejnyj byt narodov CCCR* (Moskva: Nauka, 1990), 187.
34 *Pagrindiniai 1989 metų gyventojų surašymo duomenys* (Essential Data from the 1989 Census) (Vilnius: Lietuvos Valstybinis Statistikos Komitetas, 1990), 13.
35 Francine du Plessix Gray, *Soviet Women Walking the Tightrope* (New York: Doubleday, 1989), 38.
36 Yulia Gradskova and Ildikó Asztalos Morell, eds, *Gendering Post-socialism: Old Legacies and New Hierarchies* (Global Gender) (London: Routledge, 2018), 4.
37 T. A. Ždanko, ed., *Semejnyj byt narodov CCCR* (Moskva: Nauka, 1990), 188.
38 Donald Filtzer, *Workers and De-Stalinization* (Cambridge: Cambridge University Press, 1992), 31. Lynne Haney, *Inventing the Needy: Gender and the Politics of Welfare in Hungary* (Berkeley: University of California Press, 2002), 66.
39 Dalia Leinarte, *Adopting and Remembering Soviet Reality. Life Stories of Lithuanian Women, 1945–1970* (Amsterdam: Rodopi, 2010), 149.
40 Ibid., 98.
41 Interview with Rūta Skatikaitė, 2001, Vilnius University LSC Women's Memories Archive.
42 G. Dovydaitė, 'Ką pasakoja moterys' (What Do Women Tell Us?), *Kalba Vilnius* 41 (1970), 15.

43 Interview with G. M., 2004, Vilnius University LSC Women's Memories Archive.
44 'Jūsų Jūratė. Ne vien prie lopšio' (Your Jūratė: Not Just a Mummy), *Kalba Vilnius* 15 (1968). On latchkey kids, see Barbara Alpern Engel, *Women in Russia: 1700–2000* (Cambridge, UK: Cambridge University Press, 2004), 237.
45 Interview with Natalija J., 2001, Vilnius University LSC Women's Memories Archive.
46 Interview with Janina Žižienė, 2003, Vilnius University LSC Women's Memories Archive.
47 Interview with Elena Steponavičienė, 2003, Vilnius University LSC Women's Memories Archive.
48 Interview with Petronelė-Aldona Adomaitienė, 2001, Vilnius University LSC Women's Memories Archive.
49 Donald Filtzer, *Workers and De-Stalinization* (Cambridge, UK: Cambridge University Press, 1992), 62.
50 Donald Filtzer, 'Women Workers in the Khrushchev Era', in *Women in the Khrushchev Era*, ed. Melanie Ilič, Susan E. Reid and Lynne Attwood (New York: Palgrave Macmillan, 2004), 44.
51 Interview with Angelika Grikšienė, 2001, Vilnius University LSC Women's Memories Archive.
52 Interview with Viktorija Varganienė, 2004, Vilnius University LSC Women's Memories Archive.
53 Dalia Leinarte, *Adopting and Remembering Soviet Reality: Life Stories of Lithuanian Women, 1945–1970* (Amsterdam: Rodopi, 2010), 31.
54 Ibid., 32.
55 'Dėl *respublikinių mokyklų-internatų*' (On the Republic's Boarding Schools for the Needy), LTSR Švietimo ministerijos įsakymas dėl metodinės komisijos sudarymo (LSSR Ministry of Education decree on Creating a Commission on Methods), 24 April 1978, 7–8.
56 Interview with Brone Sopienė, 2003, Vilnius University LSC Women's Memories Archive.
57 '…Ir apie vyro laiką' (… And Now Let's Talk About Men's Time), *Tarybinė moteris* 6 (1966), 4–5.
58 Vladimir Shlapentokh, *Love, Marriage and Friendship in the Soviet Union: Ideals and Practices* (New York: Praeger, 1984), 191.
59 Lynne Haney, *Inventing the Needy: Gender and the Politics of Welfare in Hungary* (Berkeley: University of California Press, 2002), 66.
60 Interview with Elena Steponavičienė, 2001, Vilnius University LSC Women's Memories Archive.
61 For more on women's conflict between state jobs and family responsibilities, see Vladimir Shlapentokh, *Love, Marriage, and Friendship in the Soviet Union: Ideals*

and Practices (New York: Praeger, 1984), 176–8 and Lynne Attwood, 'Housing in the Khrushchev Era', in *Women in the Khrushchev Era*, ed. Melanie Ilič, Susan E. Reid and Lynne Attwood (New York: Palgrave Macmillan, 2004), 195. Donald Filtzer, 'Women Workers in the Khrushchev Era', in ibid., 44.

62 Marianne Liljeström, Arja Rosenholm and Irina Savkina, eds, *Models of Selves: Russian Women's Autobiographical Texts* (Helsinki: Kikimora Publikation, 2000), 94. See also Barbara Alpern Engel and Anastasia Posadskya-Vanderbeck, eds, *A Revolution of Their Own: Voices of Women in Soviet History* (Boulder, CO: Westview Press, 1998) .

63 Dalia Leinarte, *Adopting and Remembering Soviet Reality: Life Stories of Lithuanian Women, 1945–1970* (Amsterdam: Rodopi, 2010).

64 Comsomol/Komsomol, the All-Union Leninist Young Communist League (Russian: Всесоюзный ленинский коммунистический союз молодёжи (ВЛКСМ) was a political youth organization in the Soviet Union established in every Soviet republic, including LSSR.

65 Divorce case, 1958, LCSA, F. R.-808, Ap. 2, B. 619. L. 59. Divorce case, 1953, LCSA, F. R.-808, Ap. 2, B. 141, L. 43.

66 Divorce case of Povilas and Elena M., 1948, LCSA, F. R.-808, Ap. 2, B. 27, L. 2. Divorce case, 1953, LCSA, F. R.-808, Ap. 2, B. 141, L. 1. Divorce case, 1962–3, LCSA, F. R.-808, Ap. 2, B. 1034, L. 17, 18.

67 Divorce case of M. and O.-E. Š., 1945, LCSA, F. R.-808, Ap. 2, B. 7, L. 2.

68 Divorce case, 1969, LCSA, F. R.-808, Ap. 2, B. 1405, L. 16.

69 Divorce case of Romualdas and Danutė P., 1956, LCSA, F. R.-808, Ap. 2, B. 379, L. 23.

70 Child custody case, 1968, LCSA, F. R.-808, Ap. 2, B. 1402, L. 124.

71 Divorce case, 1950, LCSA, F. R.-808, Ap. 2, B. 115, L. 36.

72 Divorce case, 1962–3, LCSA, F. R.-808, Ap. 2, B. 1056, L. 2. Divorce case, 1962–3, LCSA, F. R.-808, Ap. 2, B. 1018, L. 22. Case regarding revocation of custody, 1962–3, LCSA, F. R.-808, Ap. 2, B. 1038, L. 37.

73 Case regarding payment of child support, 1948, LCSA, F. R.-808, Ap. 2, B. 23, L. 79.

74 P. Skaisgiris, 'Dėl teisminės praktikos, išieškant alimentus nepilnamečiams vaikams išlaikyti' (On Judicial Practice in Recovering Child Support for Minor Children), *Socialistinė teisė* 2 (1969), 24.

75 'Dėl *Lietuvos TSR teritorijoje veikiančio Santuokos, šeimos ir globos įstatymų kodekso pakeitimų*' (On the Changes to the Marriage, Family and Guardianship Code of Laws in Effect in the LSSR Territory), *LTSR Aukščiausiosios Tarybos ir Vyriausybės žinios*, 12 February 1954, 2.

76 Extension of child support case, 1973, LCSA, F. R.-808, Ap. 2, B. 1470, L. 1.

77 Ikimokyklinių vaikų įstaigų–lopšelio-darželio nuostatai' (Pre-school Institution–Creche Kindergarten Regulations *LTSR Aukščiausiosios Tarybos ir Vyriausybės žinios*, 20 February 1961, 135–6.
78 Н. Н. Соловьев, *Брак и семья сегодня* (Marriage and Family Today) (Вильнюс: Минтис, 1977), 128.
79 Ibid. Nutarimas *Dėl alimentų vaikams išlaikyti išieškojimo respublikoje*, 21 July 1967 (Resolution on Recovery of Child Support in the Republic), *LTSR Aukščiausiosis Tarybos ir Vyriausybės žinios*, 30 April 1970, 234.
80 P. Skaisgiris, 'Dėl teisminės praktikos, išieškant alimentus nepilnamečiams vaikams išlaikyti' (On Legal Practice in Recovering Child Support), *Socialistinė teisė* 2 (1969), 234. Nutarimas *Dėl alimentų vaikams išlaikyti išieškojimo respublikoje*, 21 July 1967 (Resolution on Recovery of Child Support in the Republic), *LTSR Aukščiausiosios Tarybos ir Vyriausybės žinios*, 30 April 1970, 23, 24.
81 Ibid., 3.
82 Divorce case, 1957, LCSA, F. R.-808, Ap. 2, B. 530, L. 1.
83 Divorce case, 1964–5, LCSA, F. R.-808, Ap. 2, B. 1216, L. 32.
84 Alimony case, 1967–9, LCSA, F. R.-808, Ap. 2, B. 1400, L. 53.
85 Alina Zvinkliene, 'The State of Family Studies in Lithuania', *Marriage and Family Review* 22 no. 3 (2010), 223, 217.
86 T. A. Ždanko, ed., *Semejnyj byt narodov CCCR* (Moskva: Nauka, 1990), 168.

4 Household

1 Dalia Leinarte, *Adopting and Remembering Soviet Reality: Life Stories of Lithuanian Women, 1945–1970* (Amsterdam: Rodopi, 2010), 68.
2 Lina Būgienė, 'Pokario Vilnius jo gyventojų akimis (I)' (Post-war Vilnius as Seen by Its Residents), *Literatūra ir meanas*, 10 January 2020. See also, 'Didis rūpinimasis liaudies gerove', *Komunistas* 8 (1957), 3.
3 Dalia Leinarte, *Adopting and Remembering Soviet Reality: Life Stories of Lithuanian Women, 1945–1970* (Amsterdam: Rodopi, 2010), 69.
4 Case regarding eviction from one's apartment, 1948, LCSA, F. R.-808, Ap. 2, B. 48, L. 16.
5 Case regarding eviction from one's apartment, 1958, LCSA, F. R.-808, Ap. 2, B. 731, L. 1.
6 Vietų bendrabučiuose suteikimo ir sąlygų jomis naudotis nuostatai (Rules for Distributing Dormitory Rooms and Conditions for Their Use), in *LTSR Aukščiausiosios Tarybos ir Vyriausybės žinios*, 30 April 1966, 167.
7 Marija Drėmaitė, 'Apdovanotieji: masinė gyvenamoji architektūra ir sovietiniai architektūriniai apdovanojimai' (Prizewinners: Mass Produced Architecture and

Soviet Architectural Prizes), in *Masinės statybos gyvenamųjų rajonų architektūra Lietuvoje*, ed. I. Nekrošius, V. Petrušonis and E. Riaubienė (Vilnius: VGTU leidykla Technika, 2017), 50.
8 Lina Būgienė, 'Pokario Vilnius jo gyventojų akimis (I)' (Post-war Vilnius as Seen by Its Residents), *Literatūra ir menas*, 10 January 2020.
9 I. Nekrošius, V. Petrušonis and E. Riaubienė, eds, *Masinės statybos gyvenamųjų rajonų architektūra Lietuvoje* (The Architecture of Mass-produced Residential Districts in Lithuania) (Vilnius: VGTU leidykla Technika, 2017), 10.
10 Donald Filtzer, *The Khrushchev Era. De-Stalinization and the Limits of Freedom of Reform in the USSR, 1953–1964* (London: Macmillan, 1993), 34.
11 Marija Drėmaitė, 'Apdovanotieji: masinė gyvenamoji architektūra ir sovietiniai architektūriniai apdovanojimai', in *Masinės statybos gyvenamųjų rajonų architektūra Lietuvoje*, ed. I. Nekrošius, V. Petrušonis and E. Riaubienė (Vilnius: VGTU leidykla Technika, 2017), 59. Viltė Janušauskaitė, 'Masinės statybos perlai-paveldas ar palikimas? (The Pearls of Mass Production: Heritage or Legacy?)' in ibid., 12, 13, 97. S. Butkus, S. Tomas and Matas Cirtautas, 'Daugiabučių gyvenamųjų grupių kompleksinio atnaujinimo metodika: Esamos būklės tyrimas' (Restoration Methods of Residential Apartment Building Complexes), in ibid., 84–105.
12 See chapters by Susan E. Reid ('Everyday Aesthetics in the Khrushchev-Era Standard Apartment', 204), and Deborah A. Field ('Everyday Life and the Problem of Conceptualizing Public and Private during the Khrushchev Era', 163–80) in *Everyday Life in Russia: Past and Present*, ed. Choi Chatterjee, David L. Ransel, Mary Cavender and Karen Petrone (Bloomington: Indiana University Press, 2015).
13 Pranas Dičius, *Santuoka ir šeima Tarybų Lietuvoje* (Marriage and Family in Soviet Lithuania) (Vilnius: Minties Leidykla, 1974), 65.
14 A. Cibas, *Kaip pradėti ir vykdyti asmeninę statybą* (How to Start and Complete Individual Construction Projects) (Vilnius: LTSR Ministrų Taryba, 1959), 13, 14, 19.
15 'Dėl individualinės statybos nuostatų patvirtinimo' (On Confirmation of the Regulations for Individual Construction) Resolution No. 142, *LTSR Aukščiausiosios Tarybos ir Vyriausybės žinios*, 12 April 1974, 2–3.
16 *Alytaus eksperimentinio namų statybos kombinato surenkami gyvenamieji namai* (Alytus Experimental Home Construction Plant's Prefabricated Houses) (Vilnius: Mokslas, 1981).
17 Jurgis Okunis, *Gyvenamieji namai* (Residential Homes) (Freiburg: n.p., 1948).
18 Н. Н. Соловьев, *Брак и семья сегодня* (Marriage and Family Today) (Вильнюс: Минтис, 1977), 104.
19 Child custody case, 1945, LCSA, F. R.-808, Ap. 2, B. 23, L. 83.
20 Divorce case, 1944, LCSA, F. R.-808, Ap. 2, B. 5, L. 28.

21 Estate inheritance case, 1947, LCSA, F. R.-808, Ap. 2, B. 24, L. 87.
22 *Lietuva 1940-1990 m.* (Lithuania, 1940-1990) (Vilnius: Lietuvos gyventojų genocido ir rezistencijos tyrimo centras, 2005). Elena Zubkova, *Russia after the War: Hopes, Illusions and Disappointments, 1945-1957* (New York: M. E. Sharpe, 1998), 139.
23 Resolution of the LSSR Council of Ministers, *Dėl minimalaus kolūkiečių darbo užmokesčio* (On Minimum Wage for Collective Farm Workers), *LTSR Aukščiausiosios Tarybos ir Vyriausybės žinios*, 20 October 1968, 400.
24 A. Mikutis, 'Naujas valstybinių mažmeninių kainų sumažinimas' (New Reductions in State Retail Prices), *Tiesa*, 1 March 1951.
25 *Lietuva 1940-1990 m.* (Lithuania, 1940-1990) (Vilnius: Lietuvos gyventojų genocido ir rezistencijos tyrimo centras, 2005), 436.
26 Vylius Leonavičius and Eglė Ozolinčiūtė, 'Sovietinio žemės ūkio transformacija' (Transformation of the Soviet Agricultural Sector), *Sociologija. Mintis ir veiksmas* 1 no. 44 (2019), 93-131, 94.
27 Divorce case, 1964-5, LCSA, F. R.-808, Ap. 2, B. 590, L. 14.
28 Marriage annulment case, 1957-8, LCSA, F. R.-808, Ap. 2, B. 591, L. 25.
29 Donald Filtzer, *The Khrushchev Era: De-Stalinization and the Limits of Freedom of Reform in the USSR, 1953-1964* (London: Macmillan, 1993), 51.
30 See Divorce case, 1958, LCSA, F. R.-808, Ap. 2, B. 619. Divorce case, 1955, LCSA, F. R.-808, Ap. 2, B. 294, L. 5. Divorce case, 1953-5, LCSA, F. R.-808, Ap. 2, B. 290, L. 7. Divorce case, 1948, LCSA, F. R.-808, Ap. 2, B. 44, L. 49. Paternity and child support recovery case, 1973-4, LCSA, F. R.-808, Ap. 2, B. 1481, L. 1. Child support determination case, 1972, LCSA, F. R.-808, Ap. 2, B. 1459, L. 4.
31 Division of property case, 1981-2, LCSA, F. R.-808, Ap. 2, B. 1643, L. 3.
32 'Daugiau gerų ir gražių liaudies vartojimo prekių' (More Beautiful and Fine Quality Consumer Projects, *Tiesa*, 23 March 1954.
33 A. Antanaitytė, 'Maisto prekės pristatomos į namus' (Home Delivery of Food Products), *Tiesa*, 12 January 1957. J. Bazevičius, and P. Eidukevičius, 'Lietuvos TSR lengvosios pramonės plėtra', *Mokslas ir technika* 5 (1958), 4.
34 Ruth Oldeniel and Karin Zachmann, eds, *Cold War Kitchen: Americanization, Technology, and European Users* (Cambridge, MA: MIT Press, 2009), 1.
35 William Taubman, *Khrushchev: The Man and His Era* (New York: W.W. Norton, 2003), 510-11.
36 For more see Susan E. Reid, 'Women in the Home', in *Women in the Khrushchev Era*, ed. Melanie Ilič, Susan E. Reid and Lynne Attwood (New York: Palgrave Macmillan, 2004), 149-76. Deborah A. Field, 'Mothers and Fathers and the Problem of Selfishness in the Khrushchev Period', in ibid., 96-113. Deborah A. Field, 'Everyday Life and the Problem of Conceptualizing Public and Private during the Khrushchev Era', in *Everyday Life in Russia: Past and Present*,

ed. Choi Chatterjee, David L. Ransel, Mary Cavender and Karen Petrone (Bloomington: Indiana University Press, 2015), 163–80.
37 Resolution of the LSSR Council of Ministers, *Dėl standartizavimo pagerinimo ir standartų, normalių bei techninių sąlygų vaidmens gerinant gaminamos produkcijos kokybę pakėlimo* (On Improving Standardization and Raising the Role of Standards and Normal and Technical Conditions for Improving Product Quality), *LTSR Aukščiausiosios Tarybos ir Vyriausybės žinios*, 20 December 1962, 869.
38 Later known as the Pavilion of Best Examples. Starting in 1953, the Soviet government became increasingly concerned about the quality of Soviet citizens' everyday life. Because the economy of Lithuania, much like that of other republics of the Soviet Union, was isolated, and industrial technology was outdated, the branch of the Chamber of Commerce promoted peculiar, artificial replicas of Western production standards. The branch was established in order to stimulate the production of more modern consumer goods of better quality.
39 Dalia Leinarte, *Adopting and Remembering Soviet Reality: Life Stories of Lithuanian Women, 1945–1970* (Amsterdam: Rodopi, 2010), 166.
40 В. А. Сысенко, *Устойчивость брака: проблемы, факторы, условия* (Москва: Финансы и статистика, 1981), 41.
41 J. Paleckis and S. Naujalis, 'Resolution of the LSSR Supreme Soviet, *Dėl priemonių buitiniam gyventojų aptarnavimui toliau gerinti, liaudies vartojamų prekių gamybai didinti ir prekybai plėsti*' (Measures to Further Improve Household Services, Increase the Production of Consumer Goods and Expand Trade), *Tiesa*, 17 November 1962, 2.
42 LTSR Aukščiausiosios Tarybos nutarimas *Dėl priemonių liaudies vartojamų prekių gamybai respublikoje toliau didinti ir jų kokybei gerinti, vykdant XXIV suvažiavimo nutarimus* (On Measures to Further Increase the Production of Consumer Goods in the Republic and to Improve Their Quality in Accordance with the Resolutions of the XXIV Congress), *LTSR Aukščiausiosios Tarybos ir Vyriausybės žinios*, 20 July 1971, 322.
43 LTSR CK ir LTSR Ministrų Tarybos nutarimas *Dėl penkių darbo dienų savaitės įvedimo Respublikos ministerijų, žinybų, partinių, tarybinių ir visuomeninių organizacijų aparato darbuotojams* (Resolution of the Central Committee of the LSSR and the LSSR Council of Ministers on the Introduction of a Five-day Work Week for Employees of Ministries, Agencies, Party, Soviet and Public Organizations of the Republic), *LTSR Aukščiausiosios Tarybos ir Vyriausybės žinios*, 20 December 1967, 555.
44 An extended annual vacation of forty-eight workdays was given to university instructors and middle school teachers, and workers in the forestry industry were provided with a twenty-four-workday vacation. See H. Davidavičius, *Darbininkų ir tarnautojų kasmetinės atostogos* (Vilnius: Lietuvos 'Žinijos' draugija, 1972), 5.

45 Starting on 4 December 1969, women's retirement age was 55, while men's was 60.
46 Н. Н. Соловьев, *Брак и семья сегодня* (Marriage and Family Today) (Вильнюс: Минтис, 1977), 47. В. А. Сысенко, *Устойчивость брака: проблемы, факторы, условия* (Москва: Финансы и статистика, 1981), 157, 83.
47 T. A. Ždanko, ed., *Semejnyj byt narodov CCCR* (Moskva: Nauka, 1990), 168.
48 B. Liguckas and J. Legas, 'Daugiau dėmesio skundų knygoms' (Pay More Attention to the Book of Complaints) *Tiesa*, 27 April 1950.
49 A. Barauskas, 'Signalas, laiškas, žmogus' (Signal, Letter, Person), *Tiesa*, 7 March 1965.
50 Resolution of the LSSR Council of Ministers, *Dėl gyventojų, laiškų, skundų ir pareiškimų svarstymo nuostatų* (On Regulations for Analysing Citizens' Letters, Complaints and Suggestions), *LTSR Aukščiausiosios Tarybos ir Vyriausybės žinios*, 31 March 1966, 133.
51 Liuba D's letter to *Tiesa* correspondent Jūra B., 20 February 1964, Jūra B's Personal Archive (hereafter JBAM).
52 Liuba D's letter to *Tiesa* correspondent Jūra B., 1966, JBAM-168.
53 Ibid.
54 Ibid; emphasis added.
55 Liuba D's letter to *Tiesa* correspondent Jūra B., 1966, JBAM-169.
56 Alena V. Ledeneva, *Russia's Economy of Favours: Blat, Networking and Informal Exchange* (Cambridge: Cambridge University Press, 1998), 55–6.
57 Liuba D's letter to *Tiesa* correspondent Jūra B., 1966, JBAM-169.
58 Alena V. Ledeneva, *Russia's Economy of Favours: Blat, Networking and Informal Exchange* (Cambridge: Cambridge University Press, 1998), 171.
59 Ibid., 156–9.
60 Liuba D's letter to *Tiesa* correspondent Jūra B., 28 October 1968, JBAM-176.
61 Ibid.
62 Liuba D's letter to *Tiesa* correspondent Jūra B., 21 May 1973, JBAM.
63 Liuba D's letter to *Tiesa* correspondent Jūra B., 13 March 1969, JBAM-167.
64 Liuba D's letter to *Tiesa* correspondent Jūra B., 28 October 1968, JBAM-176.
65 Ibid.
66 Julie Hessler, 'Consumption and Civilization', in *Stalinism: New Directions*, ed. Sheila Fitzpatrick (New York: Routledge, 2000), 202.
67 Alena V. Ledeneva, *Russia's Economy of Favours: Blat, Networking and Informal Exchange* (Cambridge: Cambridge University Press, 1998), 167.
68 Liuba D's letter to *Tiesa* correspondent Jūra B., 1973, JBAM-170.
69 Liuba D's letter to *Tiesa* correspondent Jūra B., 21 May 1973, JBAM-16.
70 Ibid.
71 Ibid.
72 Liuba D's letter to *Tiesa* correspondent Jūra B., 31 August 1971, JBAM-35.

73 P. G.'s letter to *Tiesa* correspondent Jūra B., 5 March 1969, JBAM-24.
74 On the impact of such informal initiatives on Soviet society, see the introduction to *Bribery and Blat in Russia: Negotiating Reciprocity from the Middle Ages to the 1990s*, ed. Stephen Lovell, Alena Ledeneva and Andrei Rogachevskii (New York: Palgrave MacMillan, 2001). Sheila Fitzpatrick, '*Blat* in Stalin's Time', in ibid., 179. Vladimir A. Kozlov, 'Denunciation and Its Functions in Soviet Governance: A Study of Denunciations and Their Bureaucratic Handling from Soviet Police Archives, 1944–1953', in *Denunciation in Modern European History, 1789–1989: Accusatory Practices*, ed. Sheila Fitzpatrick and Robert Gellately (Chicago: University of Chicago Press, 1997), 140.

Bibliography

Primary Published Sources

1940 m. Santuokos įstatymas (1940 Marriage Law), *Vyriausybės žinios*, 15 August 1940.

1957 m. Liepos 17 d. Instrukcijos dėl civilinės metrikacijos tvarkos LTSR (17 July 1957 Instructions on Civilian Metrics Procedures in the LSSR), *Lietuvos Tarybų Socialistinė Respublika* (hereafter *LTSR*) *Aukščiausiosios Tarybos ir Vyriausybės žinios* (News of the Lithuanian Socialist Republic Supreme Soviet), 30 August 1958.

1958 m. August 20 d. Instrukcijos dėl civilinės metrikacijos tvarkos LTSR (20 August 1958 Instructions on Civil Metrics Procedures in the LSSR), *LTSR Aukščiausiosios Tarybos ir Vyriausybės žinios*, 31 May 1960.

1958 m. August 20 d. Instrukcijos dėl civilinės metrikacijos tvarkos LTSR, 1 ir 4 punktų pakeitimo (Changes to Points 1–4 of on Civil Metrics Instructions in the LSSR), *LTSR Aukščiausiosios Tarybos ir Vyriausybės žinios*, 20 August 1963.

1970 m. Sausio 4 d. LTSR Ministrų Tarybos nutarimas Dėl civilinės metrikacijos instrukcijos patvirtinimo (Resolution of the Council of Ministers of the LSSR on the Approval of the Instructions on Civilian Metrics), *LTSR Aukščiausiosios Tarybos ir Vyriausybės žinios*, 20 February 1970.

Aksomaitis, V. 'Kada Vilniuje bus įrengtas vaikų miestelis?' (When Will the Children's Village Open in Vilnius?), *Komjaunimo tiesa*, 5 August 1951.

Alekseičikas, A. 'Ant ko laikosi šeima?' (What Is the Foundation of a Family?), *Tarybinė šeima* 8 (1970).

Alekseičikas, A. 'Optimistinis žvilgsnis į šeimą' (An Optimistic Look at the Family), *Tarybinė moteris* 11 (1981).

Alytaus eksperimentinio namų statybos kombinato surenkami gyvenamieji namai (Alytus Experimental Home Construction Plant's Prefabricated Houses) (Vilnius: Mokslas, 1981).

Antanaitytė, A. 'Maisto prekės pristatomos į namus' (Home Delivery of Food Products), *Tiesa*, 12 January 1957.

Apie auklėjimą mokyklose-internatuose ir vaikų namuose (On Education at the Boarding Schools for the Needy and Orphanages) (Kaunas: Valstybinė Pedagoginė Literatūros Leidykla, 1960).

'Apie valstybines pašalpas daugiavaikėms ir vienišoms motinoms' (On State Assistance for Mothers of Large Families and Single Mothers), *Tiesa*, 16 November 1944.

Baltrūnienė, A. 'Ne, nefantazija' (No, It's Not a Fantasy), *Jaunimo gretos* 8 (1963).

Barauskas, A. 'Signalas, laiškas, žmogus' (Signal, Letter, Person), *Tiesa*, 7 March 1965.

Bazevičius, J., and P. Eidukevičius. 'Lietuvos TSR lengvosios pramonės plėtra' (Development of Light Industry of Lithuanian SSR), *Mokslas ir technika* 5 (1958).
Butautienė, I. 'Dar apie šeimos židinį' (More on the Family Hearth), *Tarybinė moteris* 7 (1959).
Čekalinas, V. *Meilė ir šeima* (Love and Family) (Vilnius: Mintis, 1968).
Cibas, A. *Kaip pradėti ir vykdyti asmeninę statybą* (How to Start and Complete Individual Construction Projects) (Vilnius: LTSR Ministrų Taryba, 1959).
'Daugiau gerų ir gražių liaudies vartojimo prekių' (More Beautiful and Fine Quality Consumer Projects), *Tiesa*, 23 March 1954.
Daukšas, K. 'Apie šeimos patvarumą' (On the Family's Stability), *Tarybinė moteris* 10 (1959).
Daukšas, K. 'Dar apie šeimos patvarumą' (More on Marriage Stability), *Tiesa*, 15 July 1959.
Daunoravičius, V. 'Pašalpos vaikystės invalidams' (Assistance for the Handicapped since Childhood), *Mūsų žodis* 2 (1968).
Davidavičius, H. *Darbininkų ir tarnautojų kasmetinės atostogos* (Summer Vacations for Workers and Civil Servants) (Vilnius: Lietuvos 'Žinijos' draugija, 1972).
'Dėl *Civilinės Metrikacijos Instrukcijos* Patvirtinimo' (On the Ratification of the Civil Registry Guidelines Law), *LTSR Aukščiausiosios Tarybos ir Vyriausybės žinios*, 20 February 1970.
'Dėl individualinės statybos nuostatų patvirtinimo' (On Confirmation of the Regulations for Individual Construction) Resolution No. 142, *LTSR Aukščiausiosios Tarybos ir Vyriausybės žinios,* 12 April 1974.
'Dėl kovos su girtavimu sustiprinimo ir dėl prekybos stipriausiais svaiginamaisiais gėrimais sutvarkymo' (On the Intensified Battle with Drunkenness and the Regulation of Commerce of Strong, Intoxicating Alcoholic Beverages), *LTSR Aukščiausiosios Tarybos ir Vyriausybės žinios*, 1 February 1959.
'Dėl kovos su girtavimu sustiprinimo' (On the Intensified Battle with Drunkenness), *LTSR Aukščiausiosios Tarybos ir Vyriausybės žinios*, 20 June 1961.
'Dėl kovos su venerinėmis ligomis stiprinimo' (On the Intensifying the Battle against Venereal Diseases), *LTSR Aukščiausiosios Tarybos ir Vyriausybės žinios*, 9 February 1967.
'Dėl *Lietuvos TSR Santuokos ir šeimos kodekso* įsigaliojimo tvarkos' (On the Procedure for Implementing the Marriage and Family Code of the Lithuanian SSR), *LTSR Aukščiausiosios Tarybos ir Vyriausybės žinios*, 10 December 1969.
'Dėl *Lietuvos TSR teritorijoje veikiančio Santuokos, šeimos ir globos įstatymų kodekso pakeitimų*' (On the Changes to the Marriage, Family and Guardianship Code of Laws in Effect in the LSSR Territory), *LTSR Aukščiausiosios Tarybos ir Vyriausybės žinios*, 12 February 1954.
'Dėl piktybinių girtuoklių (alkoholikų)' (On the Treatment of Alcoholics and Drug Addicts), *LTSR Aukščiausiosios Tarybos ir Vyriausybės žinios*, 31 August 1966.

'Dėl priemonių kovai su girtavimu ir alkoholizmu sustiprinti' (On the Improved Methods in the Battle with Drunkenness and Alcoholism), *LTSR Aukščiausiosios Tarybos ir Vyriausybės žinios*, 10 July 1972.

'Dėl priemonių mokykloms-internatams vystyti 1959–1965 metais' (On the Methods for Developing the Boarding Schools for the Needy from 1959 to 1965), *Tiesa*, 29 May 1959.

'Dėl *respublikinių mokyklų-internatų*' (On the Republic's Boarding Schools for the Needy), LTSR Švietimo ministerijos įsakymas dėl metodinės komisijos sudarymo (LSSR Ministry of Education decree on Creating a Commission on Methods), 24 April 1978.

'Dėl Santuokos, šeimos ir globos įstatymo kodekso, galiojančio LTSR teritorijoje, pakeitimo' (On the Changes to the Marriage, Family and Guardianship Code in Effect in the Territory of the LSSR), *LTSR Aukščiausiosios Tarybos ir Vyriausybės žinios*, 31 October 1966.

'Dėl TSRS Aukščiausiosios Tarybos Prezidiumo 1965 m. gruodžio 10 d. Įsako "Dėl tam tikro ištuokos bylų teisminio nagrinėjimo tvarkos pakeitimo"' (On the Presidium of the Supreme Soviet of the USSR on the Orders of 10 December 1965 'On a Certain Change in Procedure for Legal Proceedings in Divorce Cases'), *LTSR Aukščiausiosios Tarybos ir Vyriausybės žinios*, 30 November 1966.

'Didis rūpinimasis liaudies gerove' (Extraordinary Care for Soviet People), *Komunistas* 8 (1957).

Dovydaitė, G. 'Ką pasakoja moterys' (What Do Women Tell Us?), *Kalba Vilnius* 41 (1970).

Garmuvienė, M. 'Gerbiamoji redakcija!' (Dear Editors!), *Tarybinė moteris* 2 (1958).

Grigonis, A. 'Jaunos šeimos istorija' (The Story of a Young Family), *Komjaunimo tiesa*, 25 August 1946.

Grizickas, Č. 'Jaunystės problemos' (Problems of Youth), *Mokslas ir gyvenimas* 10 (1966).

Ickovičiūtė, L. 'Motinos ir vaiko sveikatos sargyboje' (Looking Out for the Health of Mothers and Children), *Tiesa*, 7 December 1946.

'Ikimokyklinių vaikų įstaigų–lopšelio-darželio nuostatai' (Pre-school Institution–Creche-Kindergarten Regulations *LTSR Aukščiausiosios Tarybos ir Vyriausybės žinios*, 20 February 1961.

Indrašius, N. 'Už ko tekėti?' (Who Should I Marry?), *Švyturys* 8 (1966).

'…Ir apie vyro laiką' (… And Now Let's Talk About Men's Time), *Tarybinė moteris* 6 (1966), 4–5.

'Įsakymas Dėl Lietuvos TSR teritorijoje veikiančio Santuokos, šeimos ir globos įstatymų kodekso pakeitimų' (Law: On the Changes to the Marriage, Family and Guardianship Laws in Effect in the Territory of the LSSR), *LTSR Aukščiausiosios Tarybos ir Vyriausybės žinios*, 12 February 1954.

Jie-savo mokyklos-internato šeimininkai (They Are the Directors of Their Own Boarding School) (Vilnius: Laikraščių ir Žurnalų Leidykla, 1966).

'Jūsų Jūratė. Ne vien prie lopšio' (Your Jūratė: Not Just a Mummy), *Kalba Vilnius* 15 (1968).

Kaluzevičius, A. 'Apie santuoką' (On Marriage), *Tarybinė moteris* 10 (1958).

Kancleris, A. 'Optimali žmona' (The Perfect Wife), *Jaunimo gretos* 2 (1970).

Kaniauskas, M. 'Ką davė Tarybų valdžia moterims?' (What Did the Soviet Government Provide for Women?), *Tiesa*, 20 January 1946.

'Kelias į šeimą' (Journey to Having a Family), *Jaunimo gretos* 5 (1967).

Kielienė, I. 'Priešmokyklinis auklėjimas Lietuvoje' (Pre-school Education in Lithuania), *Tarybinė mokykla* 9 (1947).

'Kilnūs ir taurūs tarybinio žmogaus jausmai' (Noble and Innocent Feelings of the Soviet Person), *Tiesa*, 10 January 1960.

Klimavičius, K. 'Meilė puošia žmogų' (Love Makes Us Beautiful), *Komjaunimo tiesa*, 25 March 1955.

'Koks turi būti šeimos gyvenimas – uždaras ar atdaras?' (Should Family Life Be Open or Closed?), *Tarybinė moteris* 6, no. 2 (1970).

'Koks turi būti tavo vyras' (What Kind of Husband Should You Choose?), *Tarybinė moteris* 12 (1956).

Kovas, K. 'Moterys įsitraukia į visuomeninį darbą' (Women Entering the Workplace), *Tarybų Lietuva*, 9 October 1945.

'Kuris teisus? Skaitytojos laiškas' (Which of Us Is Right? Letter to the Editor), *Tarybinė moteris* 4 (1958).

Levanienė, E. 'Berniukų ir mergaičių draugystė' (Friendship between Boys and Girls), *Tarybinė moteris* 11 (1954).

Levšinas, A. 'Apie šeimos laimę' (On Family Happiness), *Komjaunimo tiesa*, 22 September 1956.

Lietuva 1940–1990: okupuotos Lietuvos istorija, ed. Arvydas Anušauskas (Vilnius: Lietuvos gyventojų genocido ir rezistencijos tyrimo centras, 2005).

Lietuvos TSR Ministrų Tarybos nutarimas *Dėl mėnesinių pašalpų invalidams nuo vaikystės* (Resolution of the Lithuanian SSR Council of Ministers on Monthly Benefits for Those Handicapped since Childhood), *LTSR Aukščiausiosios Tarybos ir Vyriausybės žinios*, 20 December 1967.

Lietuvos Tarybų Socialistinės Respublikos Aukščiausiosios Tarybos Prezidiumo įsakas *Dėl Vyriausiosios Karių Šeimų Valstybinio Aprūpinimo ir Buities Sutvarkymo Valdybos prie Lietuvos TSR Liaudies Komisarų Tarybos ir Karių Valstybinio Aprūpinimo ir Buities Sutvarkymo skyrių prie miestų, miestų rajonų ir apskričių vykdomųjų komitetų sudarymo* (Order of the Presidium of the Supreme Soviet of the Soviet Socialist Republic of Lithuania On the Establishment of a Board Providing State Provisions for the Well-being of Soldiers' Families Under the Council of People's Commissars of the Lithuanian SSR and the Department for Providing State Provisions for the Well-being of Soldiers' Families at the City, City District and County Levels), *LTSR Aukščiausiosios Tarybos ir Vyriausybės žinios* 1, no. 10, 28 October 1944.

Lietuvos Tarybų Socialistinės Respublikos Aukščiausiosios Tarybos Prezidiumo nutarimas *Dėl Lietuvos TSR vietinių Darbo žmonių deputatų tarybų nuolatinių komisijų nuostatų* patvirtinimo (Resolution of the Presidium of the Supreme Soviet on the Regulations Issued by the Standing Commissions of the Deputies of the Local Councils of Working People of the Lithuanian SSR), *LTSR Aukščiausiosios Tarybos ir Vyriausybės žinios* 8-9, nos 134-5, 20 July 1951.

Lietuvos Tarybų Socialistinės Respublikos Aukščiausiosios Tarybos Prezidiumo nutarimas *Dėl papildomos socialinės pagalbos kare žuvusių karių šeimoms* (Resolution of the Presidium of the Supreme Soviet on Supplemental Social Benefits for Families of Soldiers Who Perished at War), *LTSR Aukščiausiosios Tarybos ir Vyriausybės žinios* 3, no.152 12 March 1952.

Lietuvos Tarybų Socialistinės Respublikos Aukščiausiosios Tarybos įsakas dėl veikiančių Lietuvos TSR teritorijoje *Santuokos, šeimos ir globos įstatymų kodekso* ir *Civilinio proceso kodekso* pakeitimų (Order of the Supreme Soviet of the Lithuanian SSR on Amendments to the Code of Marriage, Family and Custody Laws and the Code of Civil Procedure Operating in the Territory of the Lithuanian SSR), *LTSR Aukščiausiosios Tarybos ir Vyriausybės žinios*, 5 August 1946.

Lietuvos Tarybų Socialistinės Respublikos Aukščiausiosios Tarybos nutarimas *Dėl mokinių, gyvenančių kaimo vietovėse nemokamo vežiojimo* (Resolution of the Supreme Soviet of the LSSR on Free Travel for Pupils Living in Rural Areas), *LTSR Aukščiausiosios Tarybos ir Vyriausybės žinios*, 30 September 1965.

Lietuvos Tarybų Socialistinės Respublikos Ministrų Tarybos nutarimas *Dėl tolesnio žuvusių kare šeimų buities sąlygų gerinimo* (Resolution of the Council of Ministers of the LSSR on Further Improvements to the Well-being of Families of Soldiers), *LTSR Aukščiausiosios Tarybos ir Vyriausybės žinios*, 30 June 1970.

Lietuvos Tarybų Socialistinės Respublikos Ministrų Tarybos potvarkis *Dėl mokesčio ėmimo už auklėtinių išlaikymą mokyklose internatuose sutvarkymo* (Resolution of the Council of Ministers of the LSSR on the Issuing of Fees for Room and Board of Pupils Attending Boarding Schools for the Needy), *LTSR Aukščiausiosios Tarybos ir Vyriausybės žinios*, 30 October 1973.

Lietuvos Tarybų Socialistinės Respublikos Ministrų Tarybos potvarkis *Dėl tėvų atleidimo nuo mokesčio už vaiko išlaikymą, kai jis nelanko vaikų įstaigos eilinių tėvo atostogų metu* (Resolution of the Council of Ministers of the LSSR on Exemptions from Child Support for Fathers While Their Child Is Not Attending Childcare Institutions during Paternity Leave), *LTSR Aukščiausiosios Tarybos ir Vyriausybės žinios*, 10 June 1970.

Lietuvos Tarybų Socialistinės Respublikos Ministrų Tarybos nutarimas *Dėl pašalpų mokėjimo maitintojo netekusiems vidurinių bendrojo lavinimo mokyklų XI klasių moksleiviams* (Resolution of the Council of Ministers of the LSSR on the Payment of Assistance to Students of General Secondary Schools, Grades One Through Eleven Who Have Lost Their Breadwinner), *LTSR Aukščiausiosios Tarybos ir Vyriausybės žinios*, 21 September 1970.

Lietuvos Tarybų Socialistinės Respublikos Ministrų Tarybos nutarimas *Dėl profesinių technikos ir specialiųjų vidurinių mokyklų moksleivių našlaičių ir netekusių tėvų globos aprūpinimo* (Resolution of the Council of Ministers of the LSSR on Providing for Students Attending Vocational, Technical and Specialized Secondary Schools Who Are Orphans or Who Have Lost Their Parental Guardians), *LTSR Aukščiausiosios Tarybos ir Vyriausybės žinios*, 30 March 1970.

Lietuvos Tarybų Socialistinės Respublikos Ministrų Tarybos nutarimas *Dėl priemonių pramonei vaikams skirtų maisto produktų gamybai toliau didinti ir vaikų maitinimui organizuoti* (Resolution of the Council of Ministers of the LSSR on Measures for Industry to Further Increase Food Production for Children and to Administer Programme for Feeding Children), *LTSR Aukščiausiosios Tarybos ir Vyriausybės žinios*, 20 December 1965.

Lietuvos Tarybų Socialistinės Respublikos Ministrų Tarybos nutarimas *Dėl kaime gyvenančių mokinių pavežėjimo* (Resolution of the Council of Ministers of the LSSR on Transport of Pupils Living in Rural Areas), *LTSR Aukščiausiosios Tarybos ir Vyriausybės žinios*, 31 January 1966.

Lietuvos Tarybų Socialistinės Respublikos Ministrų Tarybos įsakas *Dėl Lietuvos TSR ministerijų ir žinybų vaikų darželių tipinių etatų patvirtinimo* (Resolution of the LSSR Council of Ministers on the Management of LSSR Ministry and Company Kindergarten Staff), *LTSR Aukščiausiosios Tarybos ir Vyriausybės žinios*, 30 June 1958.

Lietuvos Tarybų Socialistinės Respublikos Ministrų Tarybos įsakas *Dėl minimalaus kolūkiečių darbo užmokesčio* (Resolution of the LSSR Council of Ministers on Minimum Wage for Collective Farm Workers), *LTSR Aukščiausiosios Tarybos ir Vyriausybės žinios*, 20 October 1968.

Lietuvos Tarybų Socialistinės Respublikos Ministrų Tarybos įsakas *Dėl standartizavimo pagerinimo ir standartų, normalių bei techninių sąlygų vaidmens gerinant gaminamos produkcijos kokybę pakėlimo* (Resolution of the LSSR Council of Ministers on Improving Standardization and Raising the Role of Standards and Normal and Technical Conditions for Improving Product Quality), *LTSR Aukščiausiosios Tarybos ir Vyriausybės žinios*, 20 December 1962.

Lietuvos Tarybų Socialistinės Respublikos Ministrų Tarybos įsakas *Dėl Gyventojų, laiškų, skundų ir pareiškimų svarstymo nuostatų* (Resolution of the LSSR Council of Ministers on Regulations for Analysing Citizens' Letters, Complaints and Suggestions), *LTSR Aukščiausiosios Tarybos ir Vyriausybės žinios*, 31 March 1966.

Liguckas, B., and J. Legas, 'Daugiau dėmesio skundų knygoms' (Pay More Attention to the Book of Complaints), *Tiesa*, 27 April 1950.

LKP CK, LTSR Ministrų Tarybos ir Lietuvos respublikinės profesinių sąjungų tarybos nutarimas *Dėl priemonių vaikų ir paauglių vasaros poilsio organizavimui toliau gerinti* (Resolution of the LSSR Communist Party Central Committee, Council of Ministers and the LSSR Council of Trade Unions on Measures for Further

Improving the Management of Summer Recreation for Children and Adolescents), *LTSR Aukščiausiosios Tarybos ir Vyriausybės žinios*, 20 April 1973.

LTSR Aukščiausiosios Tarybos įsakas *Dėl veikiančių Lietuvos TSR teritorijoje Santuokos, šeimos ir globos įstatymų kodekso ir Civilinio procesinio kodekso pakeitimų* (The LSSR Supreme Soviet decree on Marriage, Family and Guardianship Code of Law and Civilian in Effect in the Territory of the Lithuanian SSR and Amendments to the Code of Civil Procedure), *LTSR Aukščiausiosios Tarybos ir Vyriausybės žinios* 17, 5 August 1946.

LTSR Aukščiausiosios Tarybos nutarimas *Dėl priemonių liaudies vartojamų prekių gamybai respublikoje toliau didinti ir jų kokybei gerinti, vykdant XXIV suvažiavimo nutarimus* (On Measures to Further Increase the Production of Consumer Goods in the Republic and to Improve Their Quality in Accordance with the resolutions of the XXIV Congress), *LTSR Aukščiausiosios Tarybos ir Vyriausybės žinios*, 20 July 1971.

LTSR CK ir LTSR Ministrų Tarybos nutarimas *Dėl penkių darbo dienų savaitės įvedimo Respublikos ministerijų, žinybų, partinių, tarybinių ir visuomeninių organizacijų aparato darbuotojams* (Resolution of the Central Committee of the LSSR and the LSSR Council of Ministers on the Introduction of a Five-day Work Week for Employees of Ministries, Agencies, Party, Soviet and Public Organizations of the Republic), *LTSR Aukščiausiosios Tarybos ir Vyriausybės žinios*, 20 December 1967.

Matuzevičius, E. 'Meilę reikia branginti ir saugoti!' (Love Must Be Cherished and Protected!), *Jaunimo gretos* 7 (1955).

Mikšytė, I. 'Dar kartą apie meilę' (Once Again on Love), *Jaunimo gretos* 7 (1954).

Mikutis, A. 'Naujas valstybinių mažmeninių kainų sumažinimas' (New Reductions in State Retail Prices, *Tiesa*, 1 March 1951.

Mockus, A. 'Viskas apie meilę' (Everything on Love), *Jaunimo gretos* 12 (1965).

Mokyklų-internatų vidaus tvarkos taisyklės auklėtiniams (Boarding School Disciplinary Rules for Students) (Vilnius: RTFSR santuokos, šeimos ir globos kodeksas, Švietimo Misterija, 1962).

Mokymas ir auklėjimas internatinėse mokyklose (Education and Upbringing in the Boarding Schools) (Kaunas: Šviesa, 1971).

Nutarimas *Dėl alimentų vaikams išlaikyti išieškojimo respublikoje*, 21 July 1967 (Resolution on Recovery of Child Support in the Republic), *LTSR Aukščiausiosios Tarybos ir Vyriausybės žinios*, 30 April 1970.

Pagrindiniai 1989 metų gyventojų surašymo duomenys (Essential Data from the 1989 Census) (Vilnius: Lietuvos Valstybinis Statistikos Komitetas, 1990).

Pakalnis, S. Letter from reader. *Jaunimo gretos* 11 (1955).

Paleckis, J., and S. Naujalis, 'Resolution of the LSSR Supreme Soviet, *Dėl priemonių buitiniam gyventojų aptarnavimui toliau gerinti, liaudies vartojamų prekių gamybai didinti ir prekybai plėsti*' (Measures to Further Improve Household Services, Increase the Production of Consumer Goods and Expand Trade), *Tiesa*, 17 November 1962.

Pauraitė, R. 'Būkite laimingi, Nijole ir Alfredai!' (Best Wishes, Nijolė and Alfredas!), *Komjaunimo tiesa*, 18 August 1964.

Pekelis, V. 'Meilės patarėjas' (The Love Adviser), *Mokslas ir technika* 1 (1970).
Petkevičius, V. 'Jūsų žodis, Viktorai!' (Your Message to Victoria), *Jaunimo gretos* 1 (1966).
Petrauskas, A. 'Kolūkietės-motinos laukia sezoninių vaikų lopšelių' (Collective Farm Worker and Mother Awaits Seasonal Daycare for Her Children), *Tiesa*, 23 June 1954.
Petravys, B. 'Remiamos daugiavaikės ir vienišos motinos' (Mothers of Large Families and Single Mothers Are Receiving Support), *Tarybų Lietuva*, 14 June 1945.
Poškienė, O. 'Tu ir santuoka' (Marriage and You), *Tarybinė moteris* 6 (1969).
Resolution of the LSSR Council of Ministers. *Dėl Gyventojų, laiškų, skundų ir pareiškimų svarstymo nuostatų* (On Regulations for Analysing Citizens' Letters, Complaints and Suggestions), *LTSR Aukščiausiosios Tarybos ir Vyriausybės žinios*, 31 March 1966.
Sabaliauskaitė, G. 'Tave aplankė meilė' (Love Visited You), *Švyturys* 14 (1964).
Šalčiūtė, A. 'Noriu vesti' (I Want to Marry), *Jaunimo gretos* 5 (1964).
Sidorkaitė, N. 'Motina ir sūnus' (Mother and Son), *Tarybinė moteris* 6 (1954).
Sluckis, M. 'Meilės ir fiziologiniai instinktai?' (Instincts of Love and Physiology), *Tiesa*, 18 October 1959.
Sluckis, M. 'Tegyvuoja gilus jausmas ir skaisti svajonė' (May Deep Feelings and Innocent Dreams Flourish), *Tiesa*, 13 December 1959.
Šniukas, D. 'Sutuoktuvių liudijimas Nr.1' (Witness to a Marriage No. 1), *Tiesa*, 24 July 1964.
Sodaitytė, I. 'Nepinkime meilei vainikų' (Let's Not Make Wreaths for Love), *Tiesa*, 29 November 1959.
Solovjovas, N. 'Apie šeimos laimę' (On Happiness in Marriage), 6. 'Religija nepadeda' (Religion Does Not Help), *Komjaunimo tiesa*, 24 May 1957.
Solovjovas, N. 'Meilė – tai jausmas, širdis ir protas' (Love Is a Feeling, Heart and Mind), *Komjaunimo tiesa*, 7 May 1957.
Stungurys, T. 'Vedybos – rimtas žingsnis' (Marriage Is a Serious Step), *Tarybinė moteris* 12 (1959).
'Tavo laisvalaikio valandos' (Your Leisure Time) (reprinted from the newspaper *Komsomolskaja pravda*), *Komjaunimo tiesa*, 5 August 1960.
TSRS Aukščiausiosios Tarybos Prezidiumo nutarimas dėl priemonių savalaikiam daugiavaikių motinų apdovanojimui bei ordinų ir medalių įteikimui užtikrinti (Resolution of the Presidium of the Supreme Soviet on Measures for Ensuring the Timely Honouring and Presenting of Orders and Medals to Mothers of Large Families), *LTSR Aukščiausiosios Tarybos ir Vyriausybės žinios*, no. 5 (185), 15 April 1954.
Valiulytė, J. 'Ir meilės reikia mokytis' (Even Love Must Be Learnt), *Tarybinė moteris* 1 (1960).
Varžgalys, A., and P. Mikuckas. 'Kad moteriai nereikėtų užsidaryti virtuvėje' (So Women Wouldn't Have to Hide in the Kitchen), *Tiesa*, 25 February 1960.

Veržbavičius, L. 'Motinystės ir vaikystės globa Tarybų valstybėje' (Care for Mothers and Children in the Soviet State), *Tiesa*, 8 July 1945.

Vietų bendrabučiuose suteikimo ir sąlygų jomis naudotis nuostatai (Rules for Distributing Dormitory Rooms and Conditions for Their Use), *LTSR Aukščiausiosios Tarybos ir Vyriausybės žinios*, 30 April 1966.

Vijūnas, Kastytis 'Nakties laiškai' (Letters at Night), *Tarybinė moteris* 8 (1985).

Законы о разводе православного и неправославного исповедания (Divorce Regulations of Russian Orthodox and non-Orthodox Population) (Moscow, 1909), 258.

List of literature

Andriulis, V. 'Santuokos nutraukimas ir jos pripažinimas negaliojančia senojoje Lietuvos teisėje' (The Annulment of Marriage and the Recognition of Its Invalidity in Early Lithuanian Law), *Socialistinė teisė* 1 (1975).

Ashwin, Sarah, ed. *Gender, State and Society in Soviet and Post-Soviet Russia* (New York: Routledge, 2000).

Bridger, Sue. 'Young Women and Presetroika', in *Women and Society in Russia and the Soviet Union*, ed. Linda Edmondson (Cambridge: Cambridge University Press, 1990).

Būgienė, Lina. 'Pokario Vilnius jo gyventojų akimis (I)' (Post-war Vilnius as Seen by Its Residents), *Literatūra ir menas*, 10 January 2020.

Carlback, Helene, Youlia Gradskova and Zhanna Kravchenko, eds. *And They Lived Happily Ever After: Norms and Everyday Practices of Family and Parenthood in Russia and Eastern Europe* (Budapest: CEU Press, 2012).

Chatterjee, Choi, David L. Ransel, Mary Cavender and Karen Petrone eds. *Everyday Life in Russia: Past and Present* (Bloomington: Indiana University Press, 2015).

de Rougemont, Denis. *Love in the Western World* (New York: Fawcett, 1956).

Dičius, Pranas. *Santuoka ir Šeima Tarybų Lietuvoje* (Marriage and Family in Soviet Lithuania) (Vilnius: Minties Leidykla, 1974).

du Plessix Gray, Francine. *Soviet Women Walking the Tightrope* (New York: Doubleday, 1989).

Engel, Barbara Alpern. *Women in Russia: 1700–2000* (Cambridge, UK: Cambridge University Press, 2004).

Engel, Barbara Alpern, and Anastasia Posadskya-Vanderbeck, eds. *A Revolution of Their Own: Voices of Women in Soviet History* (Boulder, CO: Westview Press, 1998).

Engel, Barbara Alpern. *Women in Russia: 1700–2000* (Cambridge, UK: Cambridge University Press, 2004).

Filtzer, Donald, *The Khrushchev Era. De-Stalinization and the Limits of Freedom of Reform in the USSR, 1953–1964* (London: Macmillan, 1993).

Filtzer, Donald.*Soviet Workers and De-Stalinization* (Cambridge, UK: Cambridge University Press, 1992.

Fitzpatrick, Sheila, ed. *Stalinism: New Directions* (New York: Routledge, 2000).

Fitzpatrick, Sheila, and Robert Gellately, eds. *Denunciation in Modern European History, 1789–1989: Accusatory Practices* (Chicago: University of Chicago Press, 1997).

Funk, Nanette, and Magda Mueller, eds. *Gender Politics and Post-Communism: Reflections from Eastern Europe and the Former Soviet Union* (New York: Routledge, 1993).

Gaidys, V. 'Demografinės situacijos Lietuvoje bruožai' (On Lithuanian Demographics) (Šeimos ir Santuokos Aspektai), in *Žvilgsnis į šeimą* (A Look at Families), ed. V. Gaidys, A. Žvinklienė and V. Dumbliauskas (Vilnius: Lietuvos mokslų akademija, 1990).

Gaidys, V. *Visuomenės pagalba šeimai: Praktika ir problemos* (Social Assistance to Families: Practice and Problems) (Vilnius: Lietuvos TSR Žinijos draugija, 1984).

Goldman, Wendy Z. *Women, the State and Revolution, Soviet Family Policy and Social Life: 1917–1936* (Cambridge, UK: Cambridge University Press, 1993).

Gradskova, Yulia, and Ildikó Asztalos Morell, eds. *Gendering Post-socialism: Old Legacies and New Hierarchies* (London: Routledge, 2018).

Haney, Lynne. *Inventing the Needy: Gender and the Politics of Welfare in Hungary* (Berkeley: University of California Press, 2002).

Ilič, Melanie, Susan E. Reid and Lynne Attwood, eds. *Women in the Khrushchev Era* (New York: Palgrave Macmillan, 2004).

Illouz, Eva. *Consuming the Romantic Utopia: Love and the Cultural Contradictions of Capitalism* (Berkeley: University of California Press, 1997).

Jankowiak, William, ed. *Romantic Passion. A Universal Experience?* (New York: Columbia University Press, 1995).

Juviler, Peter H. *Cell Mutation in the Soviet Union: The Family*, Final Report to National Council for Soviet and East European Research (New York: Columbia University Press, 1987).

Katkova, I. 'Maternal Care of Infants', in *Women, Work and Family in the Soviet Union*, ed. Gail W. Lapidus (New York: Routledge, 1982).

Lapidus, Gail W., ed. *Women, Work and Family in the Soviet Union* (New York: Routledge, 1982).

Ledeneva, Alena V. *Russia's Economy of Favours: Blat, Networking and Informal Exchange* (Cambridge, UK: Cambridge University Press, 1998).

Leinarte, Dalia. *Adopting and Remembering Soviet Reality: Life Stories of Lithuanian Women, 1945–1970* (Amsterdam: Rodopi, 2010).

Leinarte, Dalia. *The Lithuanian Family in Its European Context, 1800–1914: Marriage, Divorce and Flexible Communities* (London: Palgrave Macmillan, 2017).

Leonavičius, Vylius, and Eglė Ozolinčiūtė. 'Sovietinio žemės ūkio transformacija' (Transformation of the Soviet Agricultural Sector), *Sociologija. Mintis ir veiksmas* 1, no. 44 (2019).

Lietuva 1940–1990 m. (Lithuania, 1940-1990) (Vilnius: Lietuvos gyventojų genocido ir rezistencijos tyrimo centras, 2005).

Liljeström, Marianne, Arja Rosenholm and Irina Savkina, eds. *Models of Selves: Russian Women's Autobiographical Texts* (Helsinki: Kikimora Publikation, 2000).

Lovell, Stephen, Alena Ledeneva and Andrei Rogachevskii, eds. *Bribery and Blat in Russia: Negotiating Reciprocity from the Middle Ages to the 1990s* (New York: Palgrave Macmillan, 2001).

Marcinkeviciene, Dalia, and Rima Praspaliauskiene. 'Prostitution in Post-war Lithuania', *Women's History Review* 12, no. 4 (2003).

Marsh, Rosalind. 'Women Writers of the 1930s: Conformity or Subversion?', in *Women in the Stalin Era*, ed. Melanie Ilič (New York: Palgrave Macmillan, 2001).

Maslauskaitė, A. *Meilė ir santuoka pokyčių Lietuvoje* (Love and Marriage in Lithuania) (Vilnius: Mokslo Aidai, 2004).

Naiman, Eric. *Sex in Public: The Incarnation of Early Soviet Ideology* (Princeton, NJ: Princeton University Press, 1997).

Nekrošius, I., V. Petrušonis and E. Riaubienė, eds. *Masinės statybos gyvenamųjų rajonų architektūra Lietuvoje* (Housing Development and Architecture in Lithuania (Vilnius: VGTU leidykla Technika, 2017).

Novikova, E. E., V. S. Iazykova and Z. A. Iankova. 'Women's Work and the Family', in *Women, Work and Family in the Soviet Union*, ed. Gail W. Lapidus (New York: Routledge, 1982).

Okunis, Jurgis. *Gyvenamieji namai* (Residential Homes) (Freiburg: n.p., 1948).

Oldeniel, Ruth, and Karin Zachmann, eds. *Cold War Kitchen: Americanization, Technology, and European Users* (Cambridge, MA: MIT Press, 2009).

Putinaitė, N. *Nenutrūkusi styga: Prisitaikymas ir pasipriešinimas sovietų Lietuvoje* (An Unbroken String: Conformism and Dissent in Soviet Lithuania) (Vilnius: Aidai, 2007).

Riurikovas, J. 'Mįslingiausias jausmas' (The Most Mysterious Emotion), *Jaunimo gretos* 1 (1969), 25, 30–31.

Sagatienė, Dovilė. 'Sovietinių teismų atkūrimas ir raida Lietuvoje 1944–1956 metais' (The Founding of the Soviet Courts and Their Development in Lithuania 1944–56), *Socialinių Mokslų Studijos* 5, no.1 (2013).

Siegelbaum, Lewis H. 'Cars, Cars, and More Cars: The Faustian Bargain of the Brezhnev Era', in *Borders of Socialism: Private Spheres of Soviet Russia*, ed. Lewis H. Siegelbaum (New York: Palgrave Macmillan, 2006), 90.

Shlapentokh, Vladimir. *Love, Marriage, and Friendship in the Soviet Union: Ideals and Practices* (New York: Praeger, 1984).

Singer, Irving. *The Nature of Love, Vol. 2: Courtly and Romantic* (Chicago: University of Chicago Press, 1984).

Skaisgiris, P. 'Dėl teisminės praktikos, išieškant alimentus nepilnamečiams vaikams išlaikyti' (On Judicial Practice in Recovering Child Support for Minor Children), *Socialistinė teisė* 2 (1969).

Steckienė, Aušra. 'Šeimos politikos pokyčiai Lietuvoje pereinant iš socializmo į kapitalizmą' (Changes in Family Policy in Lithuania's Transition from Socialism to Capitalism) (Master's Thesis, Vilnius University, 2008).

Stern, M., and A. Stern. *Sex in the USSR* (New York: Times Books, 1980).

Taubman, William. *Khrushchev: The Man and His Era* (New York: W.W. Norton, 2003).
Vyšniauskaitė, Angelė, Petras Kalnius and Rasa Paukštytė-Šaknienė, eds. *Lietuvių šeima ir papročiai* (The Lithuanian Family and Its Traditions) (Vilnius: Mintis, 2008).
Woll, Josephine. *Real Images. Soviet Cinema and the Thaw* (London: I. B. Tauris, 2000).
Wood, Elizabeth A. *The Baba and the Comrade* (Bloomington: Indiana University Press, 1997).
Zakharov, S. 'Russian Federation: From the First to Second Demographic Transition,' *Demographic Research* 19, no. 24 (2008).
Ždanko, T. A., ed. *Semejnyj byt narodov CCCR* (Family Life of Nations) (Moskva: Nauka, 1990).
Zubkova, Elena. *Russia after the War: Hopes, Illusions and Disappointments, 1945–1957* (New York: M. E. Sharpe, 1998).
Žvinklienė, A., and R. Savulionienė. 'Kodėl kuriamos šeimos' (Why We Form Families), in *Žvilgsnis į šeimą* (A Look at Families), ed. V. Gaidys, A. Žvinklienė and V. Dumbliauskas (Vilnius: Lietuvos mokslų akademija, 1990).
Zvinklienė, Alina. 'The State of Family Studies in Lithuania', *Marriage and Family Review* 22, nos 3–4 (1996).
Виктор, Сысенко. *Супружеские конфликты* (Marriage Conflicts) (Москва: Финансы и статистика, 1983).
Станкунене, В. 'Vosproizvodstvo naselenija Litvy', in *Demografičeskoe razvitie Litvy: retrospektiva, sovremenye problemy, sravnitelnyj analiz*, ed. V. Kanopiene, A. Sipaviciene, V. Stankuniene and V. Januškevčius (Vilnius: Institut Ekononmiki Akademii Nauk Litovskoj SSR, 1989), 22–59.
Соловьев, Н. Н. *Брак и семья сегодня* (Marriage and Family Today) (Вильнюс: Минтис, 1977).
Сысенко, В. А. *Устойчивость брака: проблемы, факторы, условия* (Marriages: Problems, Motives, Predispositions) (Москва: Финансы и статистика, 1981).

Index

aesthetic lifestyle 6, 143–6, 163
agitprop meetings 9, 12, 17
alcoholism 78, 88, 90–3, 160, 185 n.204
alimony 101–3, 181, 186 n.228, 192 n.84
annexation 7, 47, 77, 90
archival material 2, 6

Baltic States 1, 183 n.155
bastards 83, 98
bigamy 86–8
birth certificates 35, 37, 39, 48, 100, 102, 132
birthrate 28, 30, 109, 110, 117, 160
blat 5, 146–55, 163, 165 n.5, 196 nn.56–7, 196 n.67, 74
boarding schools 111–15, 124, 171 n.59, 188 nn.12–15, 18, 190 n.55
Bolsheviks 8, 9, 60

Canon Law 47, 77
census 6, 45, 55, 117, 112, 176 n.33, 189 n.34
Central Committee, the Lithuanian Communist Party 9–13, 18, 79, 89, 113, 114, 116, 127, 140, 171 n.61, 195 n.43
centralized distribution 2, 6
child custody 79, 82, 126–30, 191 n.70, 193 n.19
child support 7, 27, 39, 76, 79, 82, 99, 101, 102, 111, 128–33, 170 n.58, 188 n.7, 191 n.73, 192 n.80, 194 n.30
child's upbringing 128
childcare 5, 21–7, 61, 109, 111–25, 161, 162, 170 n.58, 178n.7
childcare institutions 5, 27, 111, 115, 170 n.58, 188 n.7
childcare leave 5
child-rearing 39, 145
children born out of wedlock 131–3
church 37, 47–52, 56, 77, 82, 83, 86–8, 132, 135, 158
civil marriages 3, 47, 48, 87

cohabitation 87
collective farm 8, 9, 11, 15, 17, 27, 30, 31, 49, 56, 96, 103, 116, 117, 137–40, 189 n.29, 194 n.23
collectivization 8, 14, 139
communist party 3, 4, 9, 13, 20, 21, 40, 41, 79, 90, 94–6, 127–8, 140, 142–4, 147
communists 3, 21, 124
complaint 5, 11, 80, 94, 146, 147–55, 163, 167 n.16, 196 nn.48–50
Comsomol 3, 4, 56, 90, 91, 127, 147, 191 n.64
Comsomol-style wedding 56
consumer goods 140, 142–4, 147, 195 nn.38, 45–6
consumerism 153
cooperative apartment 137
Council of Ministers, Lithuanian SSR 20, 48, 112, 157
crèches 11, 24, 32, 116–18
Criminal Code 7, 8, 129

daycare centres 117, 189 n.29
delegates-activists 10, 11, 13–20
demographic policies 109, 161
deportations 1, 2, 88
disabled children 25–6, 28, 112, 123, 162
discrimination 12, 21, 157
divorce 3–7, 39, 77–107, 126–31, 137, 139, 158–60
divorce cases 4, 6, 78–87, 91–9, 106, 107, 127–30, 139, 159, 160, 183 n.163
domestic violence 89, 90
double burden 144–5
dowry 52, 53

economy 2, 16, 150, 195 n.38, 196 nn.56, 58, 67
employment 5, 7, 8, 20, 24, 26
ex-husband 103, 119, 128, 130
ex-wives 102, 104
exile 7, 19, 85, 86, 135, 139, 160, 162

family happiness 4, 52, 61, 72, 73
family members 2, 24, 55, 61, 101, 113, 118, 125, 131, 139
family policy 2, 7–45, 55, 57, 61, 72, 76, 131, 157, 158, 166, 171 n.62, 177 n.53, 187 n.3
family size 109, 110, 161
family time 2
financial maintenance 129–31
financial support 5, 7, 38, 82, 128–32
free love 58, 60, 159
friendship 4, 69, 70, 74, 149, 150, 159, 165 n.4, 178 nn.59, 75, 179 nn.77, 81, 180 nn.104, 108, 181 n.119, 190 nn.58, 61
full-time employment 1

Gender equality 2–21, 44, 157
glasnost 2
government 3–28, 33, 34, 43, 50, 51, 56, 58, 60, 83, 89–95, 110, 112, 116, 136, 140–51, 189 n.24
GULAG 1, 135, 162

Holocaust 1
homemakers 17, 122, 145
household 2, 5, 16, 17, 39, 40, 44, 75, 99, 100, 103, 104, 127, 133–59, 192
household chores 2, 144
housing 5, 6, 16, 24, 25, 57, 75, 98, 105, 110, 116, 135–9, 150, 158–9, 191 n.61

ideological upbringing 113
ideologues 3, 51, 55, 65–7, 75, 112, 159
ideology 1, 2, 3, 9, 21, 63, 64, 69, 72, 146, 163, 178 nn.60–1
imprisonment 1, 20
independent Lithuania 7, 8, 28, 61, 116
indoctrination 13
infertility 101
infidelity 88–94, 106, 160
informal economic activity 8
inheritance 83, 86, 136, 187 nn.241–2, 194 n.21
instructor 9–18, 27, 166 n.11, 195 n.44
interwar Lithuania 3, 4, 30, 52, 62–3, 83, 87, 127

Kaunaitė, M. 9, 10, 11
KGB 8, 11

Khruschevian family policies 4
Khrushchev's Thaw 44, 55, 71, 74, 109
Khrushchiovki 137
kindergartens 5, 6, 92, 96, 112–18, 131, 137, 161
Kolkhoz 14, 15, 20–5, 30, 56, 93, 111, 116, 118, 139, 157, 161
Kymantaitė, M. 29–43, 172 n.84, 173 n.94, 174 n.112

labour camp 1, 86, 135
labour laws 7
large families 3–6, 11, 14–15, 19, 22–43, 110, 111, 116, 157, 168 n.39, 169 n.41, 171 n.65, 172 n.86
latchkey children 120
8 July 1944 decree 29–31
Lazdynai 6, 136, 137
living space 5, 97, 105–10, 128, 136–7, 150, 162, 177 n.45, 186 n.223, 187 n.250
love 4, 7, 52, 58–76, 93, 98–100, 126–8, 158–9
low-income families 27

marital age 48, 50, 57, 72, 158
marital status 40, 88, 101
marriage 3–7, 25, 29, 31, 39, 47–77, 82–107, 109, 130, 132, 141, 158–60
Marriage and Family Code, LSSR 1970 3, 49, 60, 82, 101–3, 158, 175 n.14, 183 n.163
Marriage and Family Code, RSFSR 1918 49, 50, 63, 77, 82, 86, 102, 132, 188 n.16
Marriage Law 7, 47, 48, 77, 166 n.1, 175 n.2
Marriage Law, LSSR 1940 47, 48, 77, 175 n.2
Marriage, Family and Guardianship Code, RSFSR 1926 88
Marriage, Family and Guardianship Code, RSFSR 1936 63
Marriage, Family and Guardianship Law Valid in the Territory of the LSSR 1940, 49, 77, 158, 175 n.12
marriages, de facto 60, 83, 88
mass construction 6, 138, 163
material shortages 5, 88, 160
maternity leave 22, 27–8, 111–12, 122, 161–2
medical assistance 5

memory 2
Metrics Instructions, LSSR 1958 49
Metrics Instructions, LSSR 1970 50, 158
Metrics Law, 1940 47–9
MGB 19, 168 n.31
micro-districts 6
military families 16, 24
Militsiya 8, 31, 35, 36, 43, 89
Ministry of Agriculture, Lithuanian SSR 10, 117
Ministry of Labour and Social Welfare, Lithuanian SSR 6
modern society 4, 107
motherhood 39, 61, 111, 126
mothers 1–7, 11–15, 19–44, 56, 83, 98, 111–33, 145, 157–62
mothers of large families and single mothers board 15
mothers-in-law 96–8
motives for marriage 4, 56, 109

Nazi occupation 1, 175 n.9
needy families 25, 26, 113
newborns 31, 109
Nomenklatura 106, 128
nuclear family 30
nursery schools 11, 15–16

parasites 7, 8, 21
parents 2, 4, 5, 7, 26–39, 50–8, 63, 64, 96, 97, 101, 109–19
paternity 39, 82, 98–2, 132–3, 170, 121–8, 131–6, 148, 158, 162, 187
partisans 16, 19, 20, 24, 94awn.58, 186 nn.225–6, 227, 228, 229, 194 n.30
patriarchal stereotypes 18, 21, 92, 107, 157
peasant society 5
People's Commissar of Finance and Finance Ministers, Lithuanian SSR 6, 35, 40, 41
Perestroika 72, 76, 90, 111, 126, 159
pioneer camps 28
polygamy 86–8, 184 n.187
popular literature 4, 61
post-war years 78, 107, 128
pregnancy leave 26
pregnant mothers 3
private homes 137, 138
privileges 5, 23, 98, 151

propaganda 2–9, 17, 20, 50–6, 61–74, 95, 111–14, 140–7, 158, 179 nn.79, 92
Propaganda and Agitation Department, LCP (B) Communist Party 20
propagandists 3, 12, 51, 65–7, 70
property 1, 11, 19, 75, 77, 79, 82, 86, 87, 103–7, 131, 135–9, 159, 162, 187 nn.244, 247, 249
prostitution 8, 166 n.3
public 2, 10, 12, 15, 20–9, 31, 49, 50, 54–61, 70, 72, 78, 85, 89, 92, 94–5, 110, 120, 144–6, 153–9, 163

quotas 18

readers' letters 4, 51
Red Army 1, 139
regime 1–9, 15, 19–21, 44, 54, 72, 84, 85, 90, 92, 98, 157, 158–61
religious ceremonies 47, 50
religious marriages 3, 52
reproduction 4, 71
residential buildings 6
romantic love 4, 58–70, 109, 159
rural districts 10, 20, 116, 117, 138, 161
Russia, 8, 9, 25, 30, 38, 60, 61, 76, 93, 140, 141, 168 n.37, 181 n.121, 183 n.155, 187 n.5, 190 n.44, 191 nn.62, 64, 196 n.67, 197 n.74

Second World War 8, 30, 50, 77, 83, 86, 116
sexual experience 60, 71
sexual life 4, 64
sexual passion 58, 59, 61, 65, 67, 69
shortage 2, 5, 14, 29, 72, 80, 88, 97, 105, 118, 137, 139, 142, 144–50, 160
siblings 121, 162
single mothers 3, 5, 11, 15, 22–48, 93, 111, 112, 116, 131–3, 168 n.39, 171 n.65
social benefits 40
social welfare 6, 23, 25, 29, 44, 123, 153
soulmates 4
Soviet Bloc 5, 137, 143
Soviet republics 24, 25, 30, 49, 54, 76, 83, 141, 159, 160
Soviet Union 1, 2, 19, 20, 21, 28, 47, 55, 111, 116, 130, 137–49, 178 n.59, 179

n.81, 180 n.107, 181 n.119, 182 nn.137, 139, 191 n.64, 195 n.38
spouse 2, 3, 6, 48, 50–86, 90, 94–5, 102–7, 130–1, 137–8, 158, 160, 163
Stakhanovite movement 15
Stalinist family policy 4, 7, 21, 44, 63, 142, 157
stereotypes 4, 9, 18, 21, 38, 52, 54, 56, 92, 99, 100, 104, 107, 157
summer vacations 2
Supreme Soviet 3, 157, 160, 166 n.5, 172 n.86, 183 n.162
Supreme Court 6, 78–91, 97–107, 129–30, 159–60, 183 n.167, 184 n.169
Supreme Court, LSSR 4, 6, 78–130, 159, 160, 183 nn.167–8, 184 n.169
Supreme Soviet 3, 8, 13, 15, 20–34, 48, 49, 77–86, 111, 112, 132, 137, 166 n.5, 169 n.47, 169 n.50, 170 n.51, 175 n.10, 195 n.41

totalitarian ideology 1
tractor stations (ATS) 10
traumatic experience 2
tsar's decree, Russian Empire 1836 77
two-instance divorce proceedings 81, 98, 160

unpaid leave 28, 111, 112, 161
urbanization 6, 96, 124, 136
USSR 3–15, 20, 22, 27, 29, 49, 57, 61, 71, 72, 76–8, 83–4, 92–3, 97, 109, 111–18, 122, 125, 128–45, 158, 160, 168 n.35, 174 n.117, 180 n.116, 182 n.143, 194 n.29

Vilnius 6, 11, 14–15, 29–32, 35, 40, 42, 57, 63–5, 770, 73, 78–81, 84, 91, 95, 103, 106, 112, 116–19, 129, 135, 139–44, 148, 154, 167 n.22
violence against women 8, 12, 89, 157

Western feminism 12
witnesses 47–50, 78, 88, 101, 103, 135
women candidates 12
women's activism 2, 20, 157
women's councils 13–14, 32, 167 n.21
women's rights 3, 11–12, 157
Work Among Women Division 10–21, 27, 165 n.3, 166 n.12, 167 nn.16, 22, 168 n.27
workforce 2, 25

Žirmūnai 136, 137

www.ingramcontent.com/pod-product-compliance
Lightning Source LLC
Chambersburg PA
CBHW062223300426

44115CB00012BA/2200